Steps in Geography

R Bateman
and
F Martin

Stanley Thornes (Publishers) Ltd

Acknowledgements

Thanks to Jane Essex for her help with Units 4 and 8, to Stuart Jordan for his help with Unit 7, and to Mr C. Richards for his help with Unit 9.2.

Acknowledgements are due to the following for permission to reproduce photographs used in this book:

J Allen Cash, cover;

Aerofilms pp 56, 59, 65, 73; J Allen Cash pp 4, 5, 9, 40, 42, 52, 54, 56, 60, 64, 73, 89; Amey Roadstone p 68; E Bahaire p 73; Barnaby's Picture Library pp 8, 17, 56; British Airways p 93; Cambridge University Collection (copyright reserved) p 56; Camera Press p 48; Colorific p 40; University of Dundee Electronic Laboratories p 51; Robert Harding Picture Library pp 4, 12, 13, 17, 40, 48, 64, 85, 89, 93; Alan Hutchinson pp 4, 64; Mars p 72; Bob Osborne p 66; Popperfoto p 42; Sealink UK Ltd Photo Library p 93; West Air Photography pp 10, 11, 70, 74.

British Rail symbol courtesy of British Rail p 21;
Ordnance Survey symbols Crown Copyright reserved p 21.

Originally published in 1980 by Hutchinson Education
Reprinted 1980, 1981 (twice), 1982, 1983 (twice), 1984
Second edition 1987

Reprinted 1990 by
Stanley Thornes (Publishers) Ltd
Old Station Drive
Leckhampton
Cheltenham GL53 0DN

Designed and produced by SGS Education Ltd
Illustrations by Chris Evans, Marlborough Design, Raymond Turvey and Barrie Thorpe
Film set by Yale Press

Printed and bound by
Wing King Tong Co. Ltd, Hong Kong

British Library Cataloguing in Publication Data

Bateman, R.
Steps in geography.—2nd ed.
1. Geography—Text-books—1945-
I. Title II. Martin, F. (Frederick) 1948-
910 G128

ISBN 0 7487 0386 1

Note to teachers
This series has been written to introduce students to some of the basic vocabulary, ideas and skills in geography in a way which makes the teacher's classroom task straightforward. It is not however, intended that the textbooks should be the student's sole resource or that the activities included should represent the total learning strategies of a course in geography. It is expected that, in many cases, the materials will serve simply as a starting point from which to develop a variety of more active learning techniques, thus ensuring a more comprehensive and balanced set of learning experiences.

Contents

Unit 1.1

What is geography?/Places

Geography is the study of **places.**
Each of the photographs (below) shows a completely different scene. There are no two places exactly the same on the Earth. Geography helps us to describe these scenes so that we can learn about and understand the different places on the Earth.

Think of some words which you could use to describe these photographs. One shows a **city** and **factories**. Another shows a **village** with **farms**. A third is a **desert** area, and the fourth is a **forest**.

Each scene is different, but there are many other places which look very much like them in other parts of the world.

How do we study these places?

First we must learn the right words to use, for example, city or village. Next we learn how to describe the places.

Here are three ways you can use to describe the places shown in the photographs.

1 Writing
A paragraph can be written about each.

2 Maps
A map can be drawn to show where the place is and what is there.

3 Facts and figures
Exact figures could be given to say how many people live in each area, how many houses there are, how tall the trees are, or how hot the desert is. Graphs or tables of figures can show the information quickly.

Geography uses all these methods so that people and places can be both described and understood.

Things to do/Places

1 Which word best sums up what geography is about?

2 Look at the two photographs. Describe what the scenes they show have in common. Then say how they are different.

3 Describe two places you know which are nearly the same, for example. two parks, two streets or two beaches. What do they both have in common?
What is different about each one?
Say how each is different, and if possible, explain why they are different.

4 What are the three different ways which can be used to describe a place?
Which method would best show where a place is?
Which would give the most exact information?
Which could best explain the scene?

Further work

5 Think about the house you live in. Describe it by
- writing a few sentences
- drawing a sketch or simple map
- giving figures which could describe it. For example, how big it is, how many rooms it has, etc.

Say what you think are the good things and the bad things about each of these methods.

Summary
Geography is a subject which studies people and places.
There are three main ways which can be used to describe a place: writing, maps, and facts and figures.

Unit 1.2

Maps and sketches

It is important to learn how to draw and read maps. Maps are used not only in school lessons, but also by many people in their jobs. Think about how a taxi driver or a salesman would get on without maps.

Every map must have the following:

a title – to show what the map is about

a frame – a neat ruled line around the map

a scale – to show distance on the map

a key – to say what the map symbols mean.

directions – an arrow to show where North is.

The main compass directions are North, East South and West.

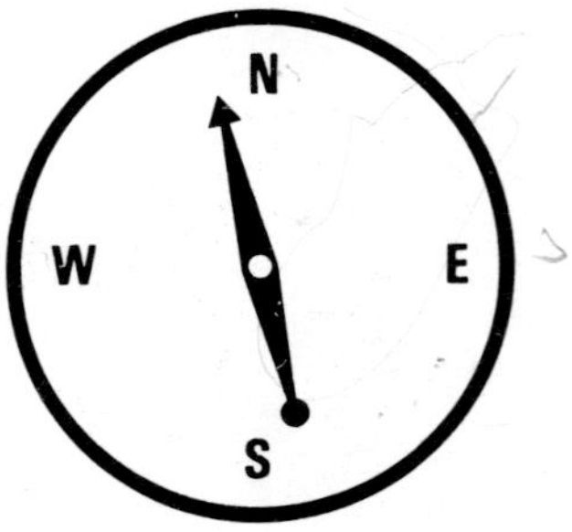

Directions diagram

You can remember this by saying 'Never Eat Shredded Wheat'.

The sketch shows a classroom during a lesson. The map shows the same classroom. The map is drawn as if looking straight down on a place.

A

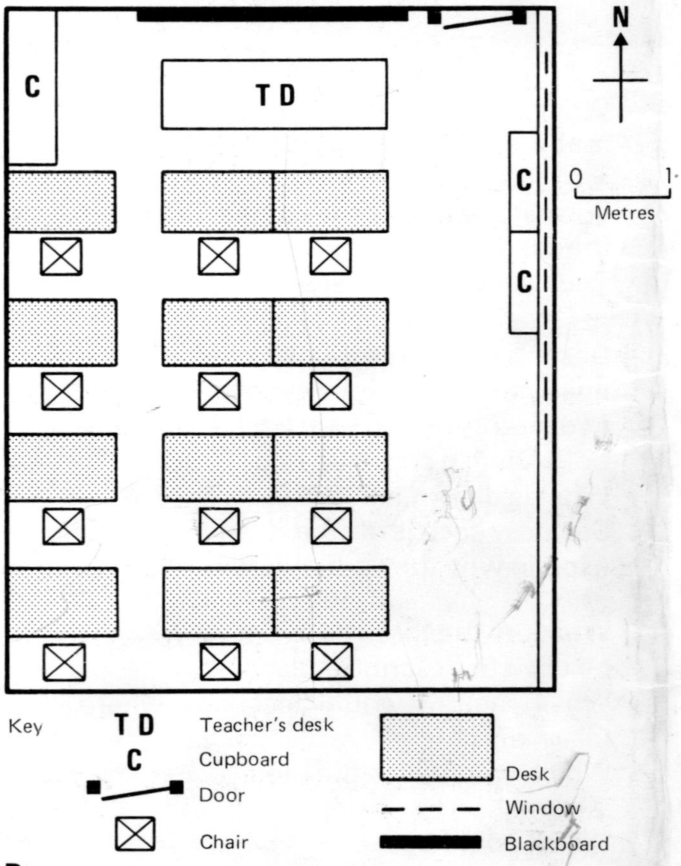

B

Things to do/Maps and sketches

policeman estate agent

soldier architect

travel agent ambulance driver

1a Write one sentence about each of the people above. Say how they could use a map.

b Make your own list of jobs where the maps can be important.

2a What does the sketch of the classroom show that the map can not?

b What can the map show that the sketch can not?

3 Copy the diagram which shows directions.

4 Copy and complete the following sentences. Choose the correct word from the two shown either/or?

a There are 12/32 desks for pupils in the room.

b The door is on the south/north side of the room.

c The window is on the east/west side of the room.

d The north to south side of the room is the shortest/longest

5 The two maps drawn below both have important things left out. State what is missing in each map.

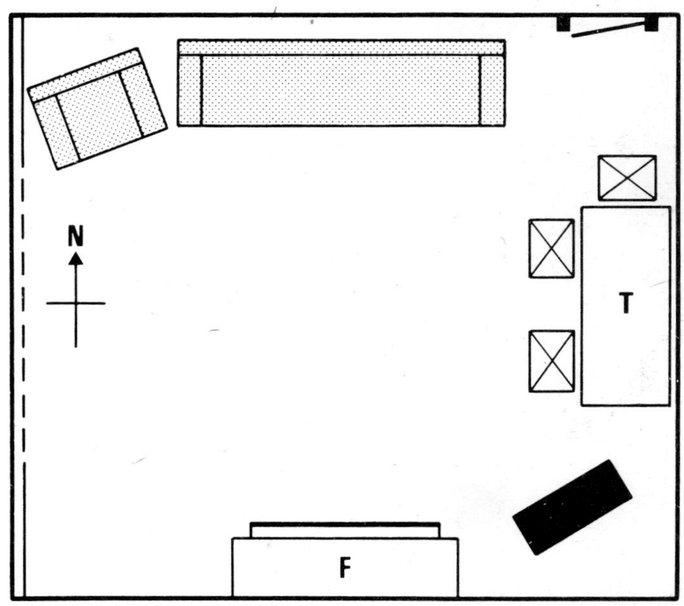

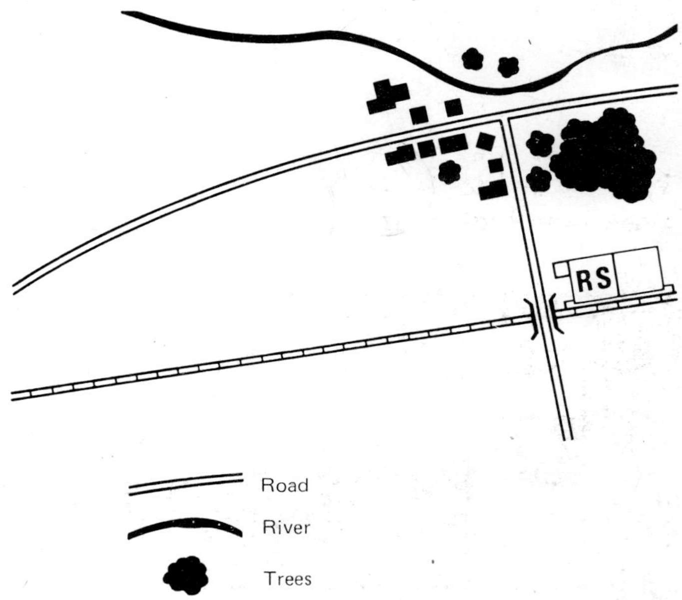

Further work

6 Draw a diagram to show the main compass points. Then draw in these extra points: north-east south-east south-west north-west.

7 Draw a map of your own classroom or one of the rooms in your house.

Summary

Maps are a good way of giving information. Good maps must have a title, frame, scale, labels or key, and directions.

Unit 1.3

Photographs and sketches

A good photograph can give a great deal of information. Making a sketch of a photograph helps to show the most important things about a place.

The photograph shows a part of Salcombe in Devon. To make a sketch from the photograph, follow the steps shown in the following diagrams.

Step 1
Rule a frame to the sketch and add a title:

Sketch of Salcombe from the South

Step 2
Draw in the main relief lines. The word 'relief' means the shape of the land.

Sketch of Salcombe from the South

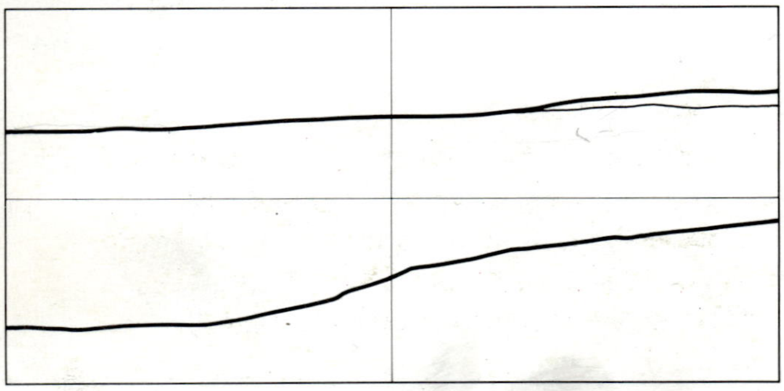

Step 3
Sketch in thinner shorter lines to show slopes and smaller relief features.

Sketch of Salcombe from the South

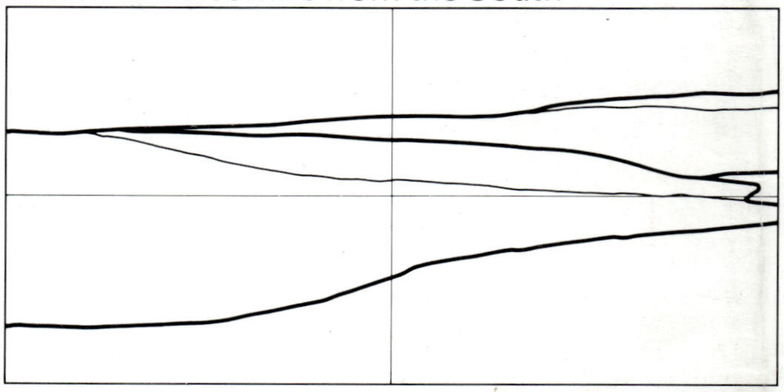

Step 4
Draw in smaller details like roads, buildings and plants. Notice how things seem smaller the further away they are.

Sketch of Salcombe from the South

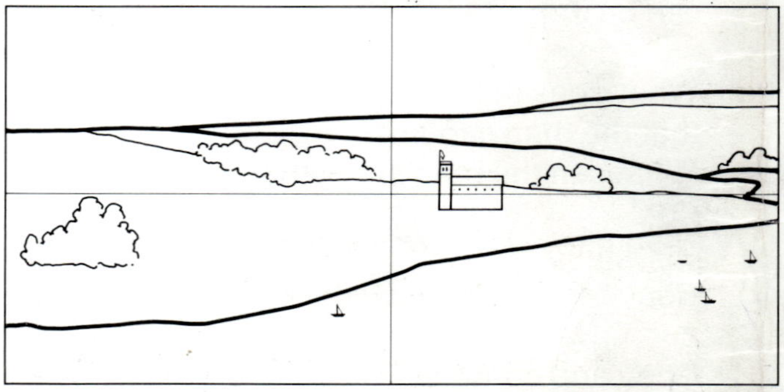

Step 5
Complete your sketch by printing labels around the box. Use thin lines to show where these things are.

Sketch of Salcombe from the South

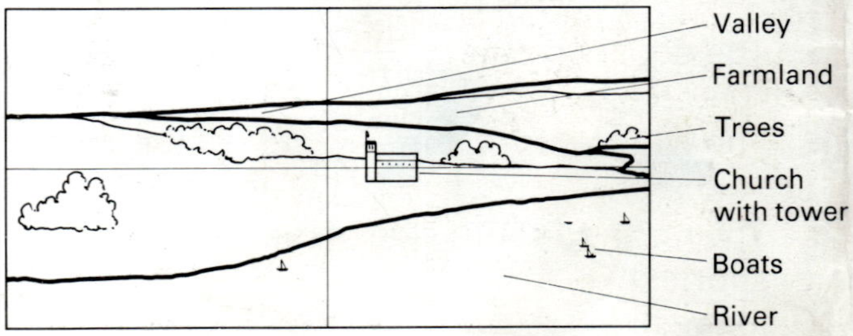

Things to do/Photographs and sketches

1a Study the photograph above.

b Make a copy of the sketch below by drawing in the main relief lines. Do this by joining up the dots.

c Draw on some shorter lines to show slopes and the smaller relief features.

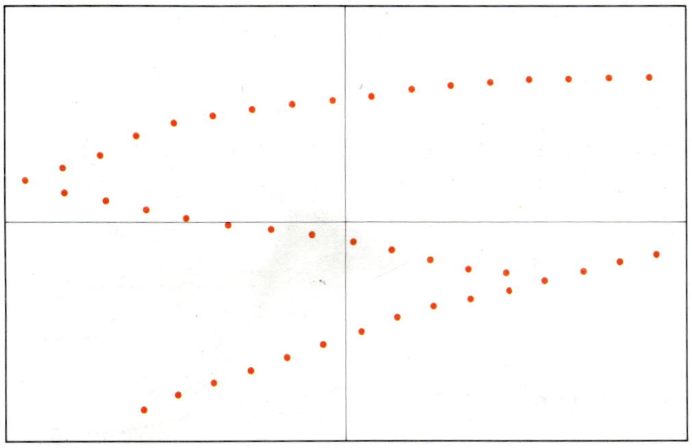

2 This diagram has been shaded over one half as if the sun was in the top left hand corner.

Copy the sketch and complete the shading on the second half.

3 This photograph shows a view of the hills of Cheshire. By following steps 1 to 5 on the opposite page, make your own simple sketch of the scene.
Label in the following things:

stone wall	road
farm buildings	trees

Further work

4 Find another photograph in this book. Make a simple sketch to show what is there.

Summary

Sketches of photographs are a simple way of showing what a place is like. Sketches are easy if drawn step by step. Your 'geographical eyesight' will improve if you practice drawing sketches.

Unit 1.4

Looking down from above

Many things on the ground can best be seen by using **air photographs**. These are taken from aircraft flying several thousand feet up. The result is a very detailed picture of what is below. Even cars and people can be seen in air photographs taken from high-flying aircraft.

This air photograph below shows the most famous rugby ground in Wales, the National Stadium. The map shows the same area. Notice that the air photograph shows everything that can be seen but the map has to select what is shown.

By using photograph **A** and map **B** together, an accurate outline sketch **C** can be drawn and information labelled in.

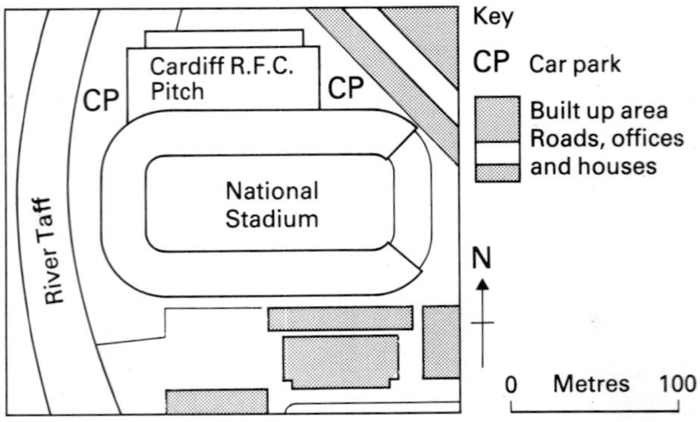

B

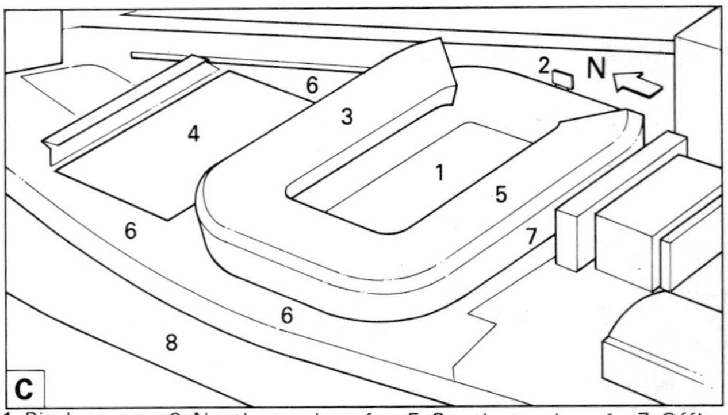

C

1 Pitch
2 Scoreboard
3 North stand roof
4 Cardiff RFC pitch
5 South stand roof
6 Car park
7 Offices
8 River Taff

A

Things to do/Looking down from above

1 Compare sketch **C** and air photograph **A** of the National Stadium.

a Make out a chart to show the good things and the bad things about air photographs and maps:

Things only shown on the photograph	Things only shown on the map

b Imagine you wanted to find the National Stadium. Would you rather be given an air photograph or a map to help find your way? Explain your answer.

2 This air photograph **F** shows a school. The map **D** shows the same area.

a Make a copy of the outline **E** of the photograph.

b Using the map, mark in and name all the buildings, street names and open space on this outline.

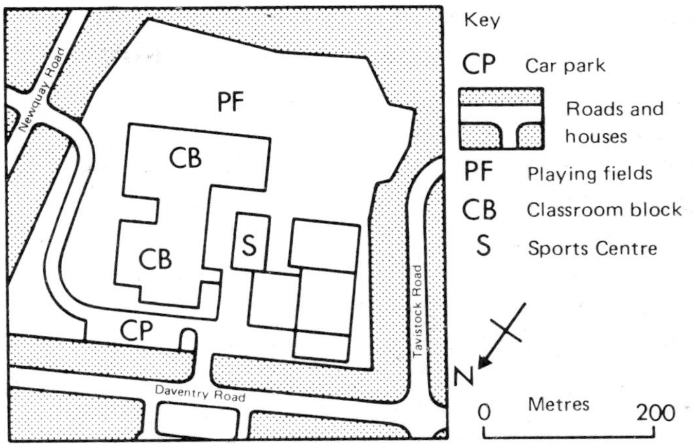

D Map of Merrywood School, Bristol

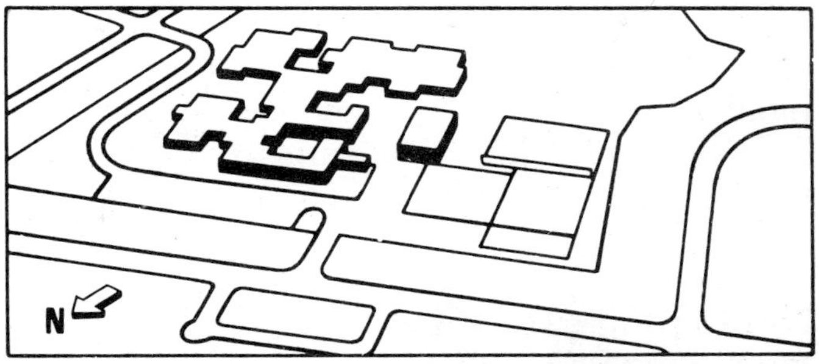

E Sketch of Merrywood School, Bristol

Further work

3 Study the photograph of the school below. Make a list of all the things which had to be left out when the map was drawn.

4 Describe any difficulties there could be in taking air photographs. Say when they can not be taken.

Summary
Air photographs show what a place looks like from above. They can be used with a map to give information about a place.

F

Unit 2.1

Useful skills/Making notes

How good is your memory? Could you write down the detailed story of a programme you saw on TV last night? What about the night before, or a programme you saw last week?
Unless you have made notes during the programme, you will soon have forgotten most of what you saw. If you want to remember, there is no need to write down every word. A list of the most important words will do. These are called the *key words.*

The following paragraph contains information about oil and gas in the North Sea. The words in italics are all important key words.

"In *1967, natural gas* began to come ashore from the *North Sea gasfields.* It is piped through *pipelines* then passed around the country to heat people's homes and run factories. By *1975, oil* had been discovered off the *East coast* of *Scotland.* The oilfields were given strange names like *Auk, Frigg* and *Piper.* Giant *oilrigs* have become a common sight. A rig can be over *200 metres high.* About *50 men* will work on a rig for up to *three weeks* at a time. They are taken to the rig in *helicopters* from the *airport* at *Aberdeen.* At the peak of oil production, in the 1980's, Britain will be getting about *120 million tonnes* of oil in one year from the North Sea."

The worlds in italics are of three types –

Places (North Sea)
Figures (1975)
Technical (gasfield)

All three types of words are needed to remember the details of the paragraph.

Things to do/Making notes

Summary
Key words are the most important pieces of information in a paragraph or film. They are a good way of remembering exactly what you have read or heard.

1 Think about one TV programme or film you have seen recently which was about Geography or Travel. Try to write down –
- **a** The names of any places or people mentioned.
- **b** What the main point of the programme was.

This will show how good your memory is.

2 Read through the passage about oil and gas in the North Sea.
List all the key words under the right heading –
Places Figures Technical terms

3 Read the passage below. When you have finished, write down what you think the key words are.

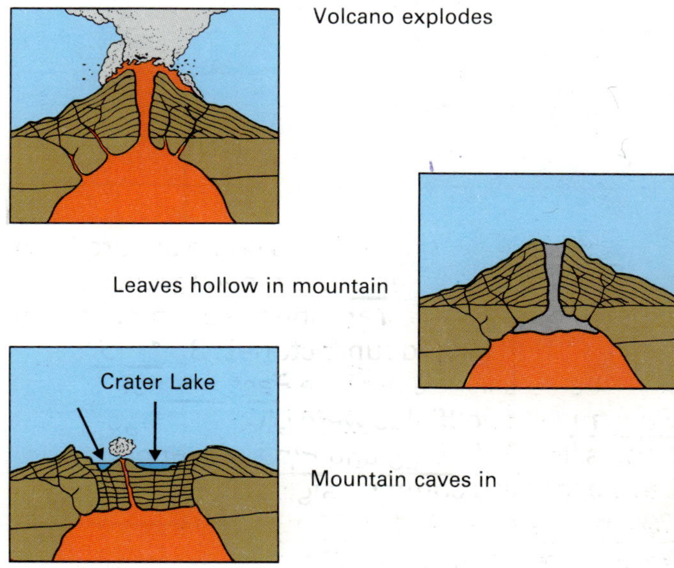

One of the world's largest volcanic explosions must have taken place in Oregon USA about 6000 years ago. Mount Mazama was one of the highest peaks in the Cascade mountains. It was 3,700 m high, four times the height of Britain's highest peak.

The explosion was so powerful that the lava beneath the mountain was drained away leaving the mountain hollow.
Rocks and cinders were blown 60 km away and the dust was carried over a thousand miles to the North.

Then the whole mountain caved in to leave a large hollow. This hollow filled with rain water and a lake was formed. This lake is called Crater Lake.

Further work

4 Listen to a TV or radio news programme. While you are listening, try to write down the key words.

Unit 2.2

Drawing maps

As well as being able to read a map, you should be able to draw one. Sometimes you need to draw a very accurate map. At other times a simple sketch map will do.

Making an accurate map

Step 1
Draw or trace a grid over the map you want to copy.

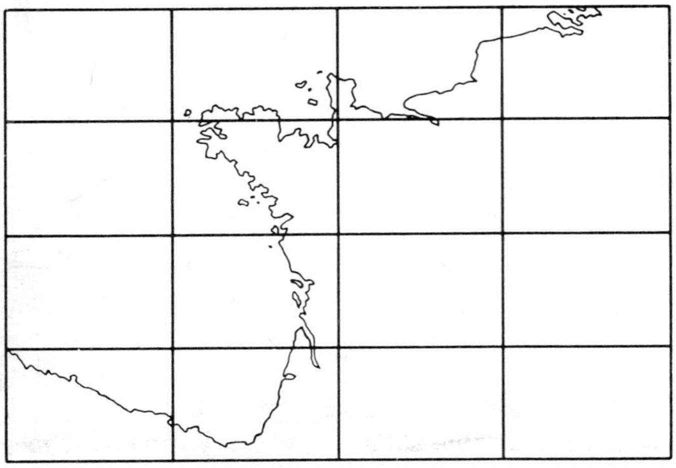

Step 2
Using the grid squares as a guide, carefully draw the outline so that it is exactly the same. Draw the outline from square to square, then fill in smaller details.

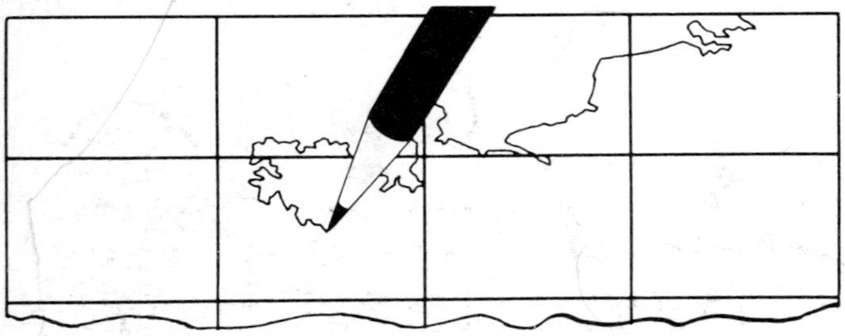

Step 3
Add in all other bits of information needed to complete the map.

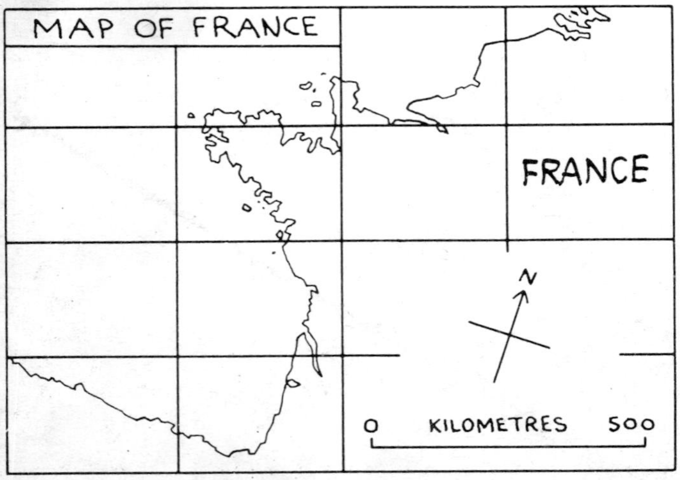

Making a sketch map

Step 1
Place dots at points where the coast or boundary change direction

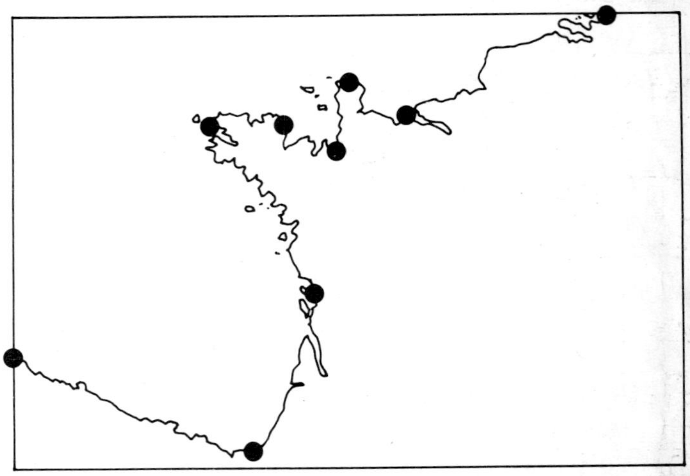

Step 2
Join up the dots with straight lines. Do not attempt to draw in all the detail. Think of the shape as being made up of circles, squares and triangles.

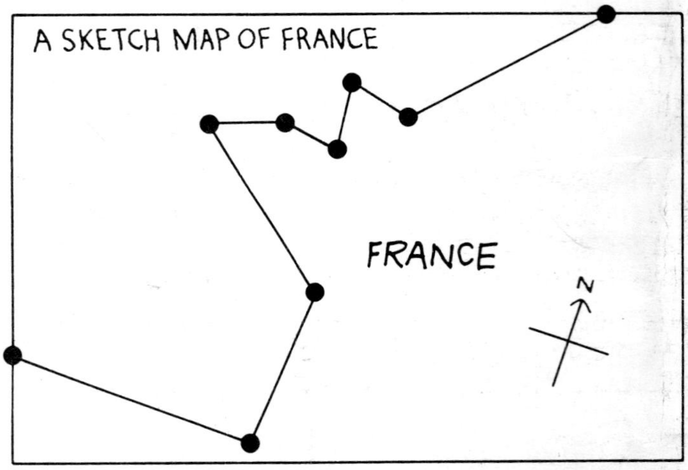

Things to do/Drawing maps

1 Study how to make an accurate map step by step.

2 Make an accurate copy of this map of Spain and Portugal.

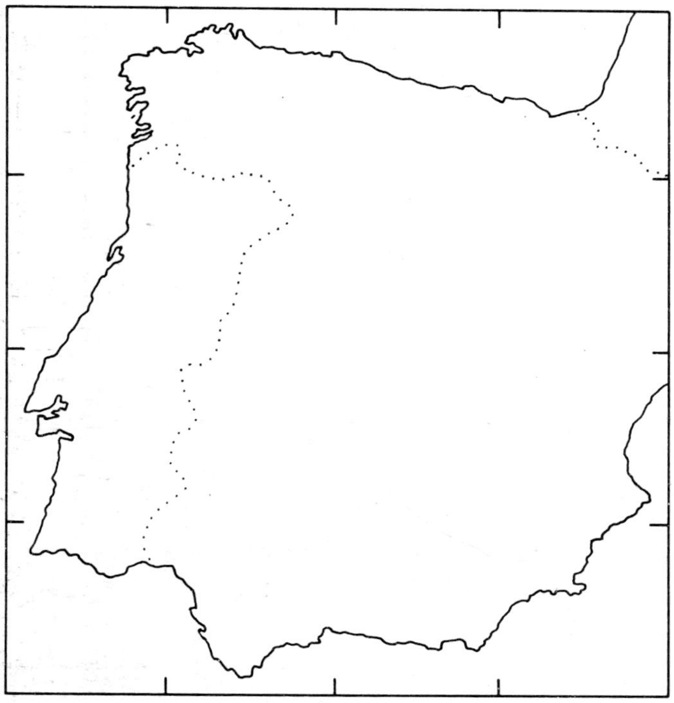

3 Study how to make a simple sketch map.

4 The maps below show accurate and simple outlines for some well known countries.
 a Draw each of the simple sketch maps.
 b Give each sketch map the correct name.

ACCURATE OUTLINES	SKETCH OUTLINES

5 Make an accurate copy or trace this map of West Germany. On your copy, place no more than ten dots at the corners. Then join up the dots to give a simple sketch map.

6 In your atlas, look up Egypt.
Draw a simple sketch map showing only the borders, the river Nile, and Cairo, its capital city.

Further work

7 Look at the map of Spain and Portugal above. Draw two more maps of the area. The first should be twice the size, the second only half the size.

Summary
Maps can be drawn accurately using a grid. A simple map may be drawn with straight lines. A simple sketch map only shows what you want it to show.

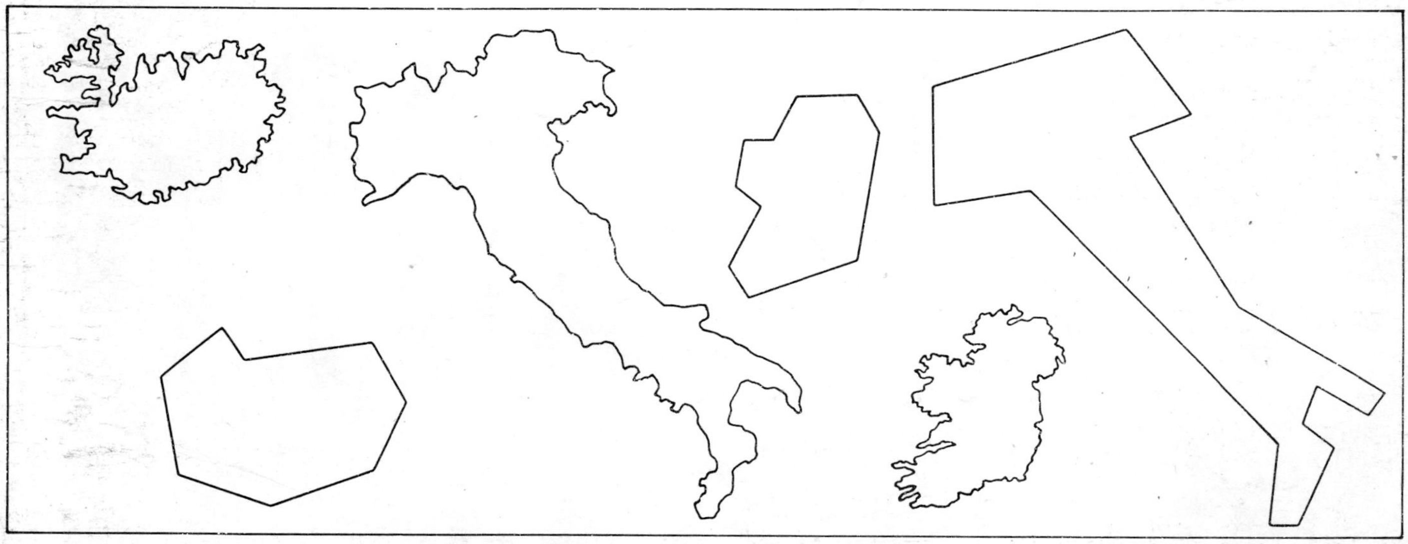

Unit 2.3

Describing places

Knowing how to describe a place is important in geography. The following terms are useful as headings for a description:

GEOGRAPHICAL TERM		MEANING
Location	–	where a place is.
Relief	–	the shape of the land.
Drainage	–	rivers and streams.
Climate	–	the present and past weather.
Vegetation	–	the plants.
Population	–	the people.
Settlement	–	where people live.
Communications	–	how people travel.
Work	–	what people do for a living.
Conclusion	–	what we think about the place.

Here is what could be said about the sketch of the Canadian lumberjack scene:

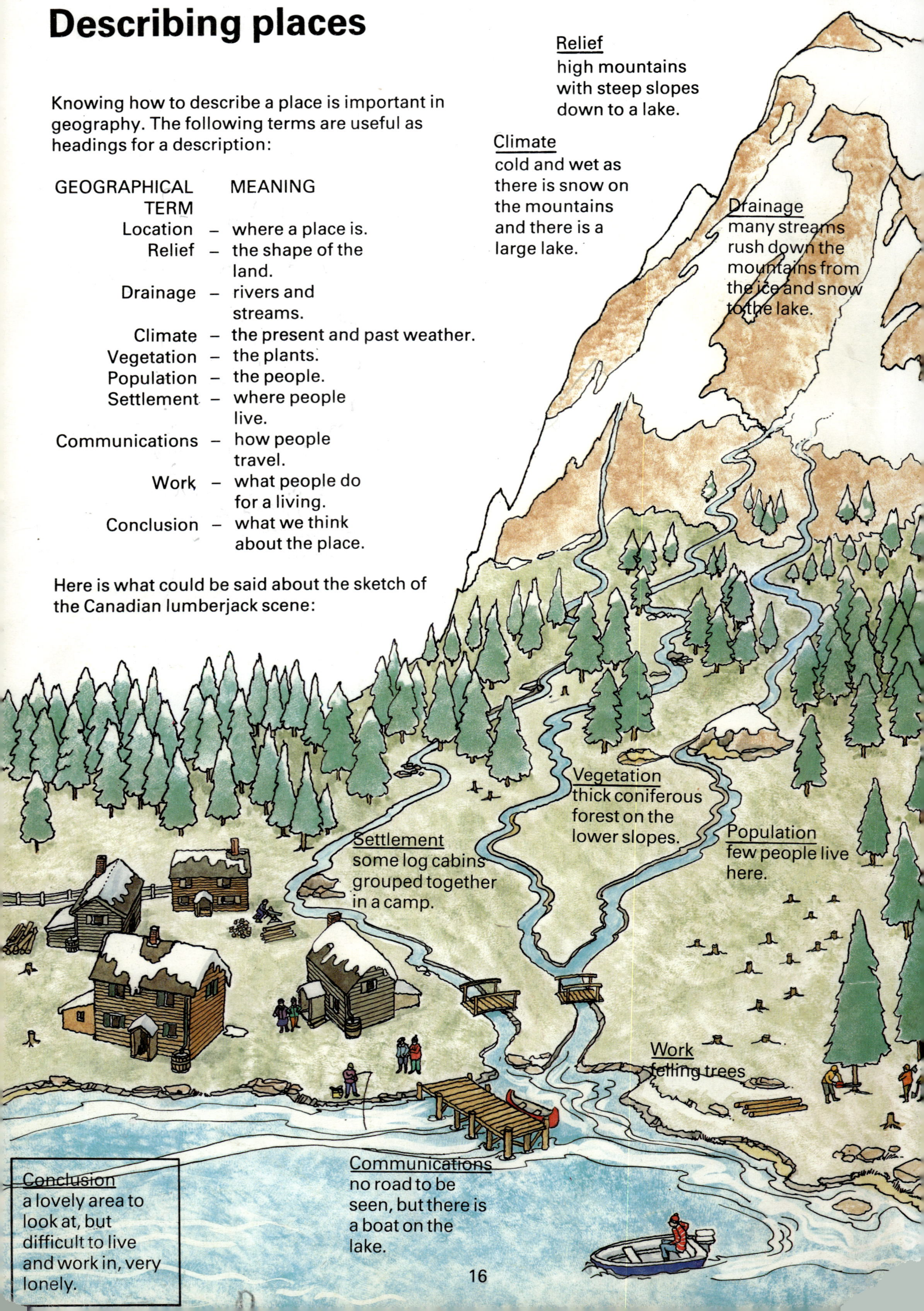

Things to do/Describing places

1 Study the sketch and the writing opposite.

2 Write down the list of ten geographical terms and what each means.

3 Try to invent a sentence you could use to remember these terms. Each word should start with the first letter –

L . . . R . . . D . . . C . . . V . . . P . . . S . . . C . . . W . . . C . . .

4a The photos below show a village in India.

b Complete the following sentences which describe the area. Select the right word from the two given – either/or?

The location is in Britain/India.

The relief is hilly/mainly flat.

The area has few/many streams.

The climate seems to be hot/cold.

The vegetation has been cleared/is mostly forest.

There are no people/many people living here.

The people live in a village/in a city.

The communications are fast and easy/slow and difficult.

The people work on farms/in factories.

Conclusion – write your own.

Further work

5 Write a description of where you live using all the geographical terms listed.

6 A photograph or sketch can not tell us everything about an area. What things might the photographs of the Indian scene not show?

Summary
A place can be described by setting out a list of geographical terms then writing about each in turn.

Unit 2.4

Using graphs

Graphs are useful in geography. They can be used to show how something changes over time, for example, how much rain falls on average in each month. They can also show how one thing is linked or related to another thing. How long people take to get to school, for example, may be linked to how far away from school they live.

Graphs are drawn using facts and figures. These are called **observations** or **data.** The observations are then plotted on the graph by looking at the numbers along the sides. The graph can be drawn as a line or a set of bars. Sometimes, a scatter of points can be plotted.

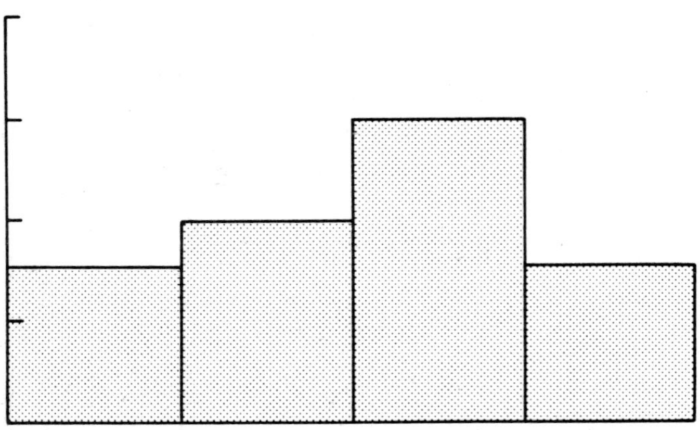

A bar graph

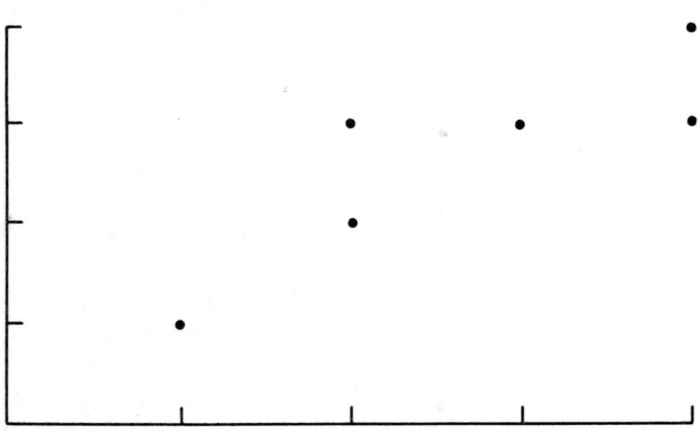

A scatter graph

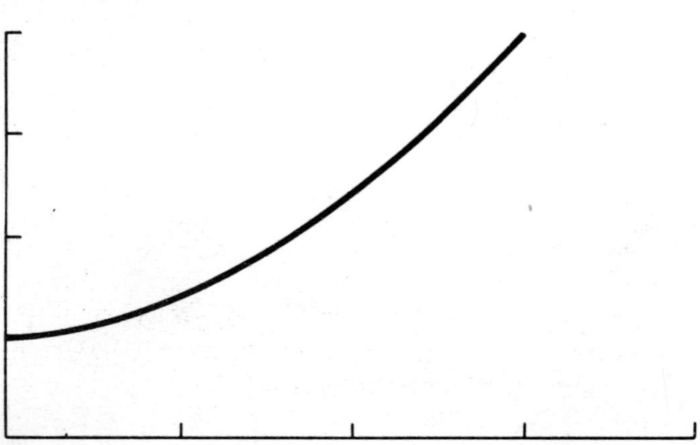

A line graph

Every graph must have

1 A title which says what the graph is about.

2 Full details of the figures along the sides.

3 Carefully plotted data.

4 A comment to say what the graph tells us.

These examples show some of the ways graphs can be used in geography.

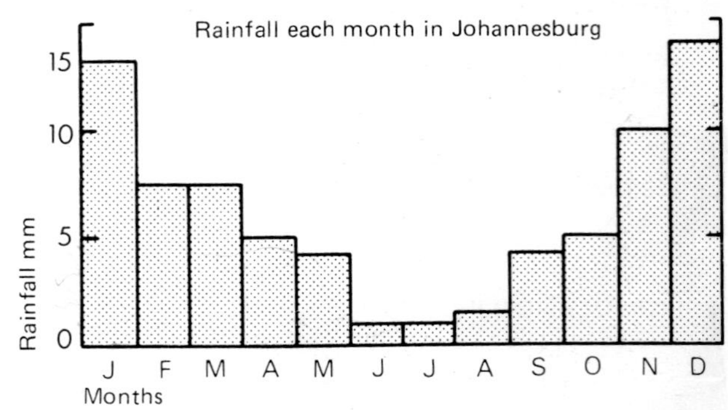

Johannesburg has some rain all year, but most of it comes between November and March.

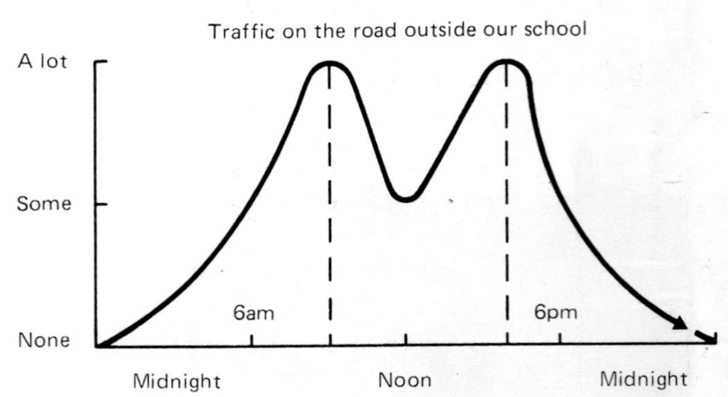

There are two busy times of the day. One is in the morning and the other in late afternoon.

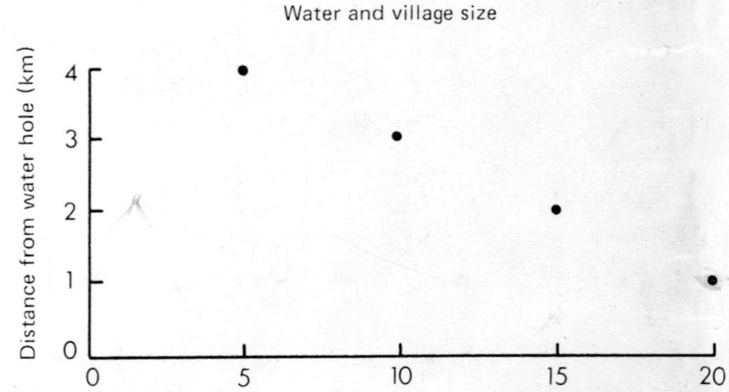

Villages near to water holes are larger than those further away.

Things to do/Using graphs

1 The graph (right) shows the results of a survey of how land was used in a town. The figures have been made into percentages. To find out what percent each bar represents, lay a ruler along the top of the bar, and read off the figure from the scale on the side line.

a Make a list of the different ways the land was used. Write down the percentage for each. For example: Open space 25%

b Now make your own outline of the graph. You should divide the base line into five equal parts and mark on the percentage scale up the side.
Redraw the bars to show each land use type but put them in order, the largest to the left and the smallest to the right.

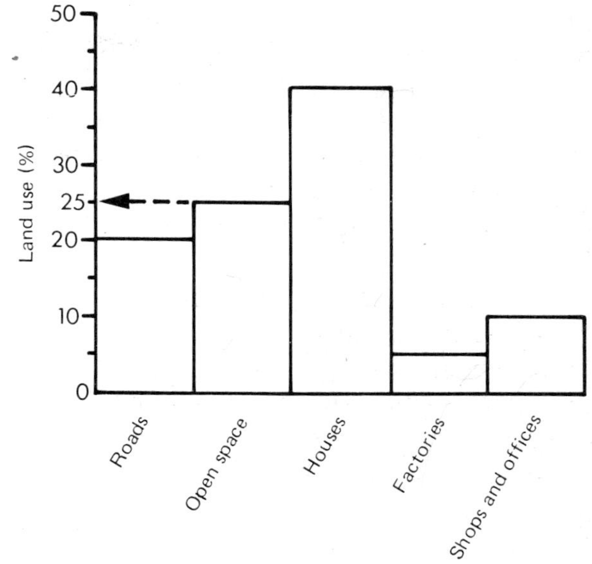

2 The figures below are the results of a survey of cars and lorries passing by a small school. These results have been plotted as a line graph.

a Complete the following sentences by filling in the right word from the list below:

The graph shows the number of . . . and . . . passing the school. There are . . . main peak periods when the traffic is busiest. The first peak comes between . . . and . . . am. The second peak between 4 and 6 pm is . . . than the first.

ten two lorries eight larger cars

b Explain what happens during the day to give the pattern shown on the graph.

Time	6-8am	8-10 am	10-12 am	12-2pm	2-4pm	4-6pm	6-8pm
No. of vehicles	25	175	75	100	75	200	100

Example: Point X shows that between 12 and 2pm, 100 cars and lorries went past

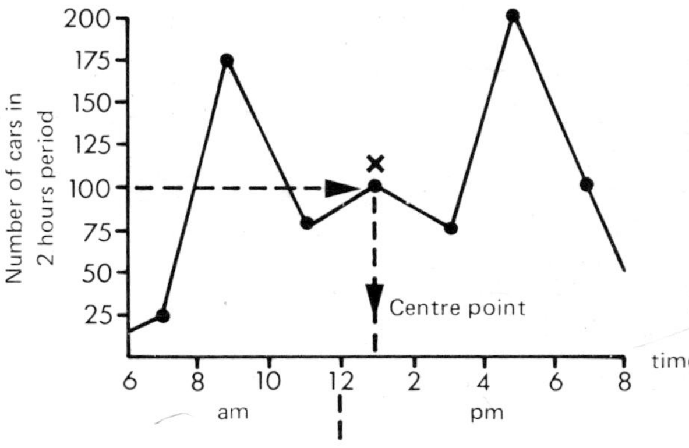

3 It is important to be able to tell when a river is going to break its banks and flood. Flooding usually happens after a period of heavy rain. The diagram (right) shows some average results for one river. As the rainfall rises, so does the depth of the river.

a What is the normal depth of the river?

b After what depth does flooding take place?

c What is the depth of the river after 5 cm of rain?

d How much rain will have fallen for the river to reach flood level?

e Try to work out what the depth of the river will be after 10cm of rain. (It may help if you lay a ruler along the line of dots.)

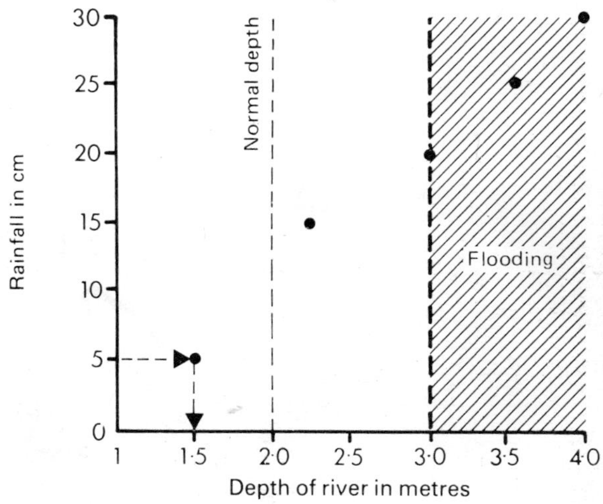

Summary
Graphs are diagrams used to show data clearly. Graphs can be used to describe a situation and to show how one thing is related to another.

Unit 3.1

Maps/Symbols on maps

A map cannot show everything that is on the ground. If it named every building, the map would become cluttered with words. It would be impossible to read. Some things could not be shown at all because they would be too small to mark on. Instead, small drawings called **symbols** are used.

Symbols can be simple drawings of the real thing. A church with a tower is a common map symbol. The square is like the church tower from above. The cross is a religious sign.

Sometimes, the symbol may look nothing like the real thing. You will have to look at the **key** to see what it stands for.

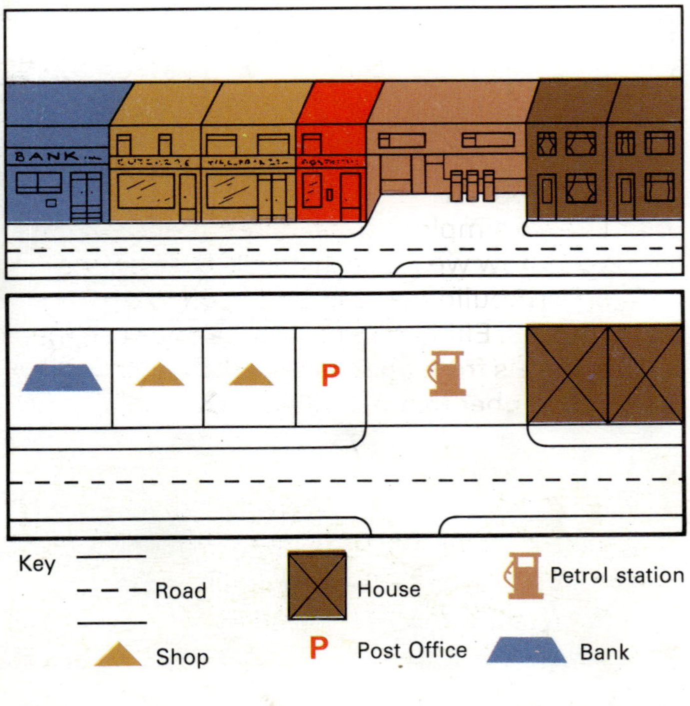

Sometimes, capital letters are used to save writing the whole word.

The map and sketch show the area around the fictitious villages of Ham and Lowton. See how important the map key is.

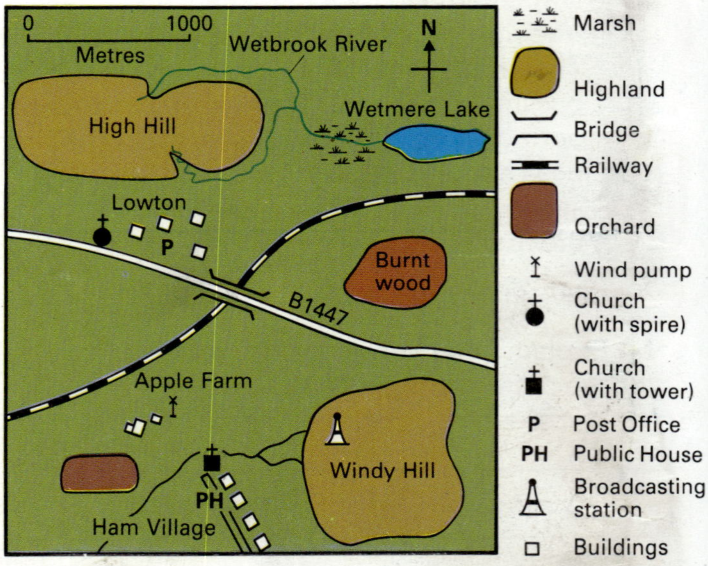

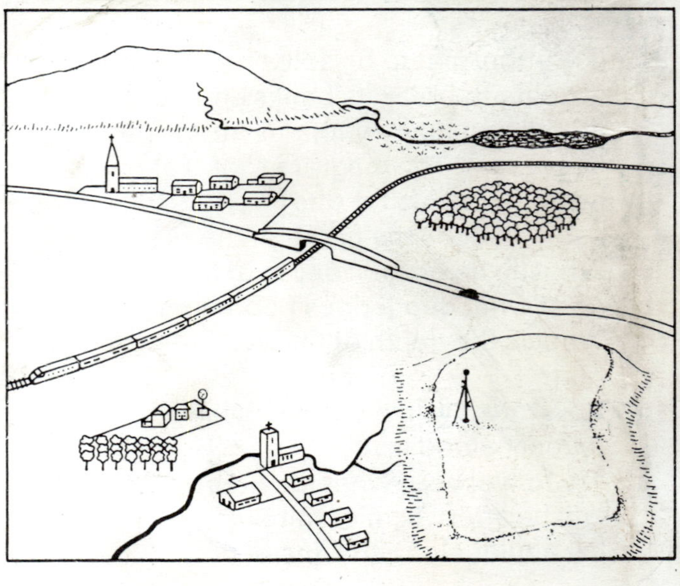

Things to do/Symbols on maps

1a Draw and write down what this common symbol means.

b Draw some other symbols which you have seen, either in the street, on shops, or on packages.

2 Study these sketches and symbols. Draw the symbols and say what you think each one means.

Sketches **Symbols**

3 Make a copy of the partly drawn map of Kirkby below. Fill in the map with symbols by looking at the sketch of the area. Use the same key that was used on the map on the opposite page.

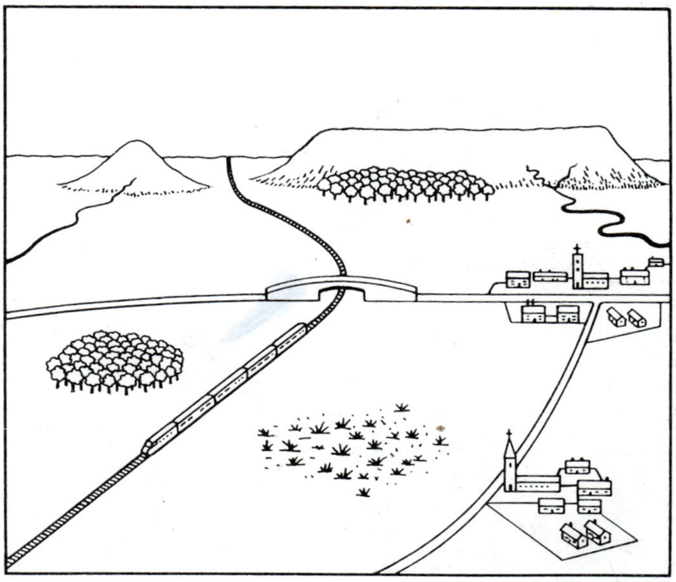

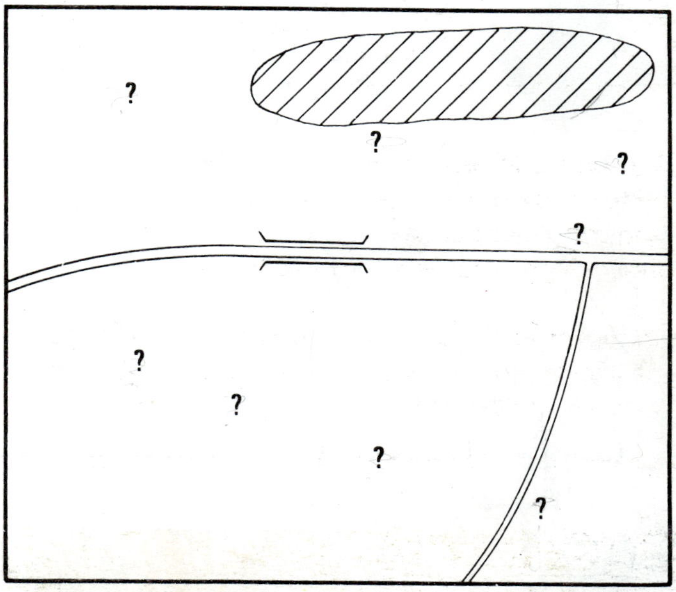

Further work

4 Draw a simple map of some streets which you know well. Use symbols to show the special buildings and other points of interest. Either invent your own, or use the symbols from an Ordnance Survey map. Remember to draw a key.

Summary

Symbols are simple drawings which show important things on a map. The symbols must be explained in a key.

Unit 3.2

Distances on maps

A map can be used to see how far one place is from another. Every map should have a **scale line.** This will tell the real distances which the map shows.

Map **A** shows part of the town where Bill and Joe live. To see how far it is from Bill's home to school, follow these simple steps.

1. Lay a piece of paper with a straight edge along the route from Bill's house to school.
2. Mark off the distance on the paper. (Diagram **B**)
3. Find the line scale at the bottom of the map **C**. Mark off the scale on the paper until the distance has been completed.

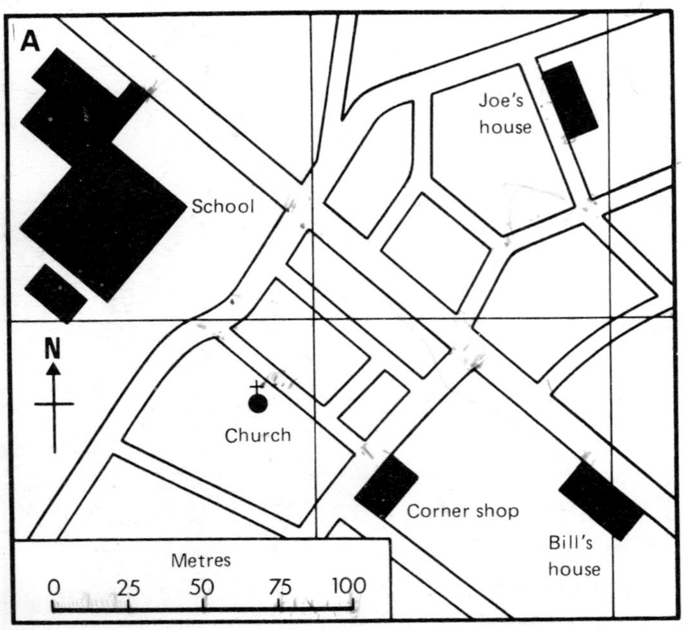

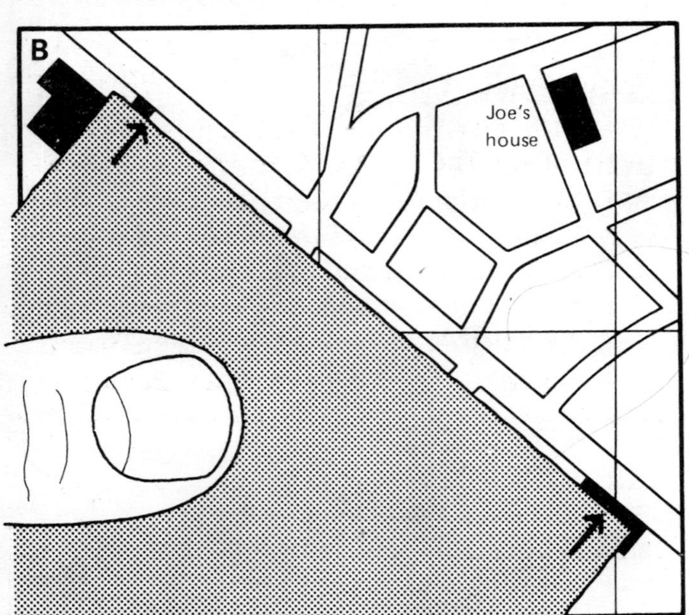

To measure from Joe's house to the school, use the straight edge but turn it each time you reach a corner. You could also use a cotton thread. Cotton is more useful if the route is winding, like along a river.

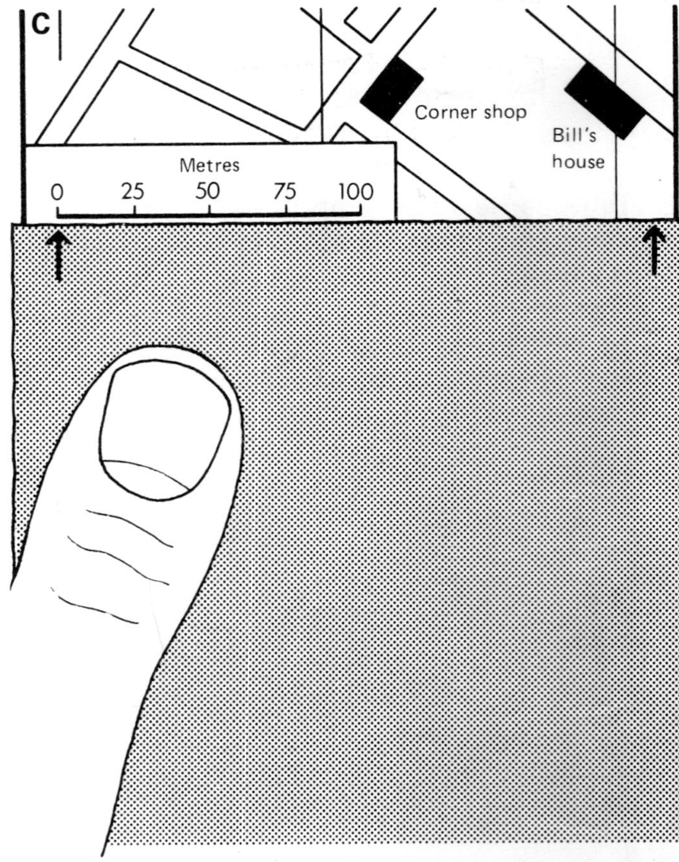

All the information about distances can be put in a simple set of boxes. This is called a **matrix.** Now you can see how near each place is to all the others.

Example: Bill's house to school is 200 metres.

	Bill's house	Joe's house	School
Bill's house			200
Joe's house			
School			

Things to do/Distances on maps

1 Study map **A** on the page opposite. Copy and complete the following sentences by working out the straight line distances:

- **a** The distance between Bill's home and the school is . . . metres.
- **b** The map measures . . . metres from North to South.
- **c** The distance from East to West across the map is . . . metres.
- **d** The corner shop to the church is . . . metres.

2 Work out the following distances by measuring along the shortest route by road.

- **a** Joe's home to the corner shop is . . . metres.
- **b** It is . . . metres from Bill's home to the corner shop.
- **c** It is . . . metres from the school to the church.

3 Copy the matrix diagram. Look back at your answers to questions **1** and **2** then fill in the matrix.

	Bill's house	Joe's house	Church
Bill's house		175 metres	
Joe's house			
Church			

4 Work out the following distances:

ROUTE	BY ROAD	BY STRAIGHT LINE	DIFFERENCE (subtract straight line from road distance)
Bill to Joe			
Joe to School			
Bill to church			

Further work

5 The table below gives the distance by road between the five towns shown in the map. Draw another table but instead measure and fill in the straight line distances between the towns. (For example, Huddersfield to Wakefield is 20 km.)

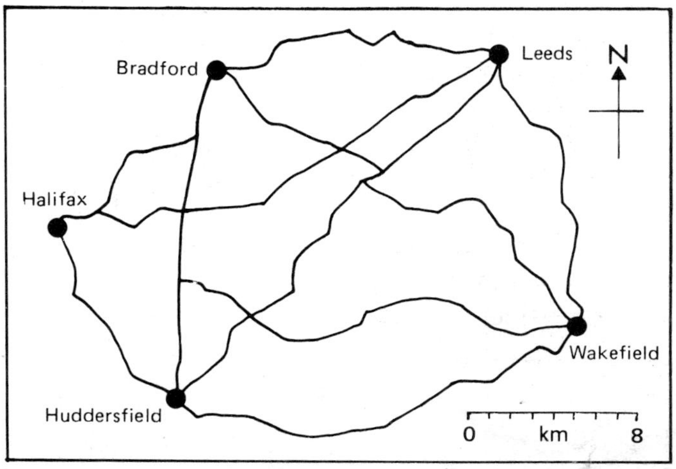

Road distances in North West Yorkshire (in km)

	Bradford	Leeds	Wakefield	Halifax
Leeds	14			
Wakefield	24	16		
Halifax	13	26	27	
Huddersfield	18	34	22	13

Summary

Distances on a map can be measured using a line scale. The scale line shows what the real distance is.

Unit 3.3

Height on maps

A map is drawn on a flat piece of paper. But the ground is seldom flat. Map makers have to find a way of showing whether the land is high or low, steep or flat.

This sketch shows an area where the ground is sloping. It is a gentle slope at first, but becomes quite steep towards the North. On a map, this can be drawn in three ways.

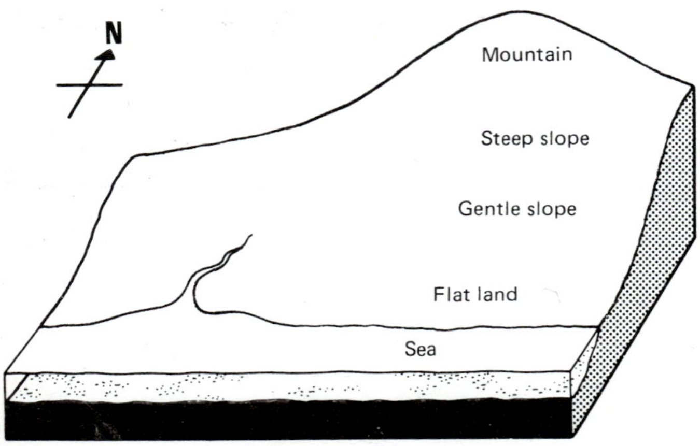

A

A surveyor can find the height at a **sample** of places. The actual height is then plotted exactly on the map. A point where the exact height is shown is called a **spot height.**

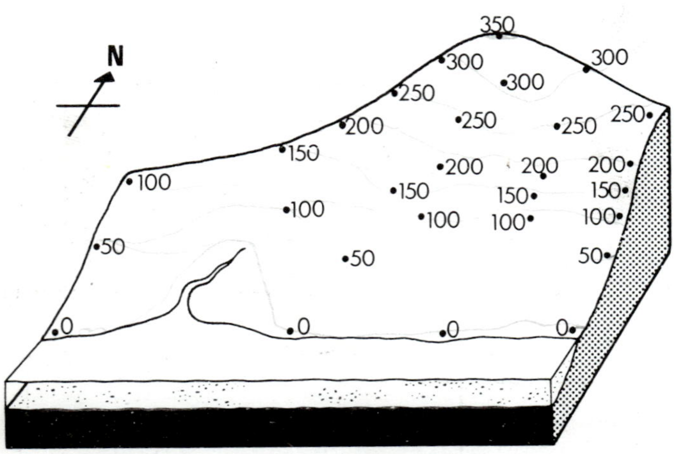

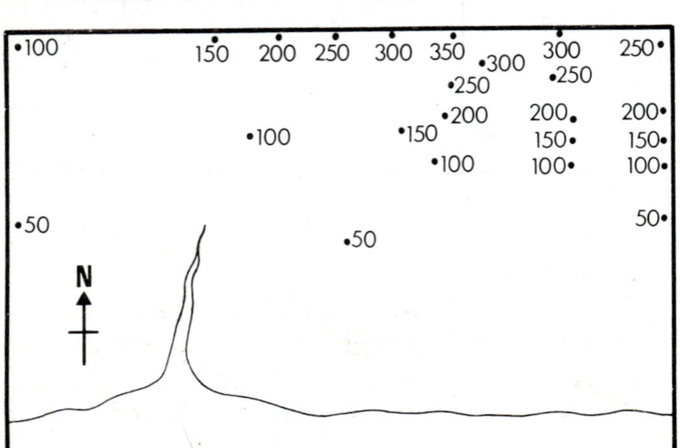

The mapmaker can then join up the places which have the same height. Lines which join places that are the same height are called **contour lines.**

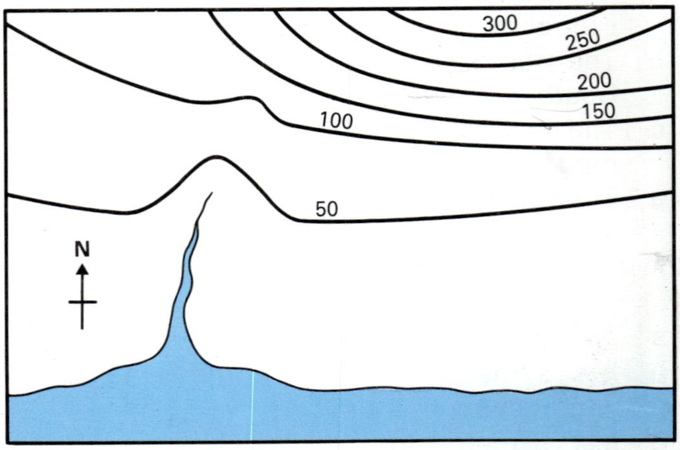

Layer shading is when large areas of high land are shaded or coloured.

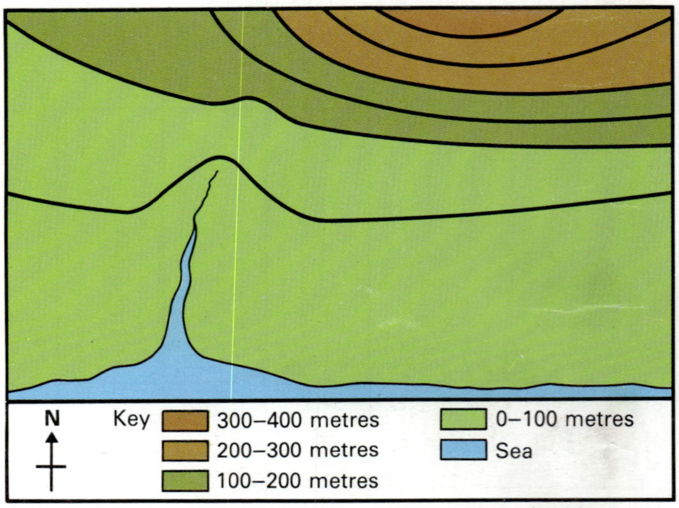

A **cross-section** is a diagram which cuts a slice out of the ground. This will show how steep the slopes are.

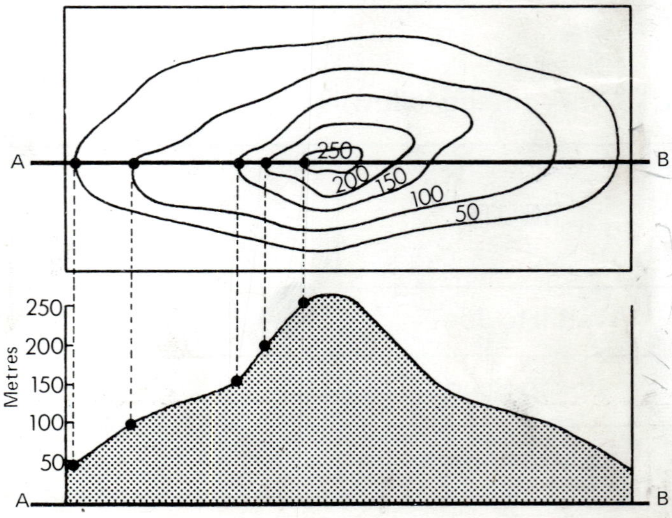

Things to do/Height on maps

1 Study sketch **A** on the opposite page. Copy the outline below and complete by filling in the following words:

mountain	flat land
steep slope	sea
gentle slope	

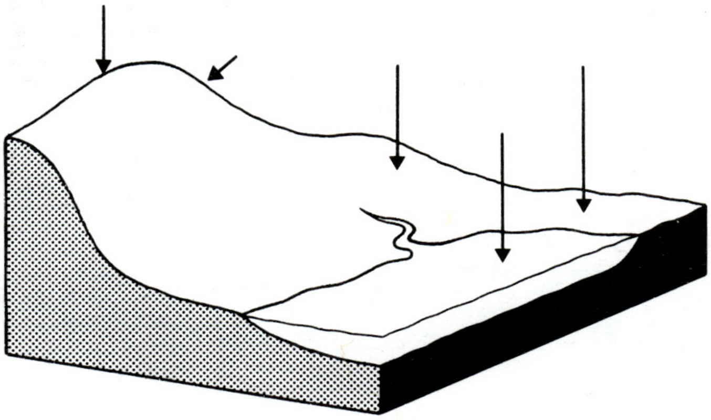

2 Write out the sentence which tells you what each of the following means:

Cross section	Layer shading
Spot height	Contour line

3 On this diagram, spot heights have been marked in.

a Draw or trace the map.

b Join up the contour lines which have been started. Note that the lines must not touch or cross each other.

c Shade in the map using different colours for land between the contours. Make a copy of the key below the map and fill it in with the colour you are using.

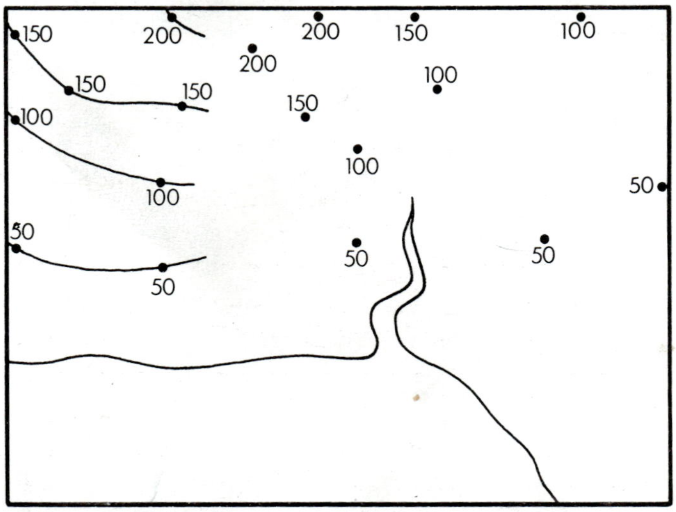

Key	
☐ 0-100 metres	☐ 200-300 metres
☐ 100-200 metres	☐ Sea

Further work

4 A railway company wants to build a line from East to West over the area shown on the maps below. They need to know which route would be the best. The best route would have the most gentle slopes.

a Draw a cross section along each of the two possible routes shown. On your diagram, label in places which have steep slopes, gentle slopes, or are flat.

b Which route would be best: **A** to **B** or **C** to **D**?

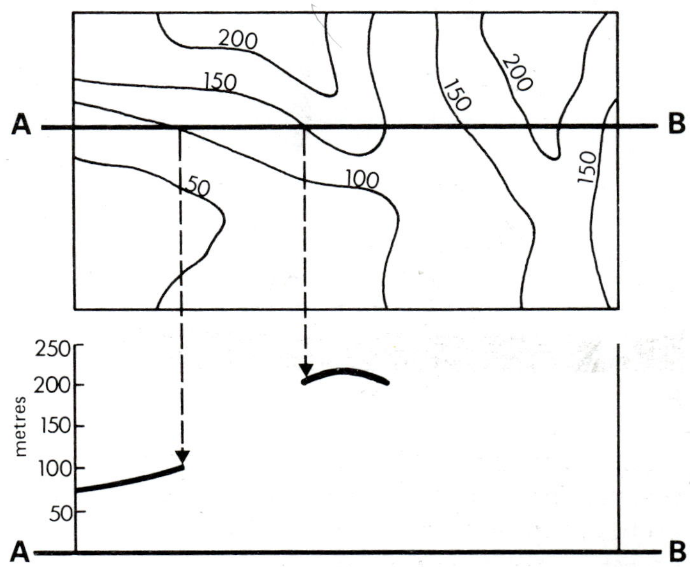

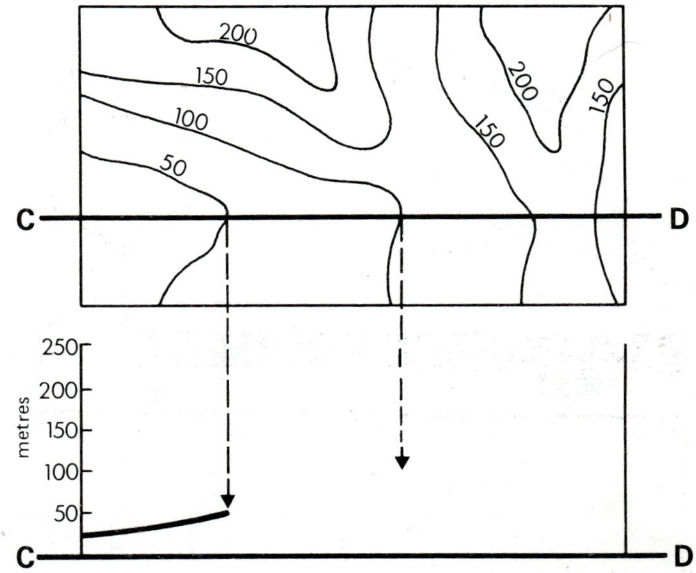

Summary

There are three ways of showing height on a map. They are spot heights, contours and layer shading. Cross section drawings can show the slope of the land.

Unit 3.4

Grid references

Most maps are divided into squares by thin lines called **grid lines.** These lines can help us find places quickly. We can also measure areas using these squares.

This map shows where Ann lives and where she keeps her pony. Ann lives in square 1510. This is called a **four figure reference.**

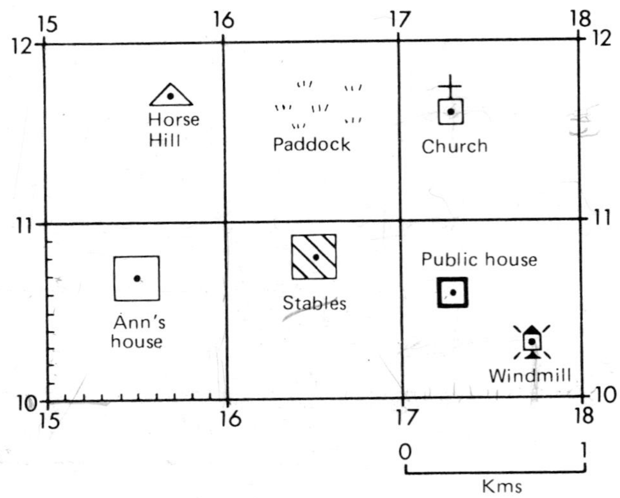

A

1 The first two numbers (15) come from the line which is the left side of the square. If you follow this line down to the bottom of the map you see the number 15.

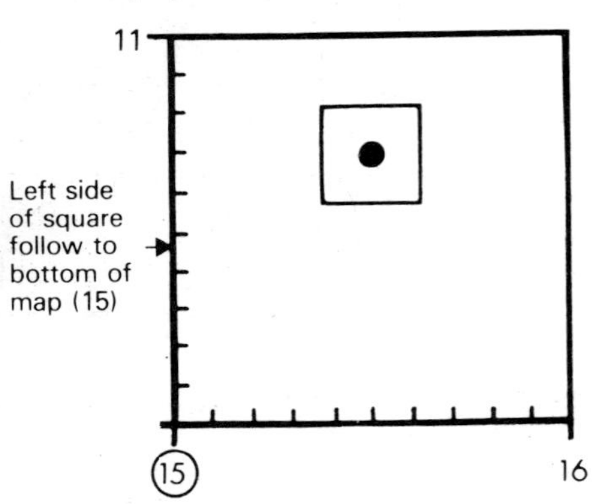

2 The second two numbers (10) come from the bottom line of the square. Follow it to the edge of the map. It is 10.

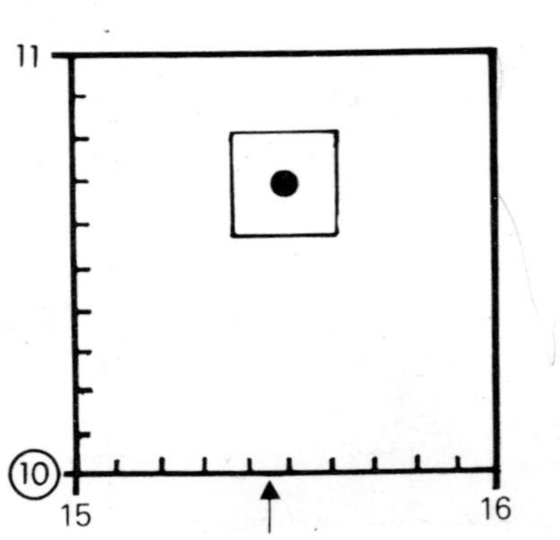

Bottom line – follow to edge of map (10)

A more exact spot on the map can be given using a **six figure reference.**

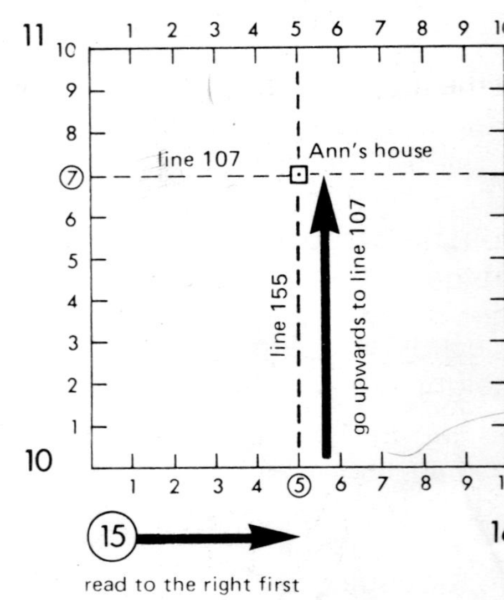

1 First write down the four figure reference, but leave two gaps: 15 – 10 –

2 Then imagine that each side of the square is divided into 10 parts.

3 The house is half way along, or $\frac{5}{10}$ths towards line 16.

4 It is almost $\frac{3}{4}$ way along, or $\frac{7}{10}$ths towards line 11.

5 So the six figure grid reference is written 155 107.

Remember, go 'along the corridors' to 155, then up the stairs to 107.

Area

If we know the scale of the map, the squares can be counted to give the area. On map **A** each grid square would be 1 sq. km in area. The area of the whole map would be 6 x 1 sq km = 6 sq kms.

Things to do/Grid references

1a Make a copy of the grid diagram below.

b Fill in the correct grid numbers in the spaces.

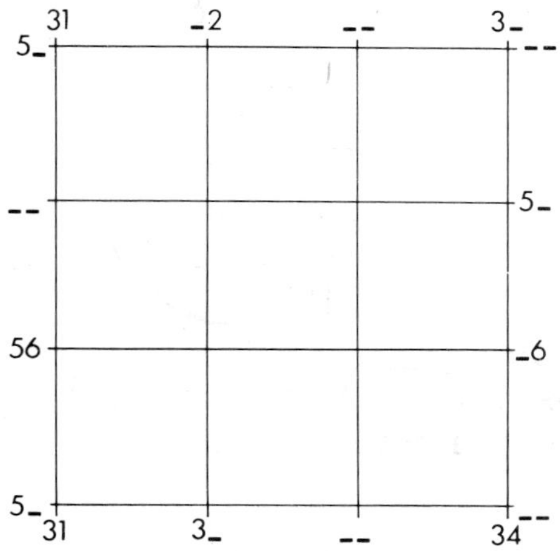

2 Study the map on the opposite page. (**A**) Write out the passage below filling in the spaces with the grid numbers.

Ann's house is in square 15 – –
She keeps her pony in the stables in square – – 10. The stables are beside the paddock in square – – – –
Every day she rides her pony to the church at 173 11 – Then she gallops to the windmill at 17 – 10 – Finally, she walks the pony back to the stables, passing a public house (P.H.) at grid reference – – – – – –

3a Draw the simple map below.

b Copy and complete the two charts by writing down what is at the grid references.

c How many square kms does the map show?

Further work

4 Using a 1:50,000 scale Ordnance Survey map, write down a 6 figure grid reference for as many of the following that you can find:
church with tower – church with spire – mile stone – telephone box – post office – youth hostel – railway station – bus/coach station – windmill.

Summary
Grid lines can help you describe where a place is on a map. They also help measure area.

CHART 1	
Reference	What is there
0922 0622	

CHART 2 6 figure references	
Reference	What is there
055225 063217	

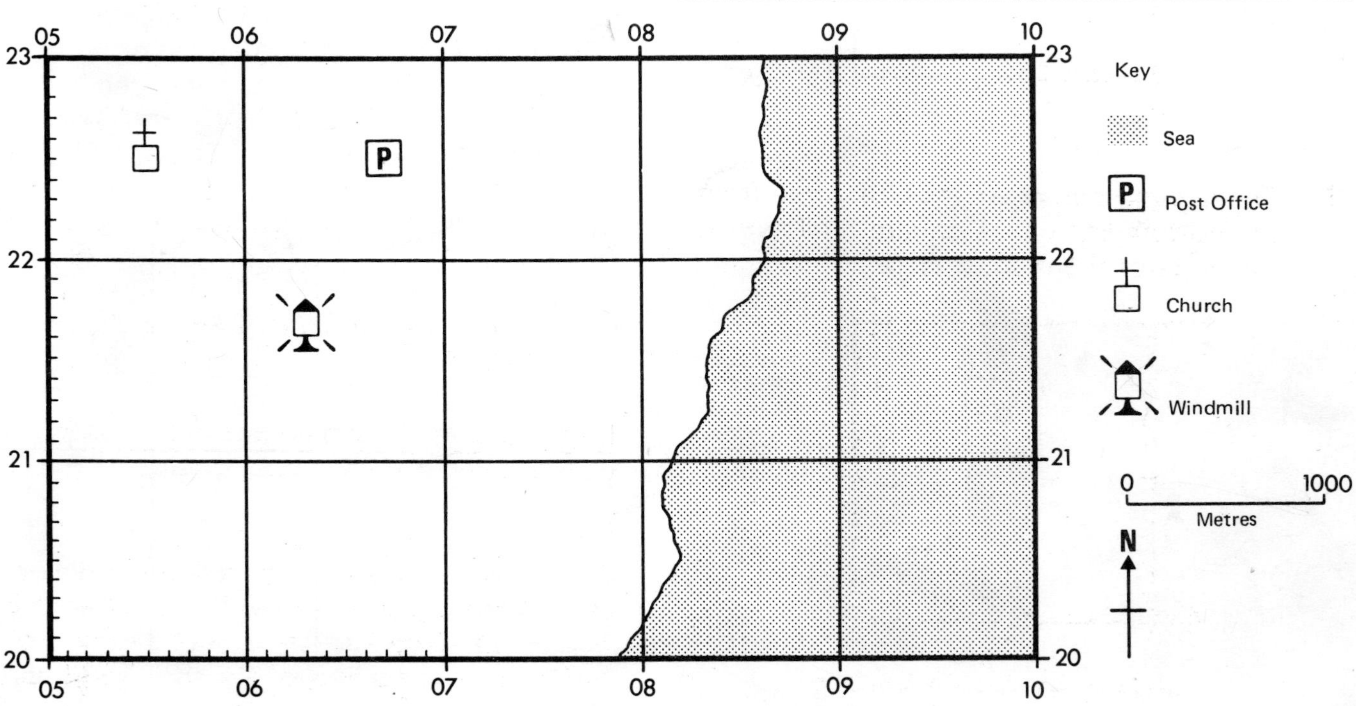

Unit 4.1
Physical maps

Some of the things you see in the landscape are made by people. Towns, roads, bridges, and factories are examples. These are called **human features.**

Other things are the work of nature. The rain, rivers, the sea, volcanoes have made these features. These are called **physical** features.

These diagrams show some examples of both human and physical features.

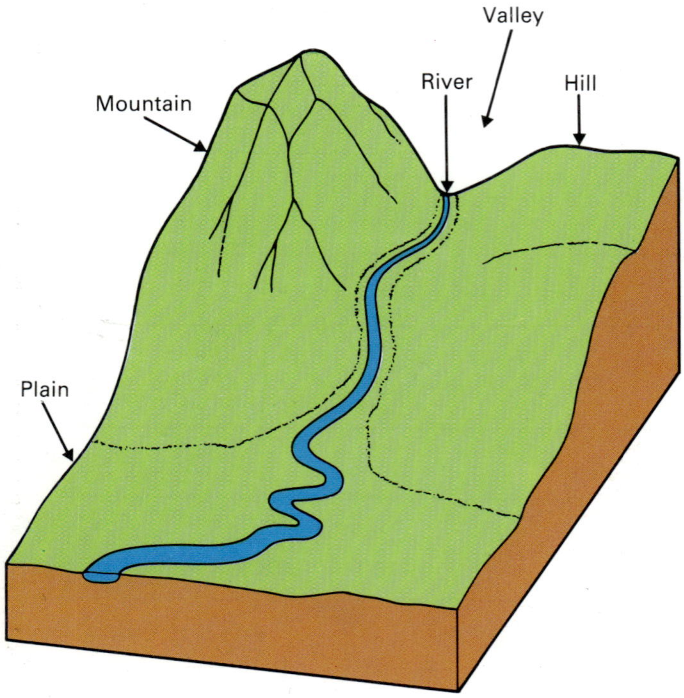

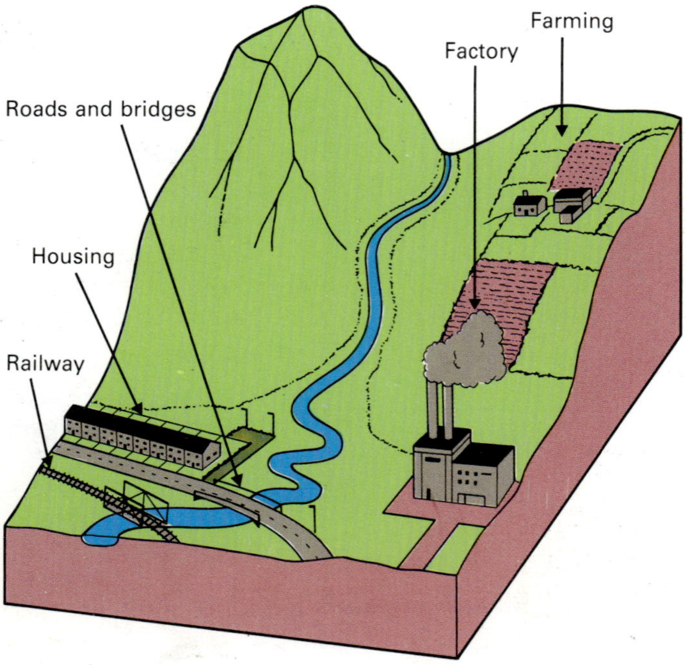

A physical map shows only the features which nature has made. The map shows the physical geography of England and Wales.

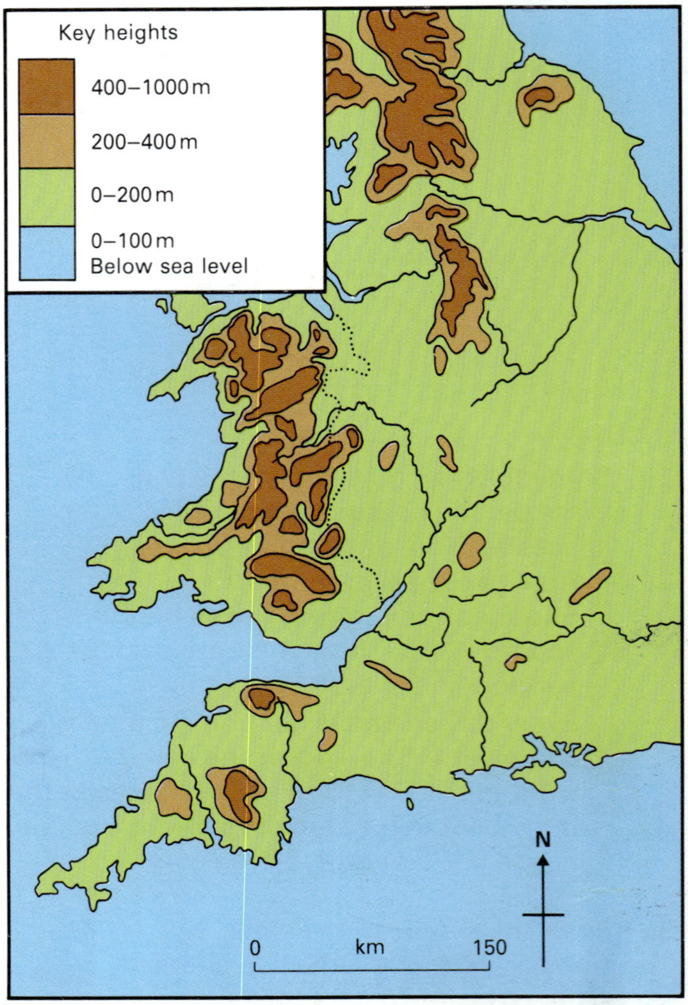

The Atlas uses different colours to show how high the land is. The usual colours used are given below. With a little imagination, you should see why these colours are used.

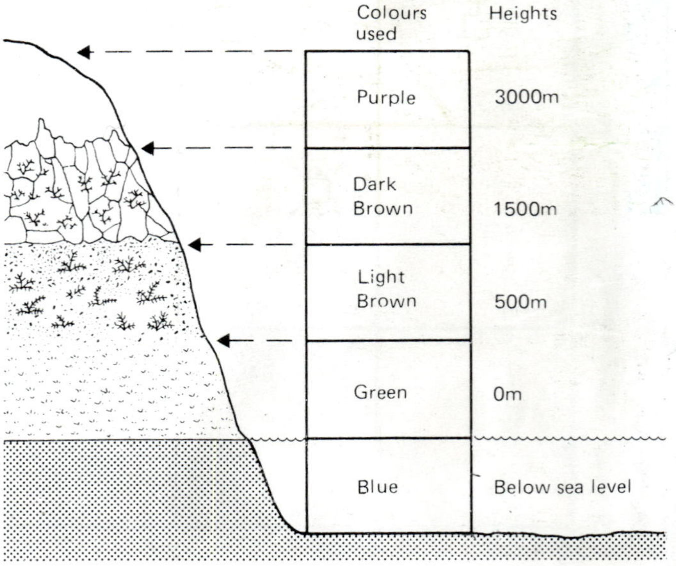

Things to do/Physical maps

1 Which of these three maps shows the physical landforms of the area? Explain your answer.

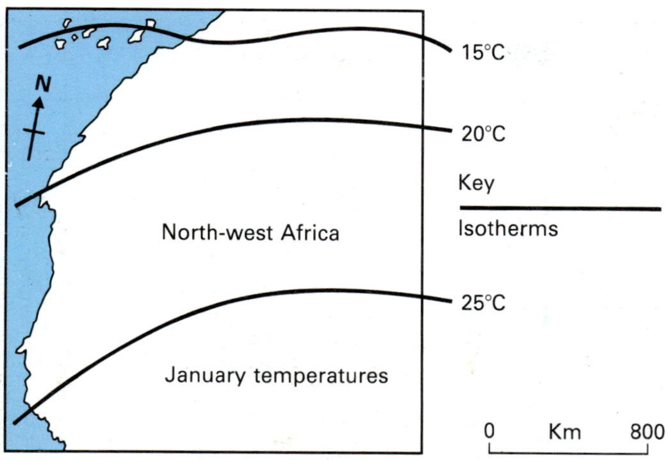

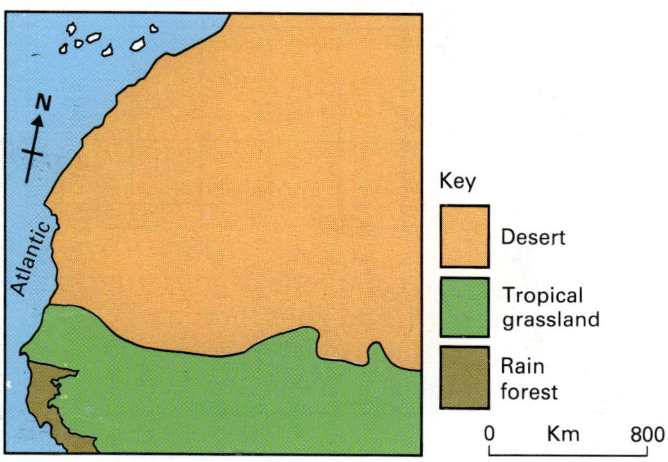

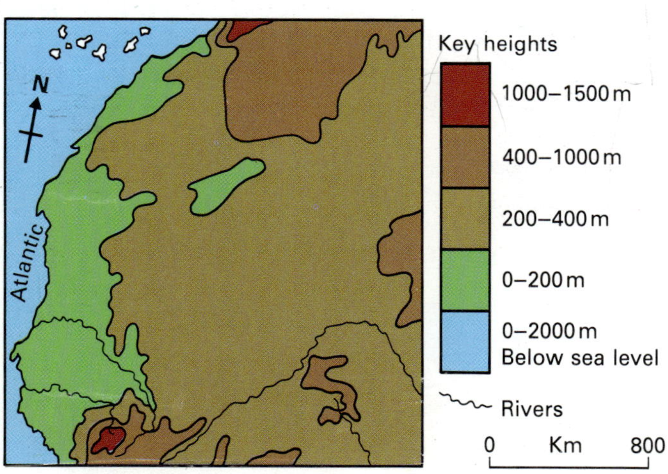

2 Copy out the words below. By the side of each, write down whether it is a human (man-made) or a physical (made by nature) feature.

a	River	f	Beach
b	Canal	g	Swimming pool
c	Plain	h	Hill
d	Valley	i	Sea
e	Village	j	City

3 Write down the page number in your Atlas where the following maps are found. Look them up in the contents page.

a North America: Physical
b South America: Physical
c Asia: Physical
d Europe: Physical
e Africa: Physical
f The World: Physical

4a Trace or copy this map of India. Draw the key outline as well.

b Shade in the map using the colours suggested in the key.

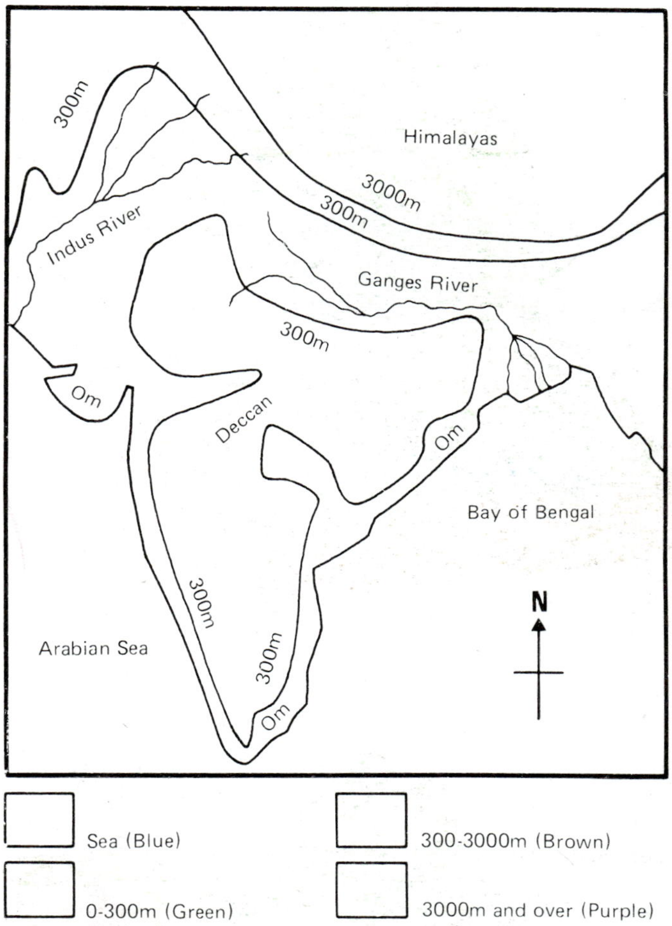

Further work

5 Find a physical map of one country in your Atlas. Draw a cross-section from one side to the other to show the main physical features. Name in the rivers, hills, plains and the mountains that the line crosses.

Summary

Physical maps show things that have been made by nature.

Unit 4.2

Latitude and Longitude

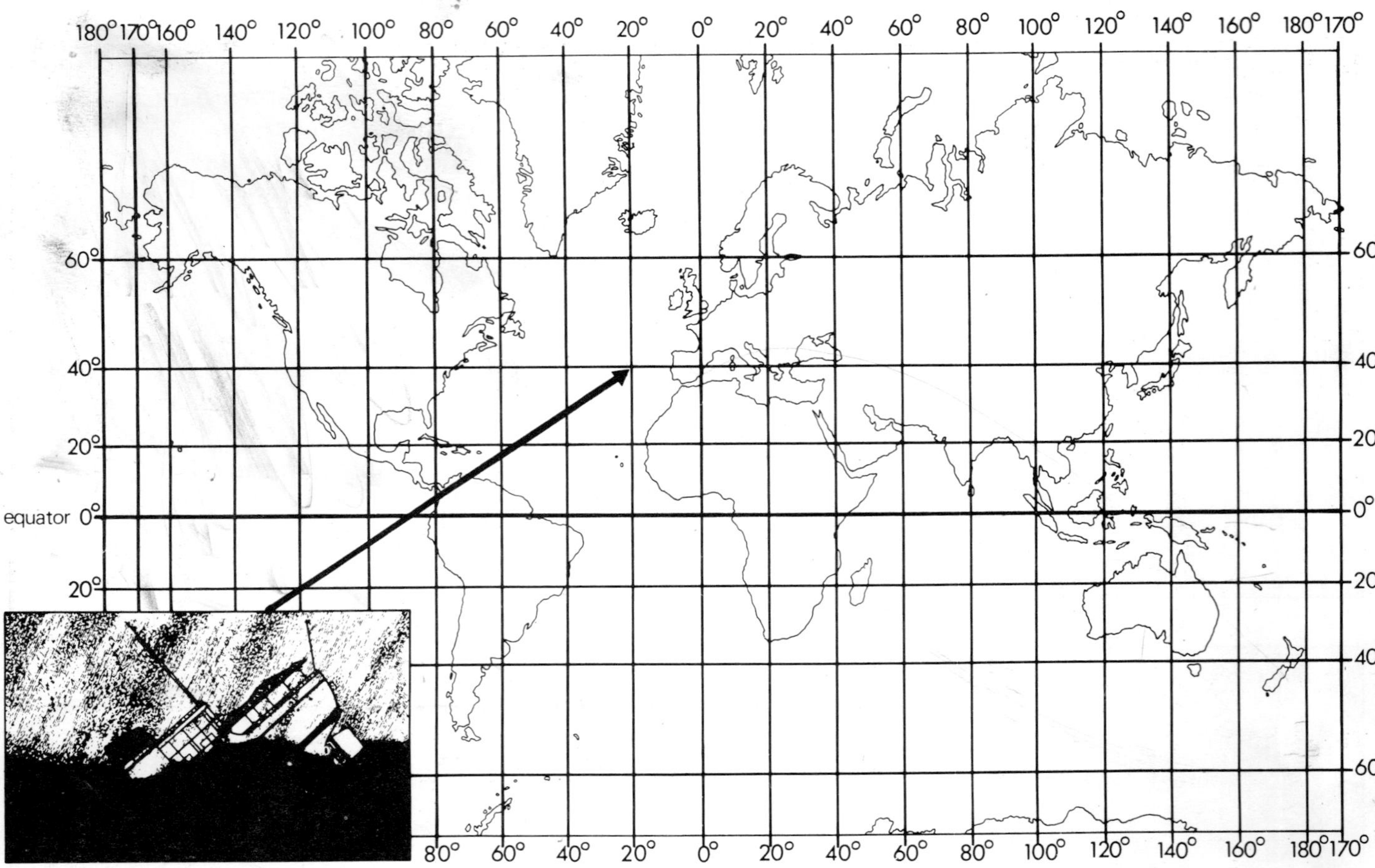

'Mayday, Mayday, Mayday – 40°N 20°W'. This was the message that came over the radio receiver. It meant that a ship was in distress, sinking somewhere in one of the world's oceans.

Mayday sounds like 'm'aider' which means 'help me' in French. But where is 40°N and 20°W and what does it mean?

The message is a short way of saying:

'40° north of latitude 0°'
and
'20° west of longitude 0°'

To help pinpoint ships and aeroplanes, lines of latitude and longitude are drawn on the world map until it looks like a grid. Latitude 0° is a line which goes round the middle of the earth and is

called the Equator. Longitude 0° goes from top to bottom on the earth and goes through Greenwich. Other lines of latitude and longitude are drawn on parallel to these two. Look at the diagrams.

By finding where latitude line 40°N meets longitude 20°W, the ship's position can be found. Now at least other ships will know where to start looking for the survivors.

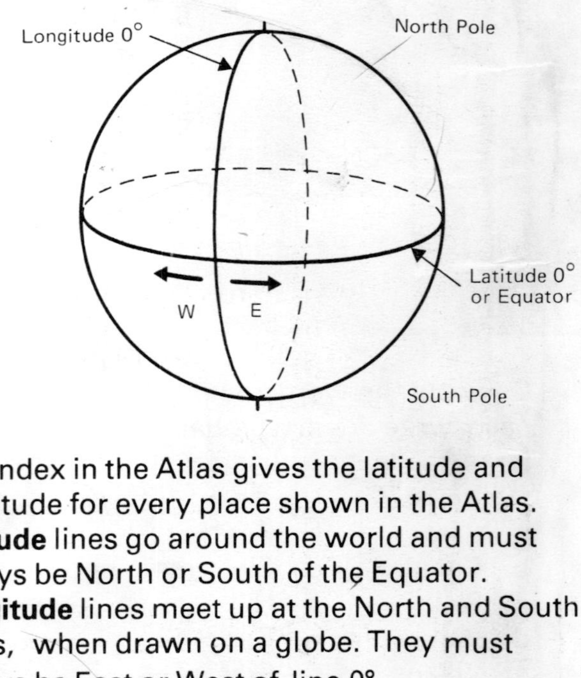

The index in the Atlas gives the latitude and longitude for every place shown in the Atlas. **Latitude** lines go around the world and must always be North or South of the Equator. **Longitude** lines meet up at the North and South Poles, when drawn on a globe. They must always be East or West of line 0°.

Things to do/Latitude and Longitude

1a Copy this map.

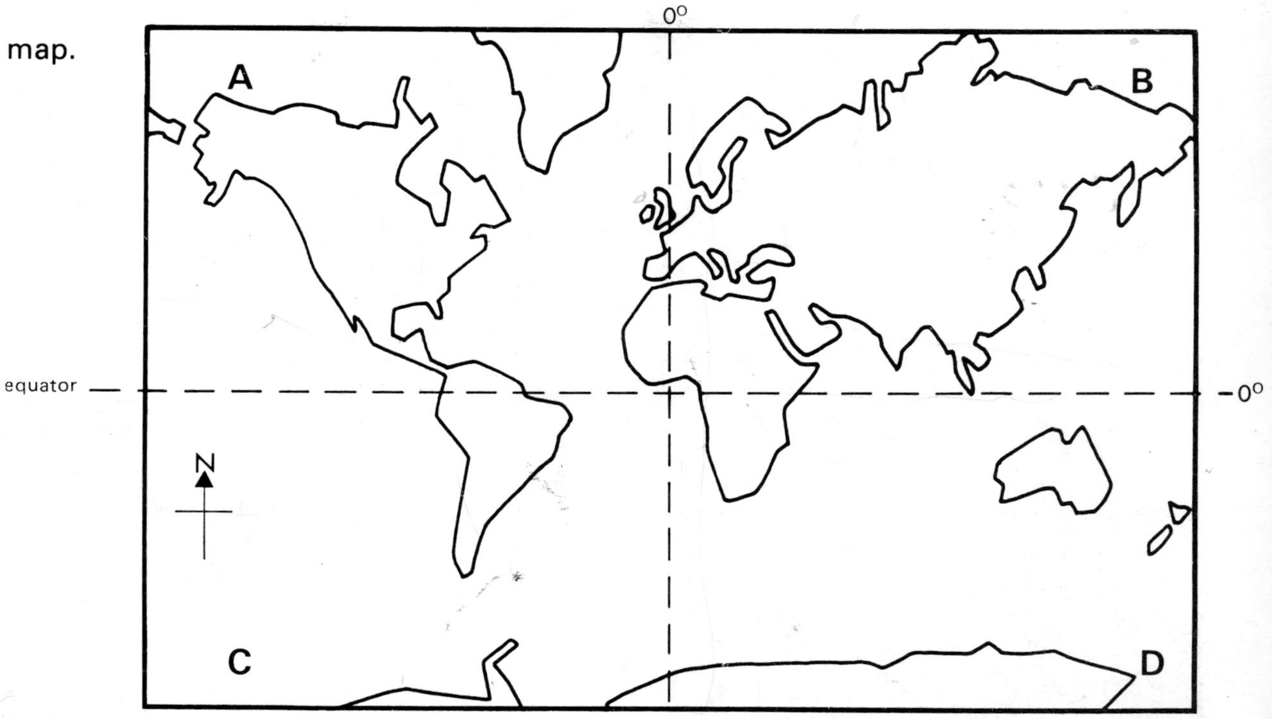

b In which quarter of the world would the following places be – answer either **A,B,C** or **D**:

10°N 15°W　　5°S 1°W
20°N 90° E　　60°S 170°W
80°S 150°E

2 Complete the following sentences:

a Lines of latitude are always . . . . of the Equator

b Lines of longitude are always . . . . of Greenwich

c Latitude 0° is also called . . . .

d Longitude 0° passes through . . . .

Use these words to fill in the gaps.
East or West, Greenwich, the Equator, North or South.

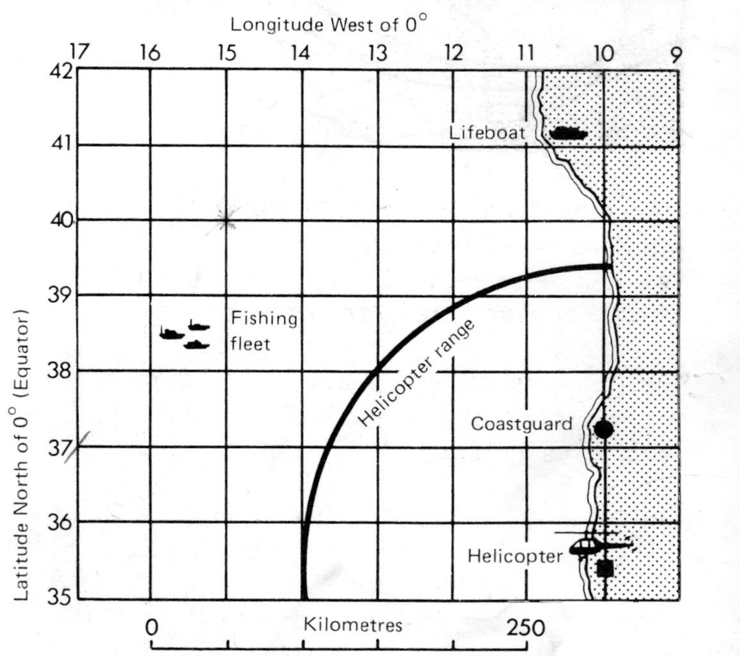

3 The coastguard receives an SOS call. A small aeroplane has come down at sea. The pilot manages to give his position. It is 40°N 15°W.

a Either trace or copy the map.

b Mark in where the aeroplane has come down.

c Now work out what you would do.
Call out the helicopter?
Send out the lifeboat?
Contact the fishing fleet?
Ask a cargo ship at 37°N 13°W to go to the rescue?

Measure the distance between each possible rescuer and the crash site. Then say which you think the coastguard should call.

Further work

4 Using an Atlas, look up the exact figure for the following lines of latitude:
Tropic of Cancer – Tropic of Capricorn – Arctic Circle – Antarctic Circle – the North Pole – the South Pole.
What degree of longitude is the international date line?

Summary
Lines of latitude and longitude help pinpoint places around the globe. They work like a giant grid.

Unit 4.3

Political maps

There are many kinds of map in an Atlas. **Political** maps only show countries with their main towns and cities. Sometimes, main roads and railways are also drawn.

This map shows part of Europe. It is a political map because only the countries and most important cities are shown.

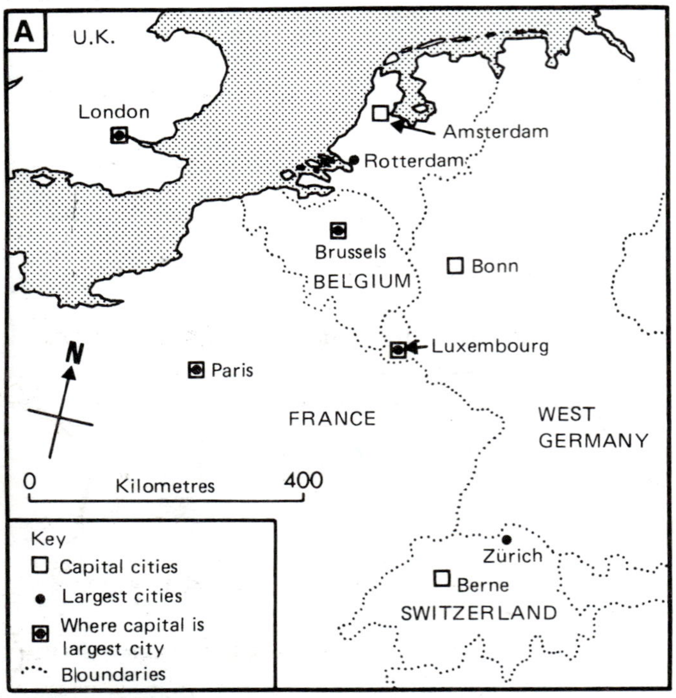

Every country has a **capital** city. This is where the government works from. The capital city is often the largest city in the country, but this is not always true.

Sometimes, countries make **agreements** so that people and goods can move more easily between them and so that they can help each other. They can also join together to defend themselves.

The map below shows countries in Europe which have joined together to trade more easily. This union is called the Common Market (E.E.C.). Each has kept its own government so they are still separate countries.

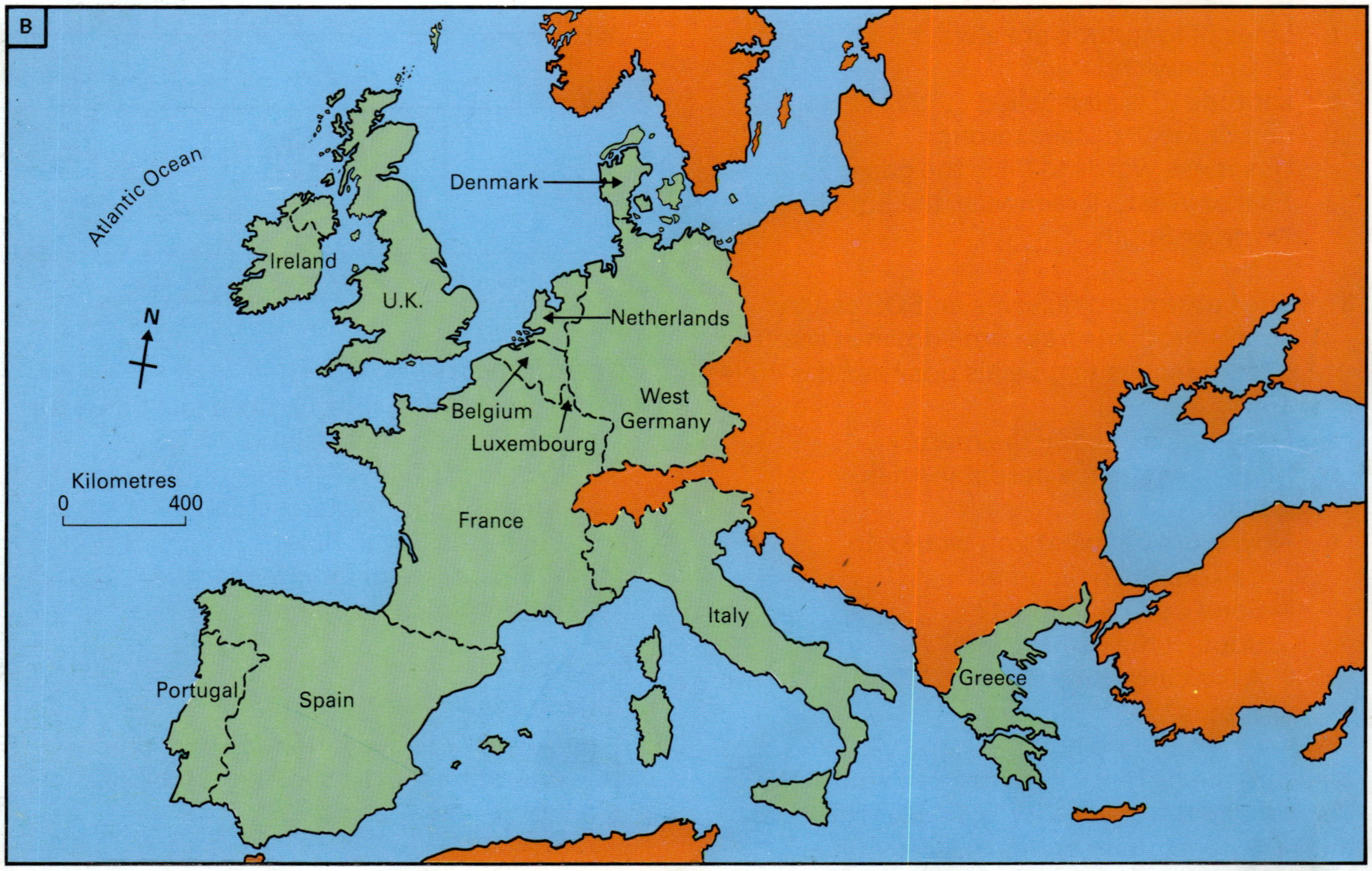

Things to do/Political maps

1 One of the three maps drawn below is a political map. Say which one it is and explain why.

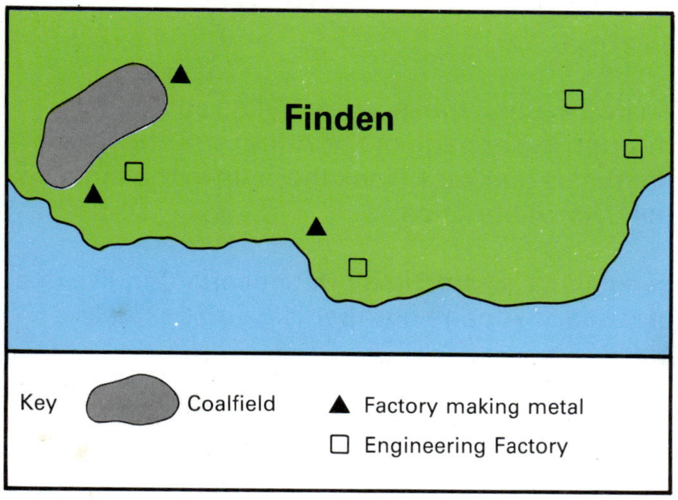

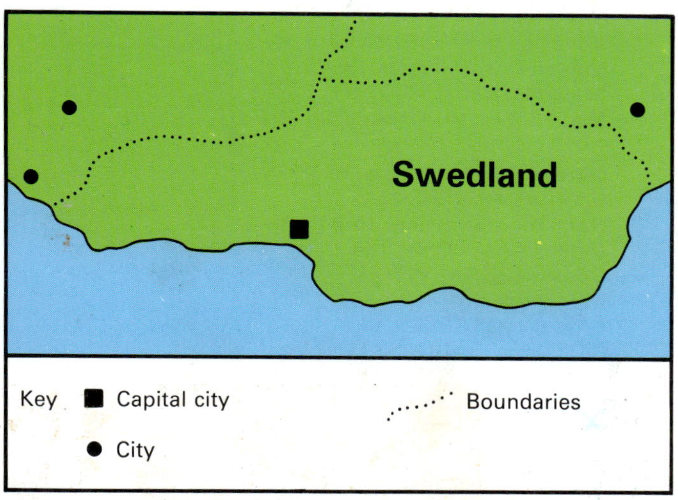

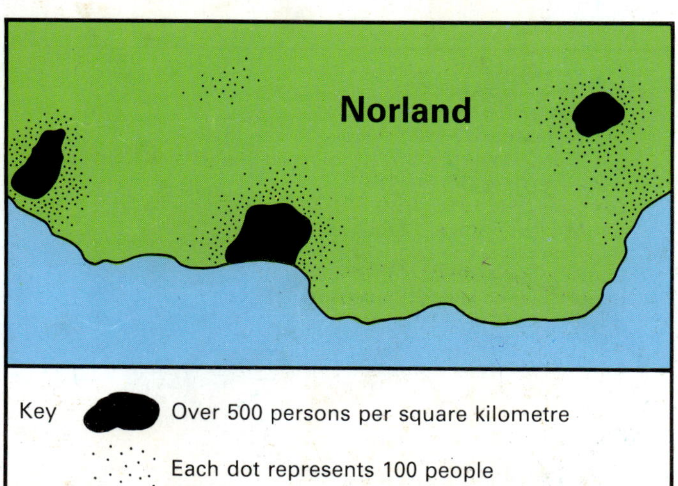

2 Study map **B** of Europe on the opposite page.
Answer the following questions:

a Which two countries in Europe are islands?

b How many countries on the map are in E.E.C?

c List the countries below. For each, write down the names of all the countries which directly touch them:

Country	Other countries which touch them
France	Belgium ....
Netherlands	....
Switzerland	....
Denmark	....

d In which countries is the capital city not the largest city?

3 Look up a political map of South America in your Atlas.

a What colour is used to show the boundary lines between the countries?

b How many countries are there in South America?

c For each country, name one large city.

Further work

4 This map shows part of South America.

a Copy or trace the map.

b Using no more than three colours or different types of shading, shade in the map. Make sure that no countries shaded the same touch each other.

Summary

Political maps show countries and their main cities. Every country has a capital city. Countries sometimes make agreements to help each other.

Unit 4.4

The Atlas/Looking up places

Meet Henri, a chef and restaurant owner. He has become world famous for cooking the foods of different countries. His menu looks like this:

Henri's daughter Sylvia wants to know where these countries are in the world. The **Atlas** will give the answer.

The **contents** page will give a page number for either the country or the continent.

CONTENTS ③

SOUTH AMERICA

Mountains, Lowlands and Rivers	32
Countries, Towns, Roads and Railways	33
Types of environment	34
Discovery and exploration	34
Farming, mining and fishing	35
Population and language	36

AFRICA

Mountains, Lowlands and Rivers	37
Countries, Towns, Roads and Railways	38
Types of environment	38
Population, peoples and religions	39
Farming, mining and industrial regions	40
Exploration and colonialism	41

Henri owns restaurants all over the world. His restaurants are in:
Bombay – Birmingham – Madrid – Tennessee – Caracas – Verdun – Osaka – Athens – Toronto – Lagos.

To find each of these cities, Sylvia could look through every page of the Atlas until she found them. It is quicker to look them up in the **Index** at the back of the Atlas.

Each place is listed in alphabetical order, like in a dictionary. A page number is given beside each place.

Norway (Europe) 19 E1
Nouakchott (Mauritania) 37 A2
Nouméa (New Caledonia) 41 D3
Novaya Zemlya (island; Asia) 22 C1
Novolazarevskaya Base (Antarctica) 45 16
Novorossiysk (USSR) 25 B1
Novosibirsk (USSR) 23 E2
Nubian Desert (Africa) 36 C1
Nuevitas (Cuba) 30-31 B1
Nullarbor Plain (Australasia) 40 B3

Oates Land (Antarctica) 45 9
Ob (river; Asia) 22 D1
Ocho Rios (Jamaica) 30-31 C1
Oder (river; Europe) 18 F2
Odessa (USSR) 19 H3
Ohio (river; North America) 26 F3
Okhotsk (USSR) 23 H2
Oklahoma City (USA) 27 E-F3
Okovango Marshes (Africa) 36 C4
Old Harbour (Jamaica) 30-31 C2

If two or more places have the same name, make sure you look up the right one.

San Cristóbal (Venezuela) 33 B1
San Diego (USA) 27 E3
San Fernando (Trinidad) 30
San Francisco (USA) 27 D3
San Francisco de Macoris (Dominican Republic) 30-31 B-C2
San José (Costa Rica) 27 F4
San Juan (Puerto Rico) 30-31 C2
San Marino (Europe) 19 F3
San Pedro Sula (Honduras) 30-31 A2
San Salvador (El Salvador) 27
Santa Catarina Island (South America) 34
Santa Clara (Cuba) 30-31 B1
Santa Cruz (Bolivia) 33 B2
Santa Cruz (island; Caribbean) 30-31 C2
Santa Cruz (Jamaica) 30-31 B1
Santa Cruz Mountains (Jamaica) 30-31 B2
Santa Fé (Argentina) 33 B3
Santa Marta (Colombia) 33 B1
Santarém (Brazil) 33 C2
Santiago (Dominican Republic) 30-31 B2
Santiago (Chile) 33 B3
Santiago de Cuba (Cuba) 30-31 B2
Santiago del Estero (South America) 34
Santo Domingo (Dominican Republic) 30-31 C2
Santos (Brazil) 33 C3
São Francisco (river; South America) 32 C2
São Luis (Brazil) 33 C2
São Paulo (Brazil) 33 C3
São Tomé (island) 36 B2
Sapporo (Japan) 23 H2

Things to do/Looking up places

1 Pair up the following foods with the country they come from:

oranges	Ireland
stew	Spain
spaghetti	Scotland
haggis	Denmark
bacon	Italy

2 List the countries which Henri includes in his menu. Look up the contents page in the Atlas and write down the page which has the largest political map of each country.

a Arrange the cities where Henri has a restaurant in alphabetical order.

b Write down the page number from the index in your Atlas where each city can be found.

3 Look up a political map of Europe in your Atlas. Write down which country Henri is in at each of the numbered places on the map below.

Further work

4 Make a list of at least five places which have the same name but are in different parts of the world. For each, state which country it is in, and the page number it is shown on.

Summary

An Atlas can be used to find where places are. The easiest way to find a place is to look them up in the contents or the index.

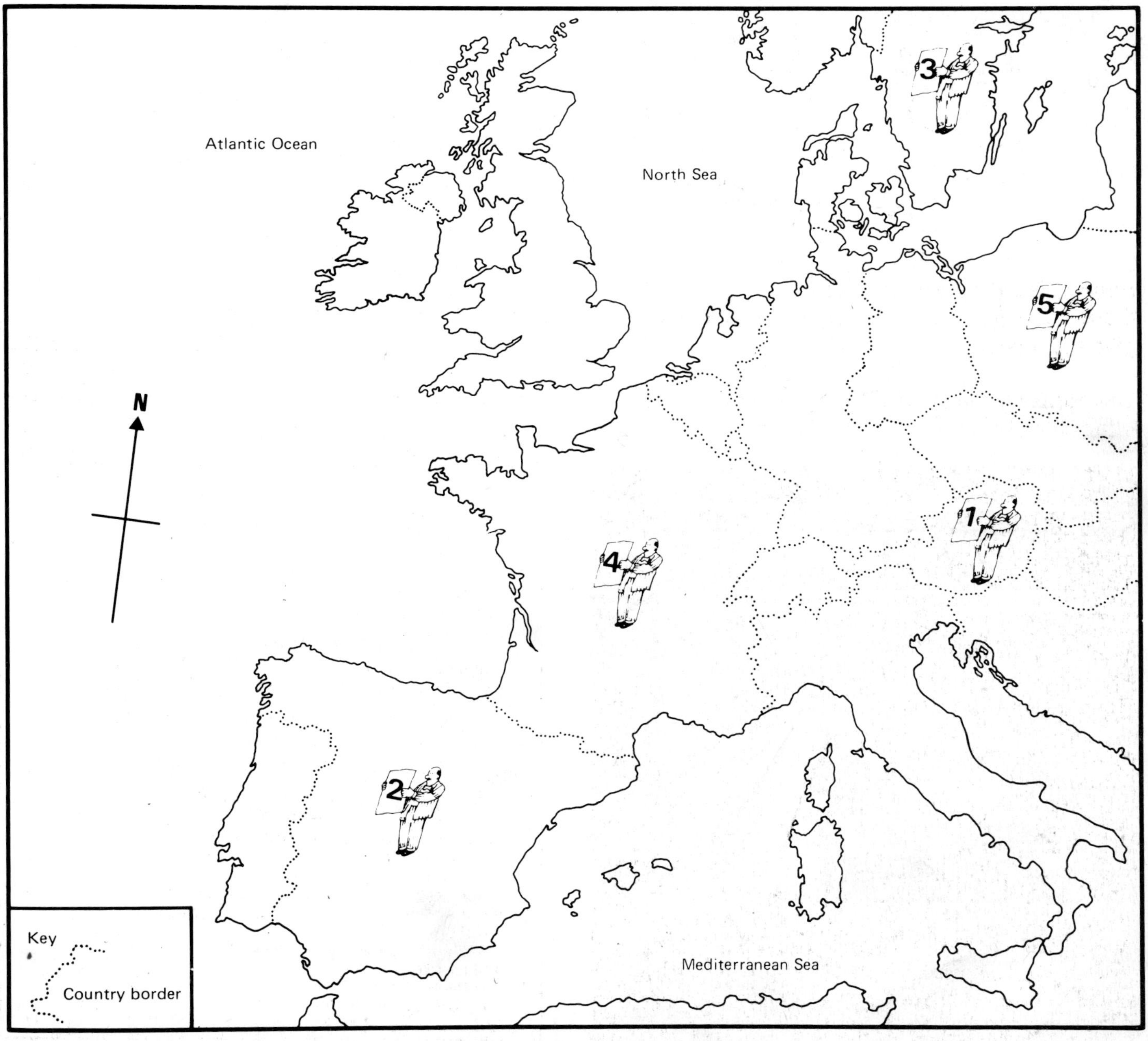

Unit 5.1

Continents and oceans/The continents

This flag is flown at the Olympic Games. Each circle stands for a continent where the athletes come from. There is no circle for the Antarctic and only one for the Americas.

Continents are very large areas of land. Most of the seven continents are divided into many different countries. The continents take up about 29% of the Earth's surface. The remaining 71% is water.

Most of the Earth's people live on only 30% of the land. Very few people live in the other 70%. Some areas are very crowded, while other areas are empty. The **distribution of population** is very uneven. People do not like to live in places which are too wet or too dry, or too cold, or too high.

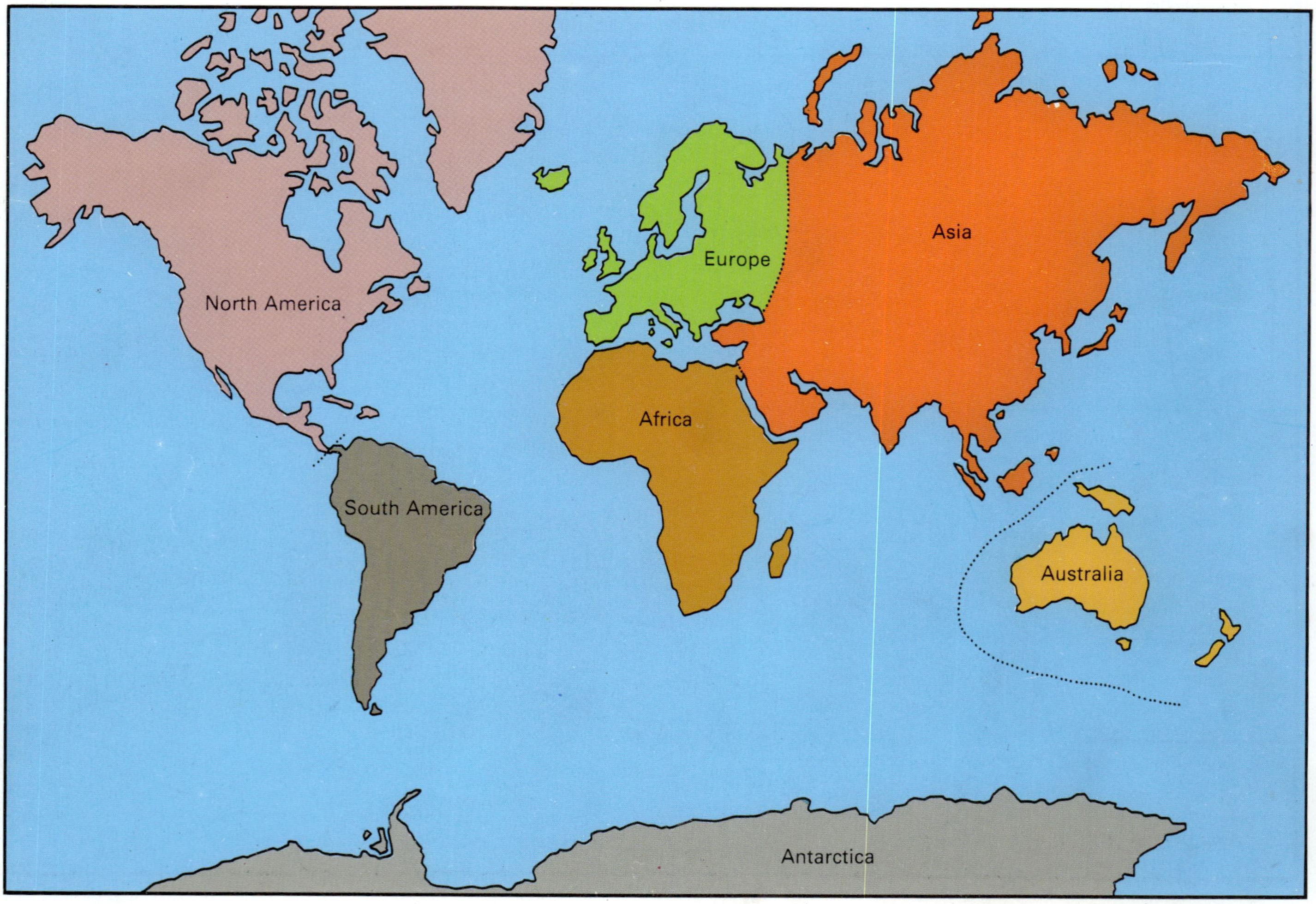

Things to do/The continent

1 The sketch maps below show each of the seven continents. Copy each map and label in the correct name of the continent.

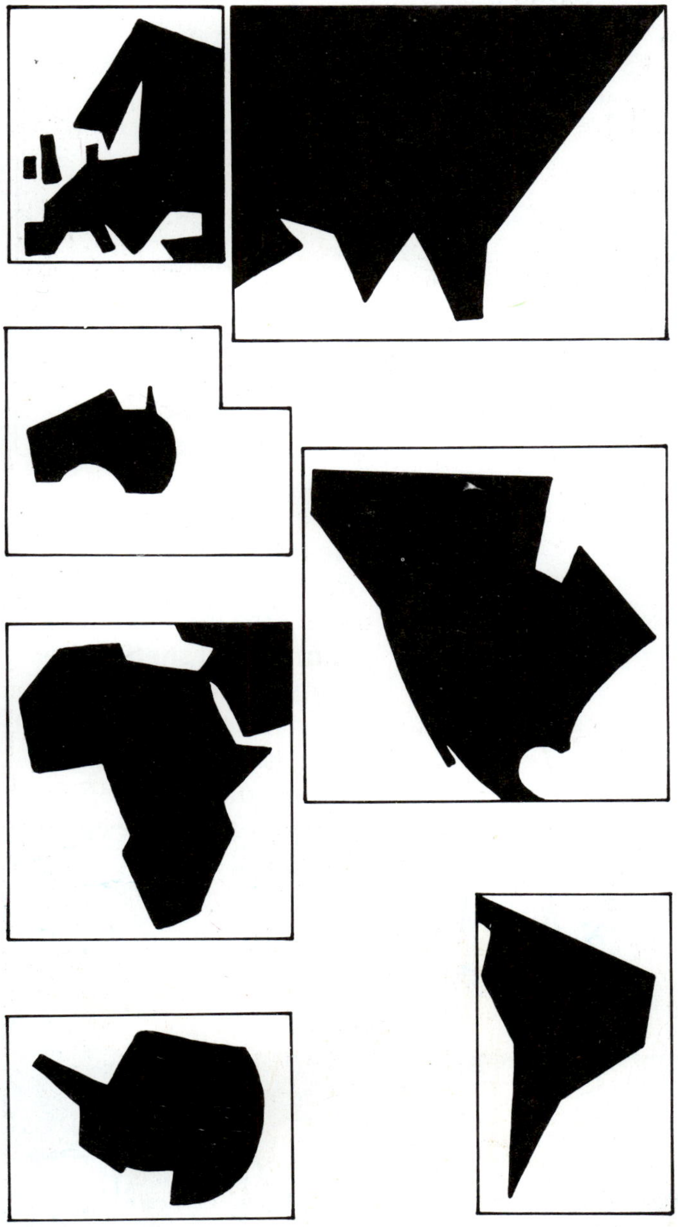

2 Answer these questions by selecting the right words.

a There are $\frac{5}{7}$ continents in all.

b The largest continent is $\frac{\text{Asia}}{\text{Africa}}$.

c There is more $\frac{\text{land than sea}}{\text{sea than land}}$ on the earth.

d France is part of the continent of $\frac{\text{Asia}}{\text{Europe}}$.

3 Explain in a paragraph why large areas of the continents have few people living there.

Further work

4 Copy and complete a bar graph to show the size of each of the continents.

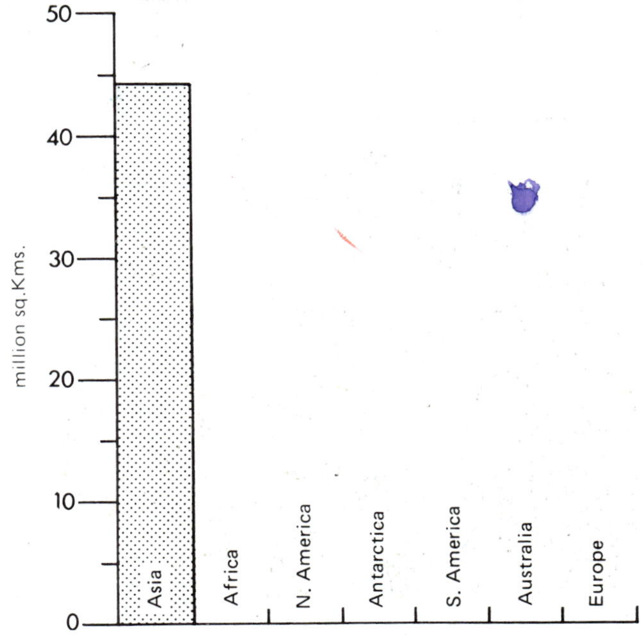

Asia 44 million km².
Africa 30 million km².
N. America 18 million km².
Antarctica 14 million km².
S. America 12 million km².
Australia 8 million km².
Europe 5 million km².

5

Asia 3000 million people.
Africa 380 million people.
N. America 400 million people.
Antarctica 0.
S. America 300 million people.
Australia 20 million people.
Europe 400 million people.

Draw a bar graph to show the number of people in each of the continents shown above. Arrange the columns in order of size, with the biggest on the left and the smallest on the right.

Summary
A very large area of land is called a continent. There is a very uneven distribution of population in the continents.

Unit 5.2

The oceans

We seem to know more about the moon than about our **oceans.** The oceans are great sheets of salt water which cover almost three quarters of the earth. They can be as difficult to explore as outer space.

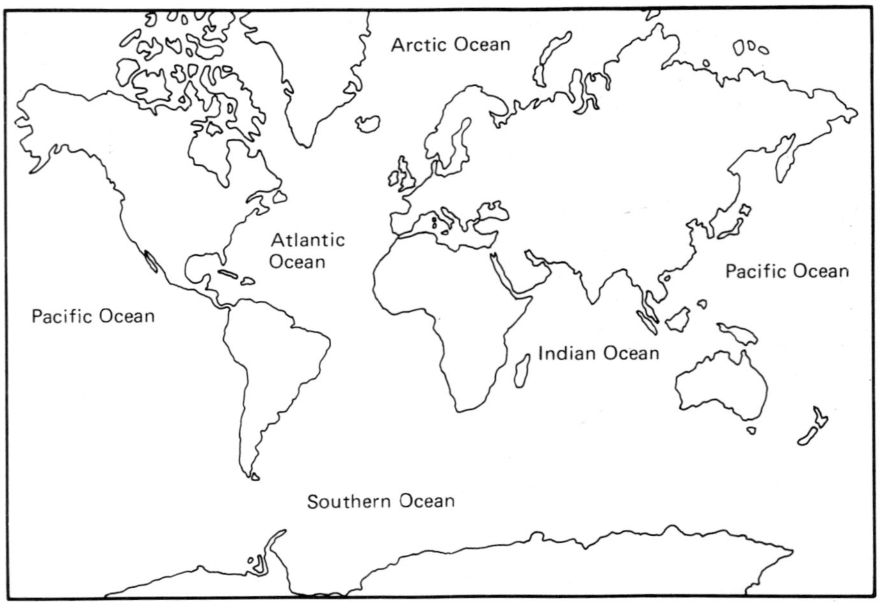

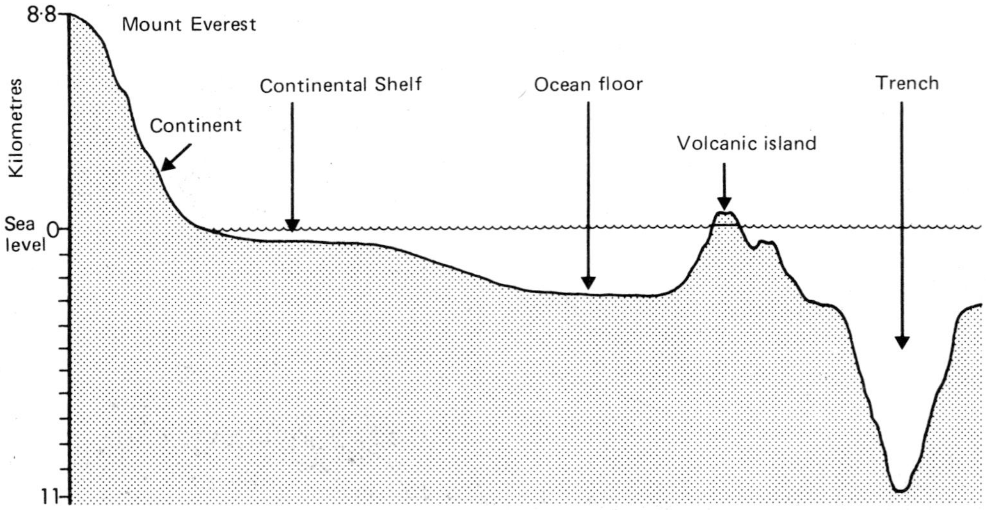

Near the continents, the oceans are quite shallow. This area is called the **continental shelf.** Other parts of the oceans are over 10 kms deep. Mount Everest would fit easily into a hole this deep. The deepest areas are called **trenches.**

Water in the oceans moves in circles. These movements of water are called **currents.** Ocean currents can be warm or cold. When they move from the Equator they are warm. Currents returning from the Poles are cold.

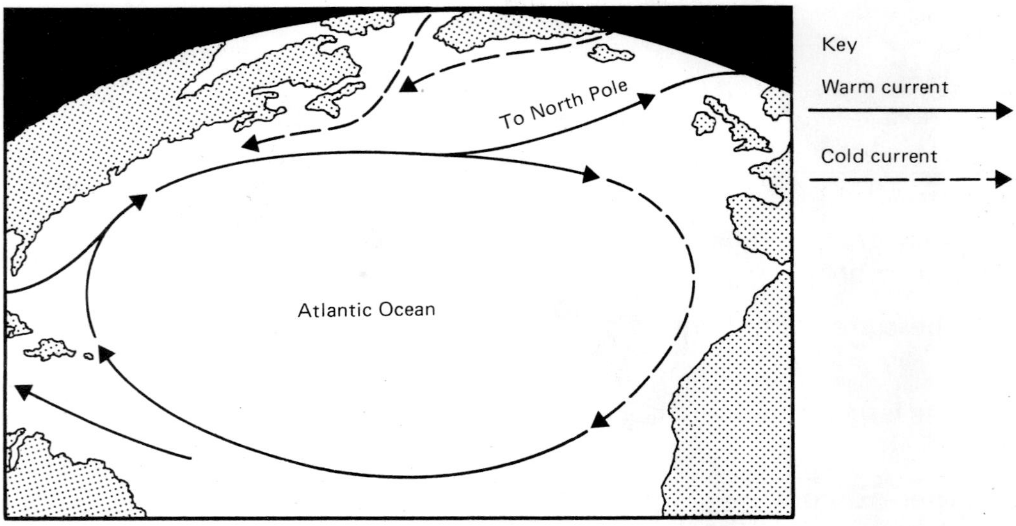

The ocean floor is dark and dangerous. Sunlight does not reach the bottom except in shallow water. In deeper areas, the weight of the water can crush a submarine.

There are many more plants and animals in the oceans than on the land. There are also important rocks and minerals as well as oil under the oceans. Perhaps one day we may find ways of using all these things.

Unit 5.2

Things to do/The oceans

1 Study the information in the diagrams on the opposite page.
Then copy and complete this crossword:

a Deepest part of the ocean.
b The world's highest mountain.
c The ocean between Africa and Australia.
d The world's largest ocean.
e Found in oceans and electric wires
f The ocean between America and Europe.

2a Explain why it is so difficult to explore the oceans.
b Give two reasons why the oceans should be studied.

3 Draw the cross section below and label in the terms in the correct place.

Continent	Ocean floor
Continental shelf	Trench

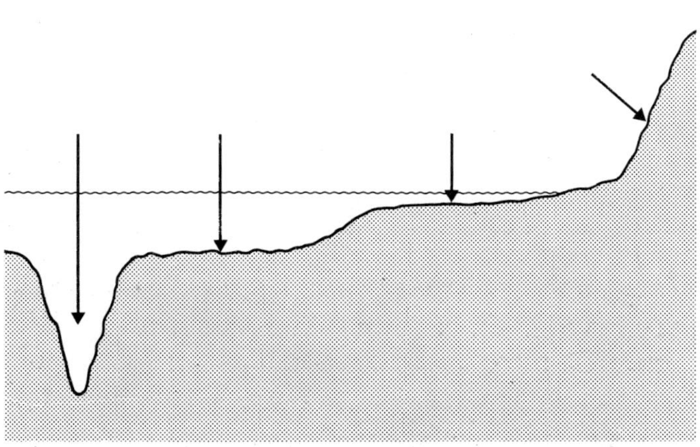

Further work

4 Find a map of the world which shows ocean currents. Make a list of the named currents you can find. Beside each current, say whether it moves clockwise or anticlockwise, and whether it is warm or cold.

Summary

Oceans cover the largest part of our planet, yet we know very little about them. They are difficult to explore, but may become important in the future.

Difficulties
e.g. Waves and wind

Remoteness

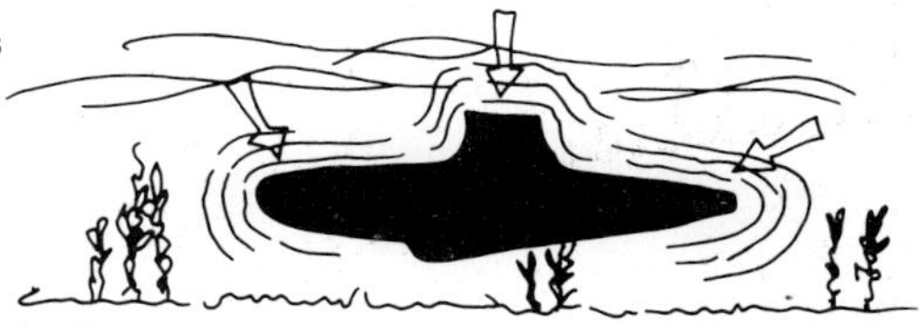

Pressures at depth

Reasons for oceans to be studied
To learn more

Valuable minerals on ocean floor

To see way of life of ocean animals and plants

Unit 5.3

South America – physical

South America is one of the smallest continents. But it has the world's biggest river, the driest desert, the largest area of jungle and the highest volcanoes.

This physical map of South America shows the main types of landforms: mountains, plateaux and river basins. The British Isles would fit easily into a small corner of South America.

South America has many different kinds of scenery. It stretches from the Equator to over half way towards the South Pole. Over the continent, there are great differences in the temperatures and the amount of rain. As a result, there are many kinds of vegetation.

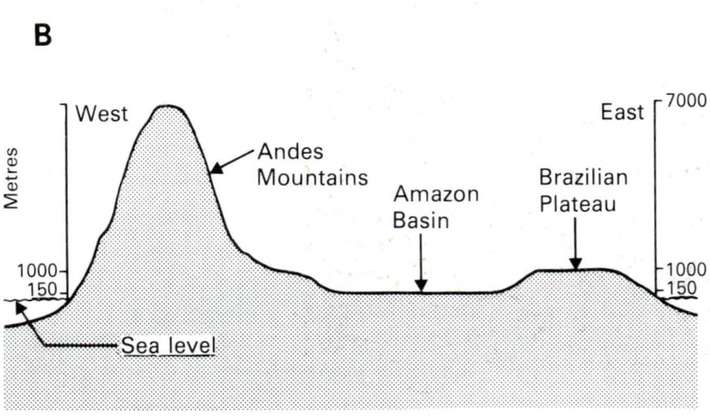

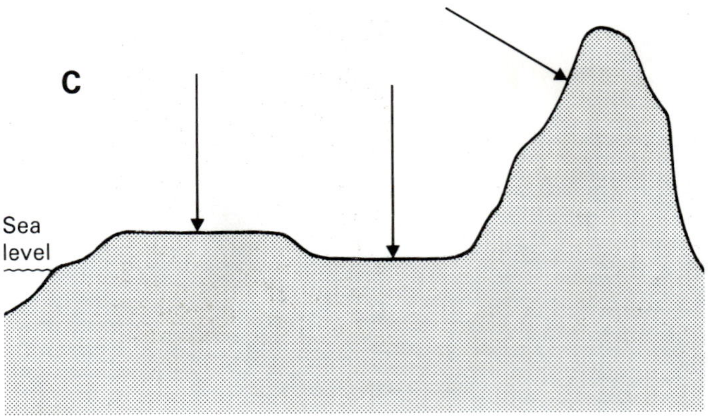

Things to do/South America – physical

1 Write out and complete the following sentences after looking at map A.

- **a** S. America lies between latitude . . . N and . . . S.
- **b** This is a distance of about . . . km.
- **c** At its widest, it measures . . . km.
- **d** The British Isles measures . . . km North to South and . . . km East to West.
- **e** The largest river in South America is the . . .
- **f** The mountain range is called the . . .
- **g** The . . . ocean lies to the East and the . . . ocean lies to the West.

2 Study diagrams B and C. Copy diagram C and label in where you would find:
Mountain, Plateau, River Basin.

3a Draw the five photos which show different kinds of scenery in South America. (Map **D**)

- **b** Write a description of what you would see in each area.
- **c** Which type of area do you think would be
  - – the most difficult to live in
  - – the most interesting to live in
  - – the easiest to live in
  - – the most beautiful to live in?

  Give reasons for your answers.

Further work

4 Find a map of South America with annual rainfall in your Atlas. (It may be under 'World-climate' or 'precipitation'.)

- **a** Draw a sketch map to show the rainfall distribution (where most rain falls).
- **b** Compare the rainfall map with the vegetation map and write a comment on what you notice.

> **Summary**
> The continents are made up of different kinds of landform. Continents have a great variety of scenery.

D

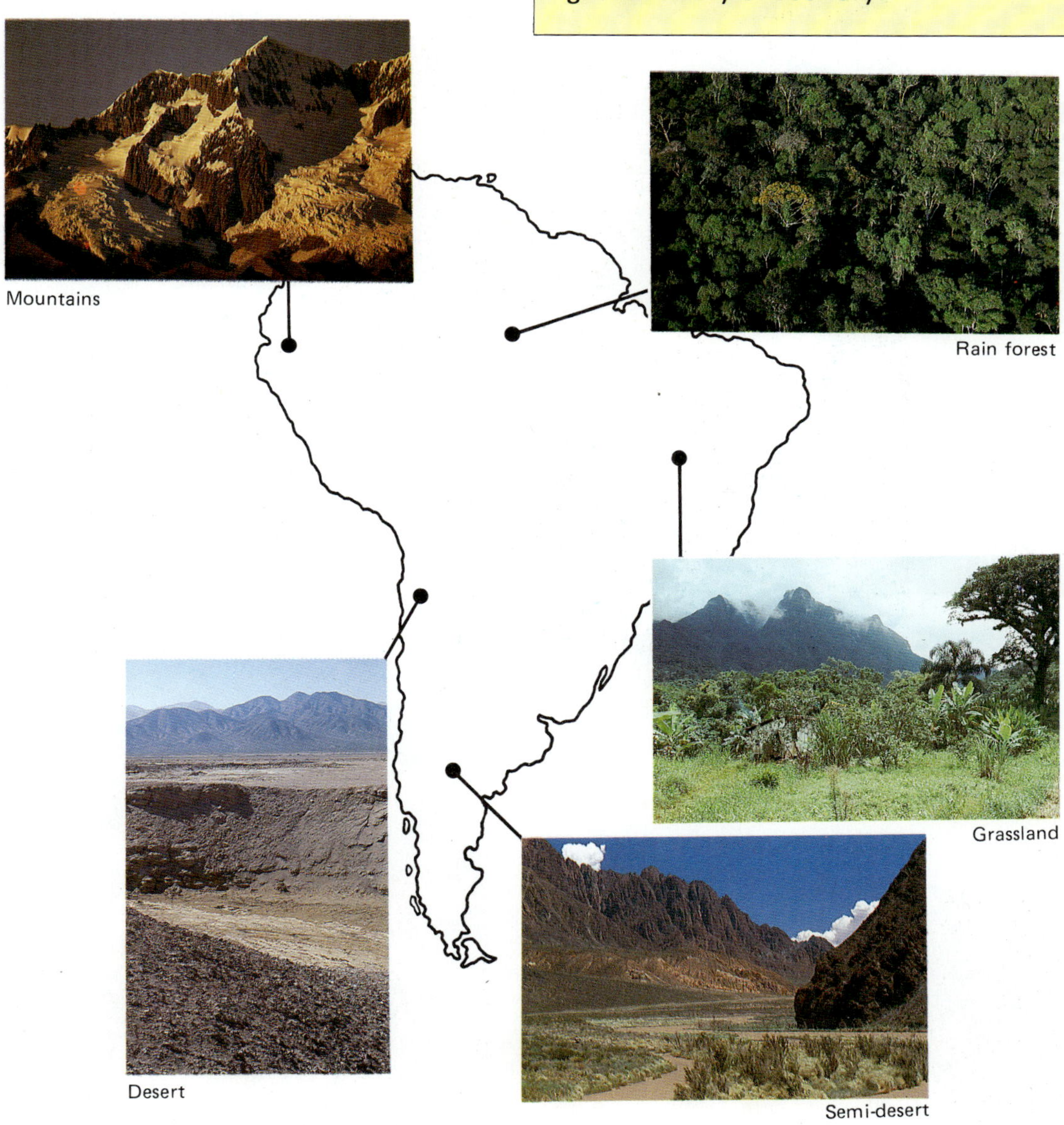

Unit 5.4

South America – human

South America is made up of 13 countries. In these countries there are 244 million people. In the British Isles, there are only 56 million. The map A shows the **distribution of population** in South America.

There are large areas where hardly anyone lives. These areas are in the centre and in the far south. Most of the people seem to live near the coast where the towns and cities are. They live in **clusters** rather than being evenly spread out. Areas like these are densely populated.

The South American countries are not yet as **developed** as the European countries or North America. This means that the people do not earn as much money, there are not as many factories making goods, and the farmers do not have machines. Every year, these countries are becoming more developed and old ways of doing things are changing.

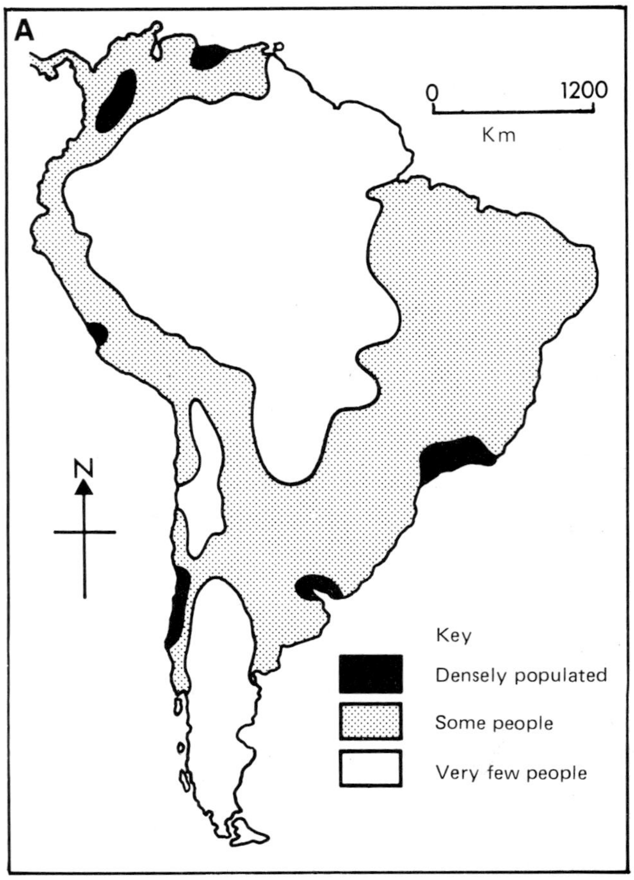

Things to do/South America — human

1 Make a copy of both of the maps below. For each, write a description of the population distribution. Use as many of the following words as you can:

distribution	coast
population	inland
even	North
uneven	South
clustered	East
densely	West

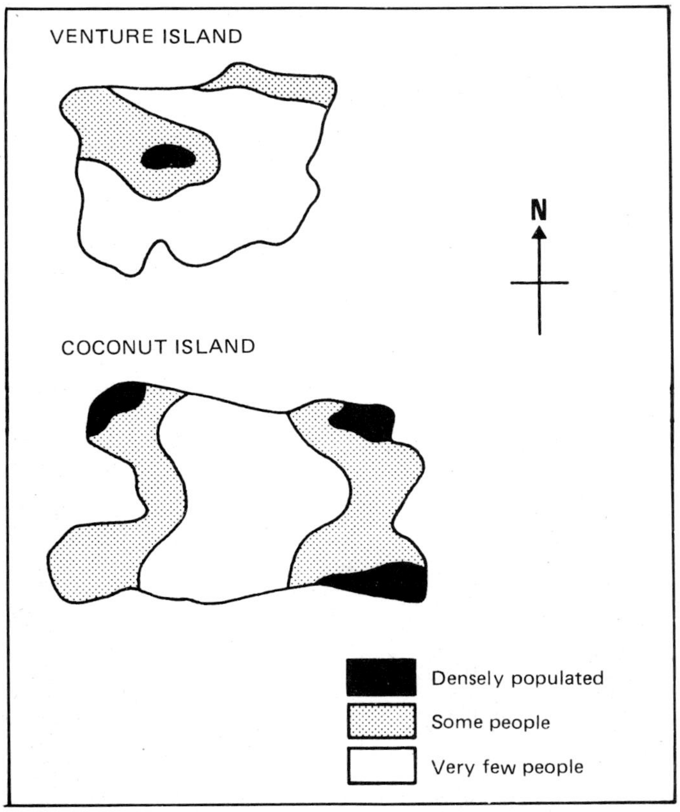

2 Each of these outlines shows a South American country. Find a political map of South America in your Atlas. For each letter, state which country you think it is.

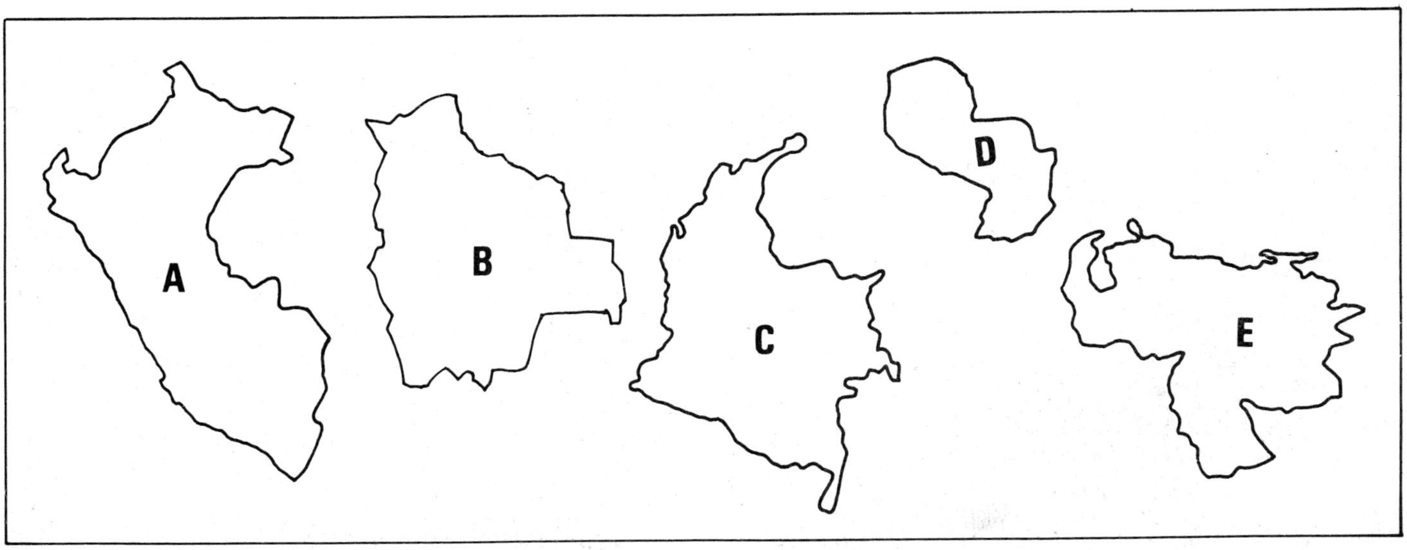

3 Under the headings below, say how South America is different from Britain:
- Farming
- Transport
- Houses

Further work

4 These figures show how many people live in each of the South American countries.

a Rule a grid of squares measuring 15 cms wide and 20 cms down. Each square should be 1 cm by 1 cm.

b Find a political map of South America in your Atlas. Imagine that each grid square represents two million people. Using different colours, shade in the right number of squares to make up the shape of each country.

Brazil	124 million	Chile	11 million
Argentina	28 million	Paraguay	3 million
Ecuador	9 million	Uruguay	3 million
Peru	17 million	Guyana	Count as one square with 2 million
Bolivia	6 million	Surinam	
Venezuela	14 million	French	
Colombia	27 million	Guiana	

Summary
People do not live evenly all over South America. Some areas are empty while others are densely populated. The South American countries are not as developed as Europe.

Unit 6.1

The sky/The atmosphere

We all breathe in oxygen, and without the oxygen in the air, we would die quickly. In high mountain areas, climbers carry oxygen bottles to help them breathe. This is because the air is thin higher up. Beyond about 20 kms up, there is no air at all to breathe in.

There is a thin layer of gasses around the earth which we can breathe. This layer is called the **atmosphere.** Above the atmosphere is **outer space.**

There is a lot to be seen in the atmosphere. Look at the sky and you will see something different every day.

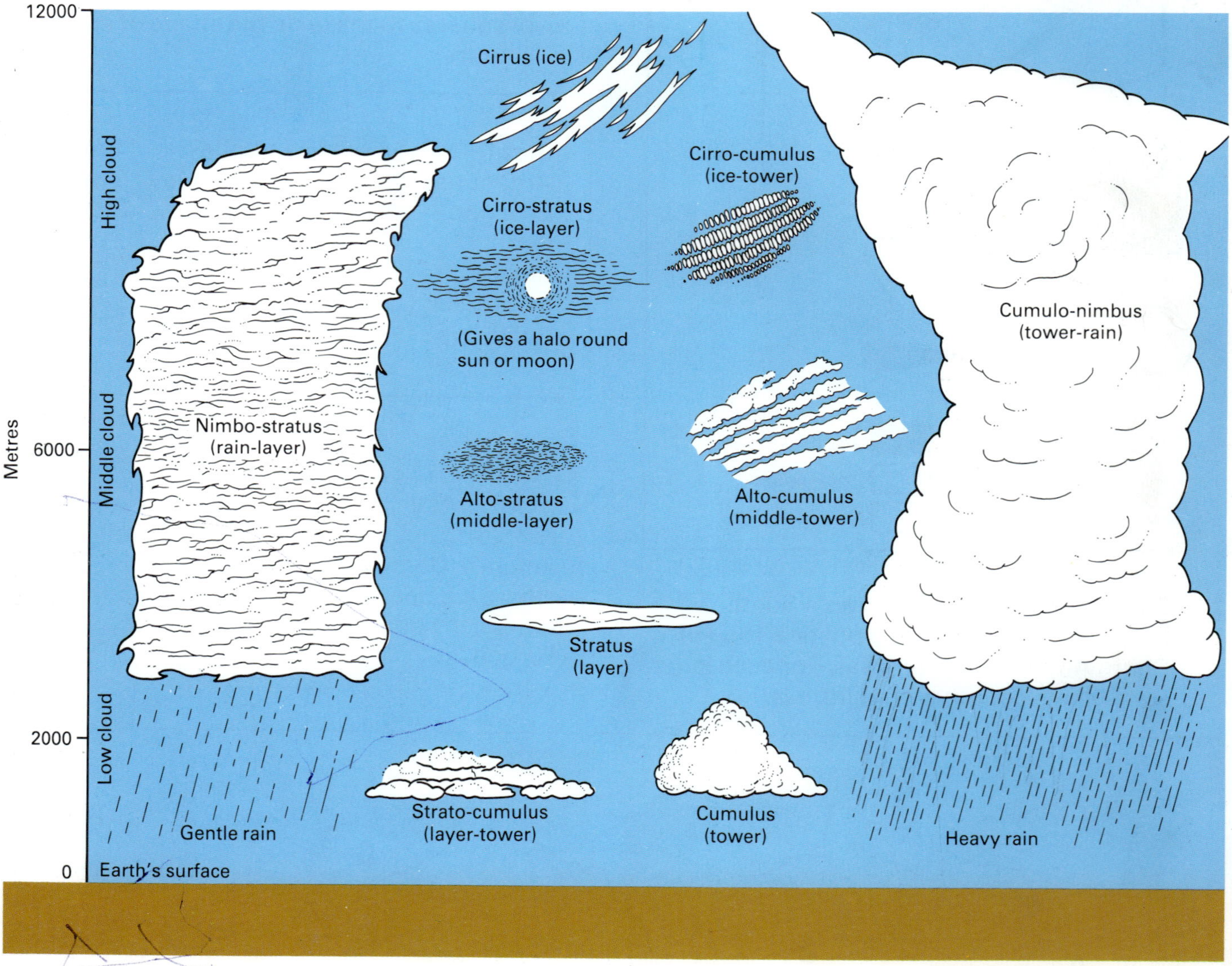

There are **clouds** which have different shapes and are at different heights. They move in different directions, and at different speeds. Clouds are patches of air which have millions of tiny rain drops in them. Some clouds cover the sky like a blanket – these are called **Stratus** clouds. Sometimes clouds look like bubbles or balls of fluffy cotton – these are the **Cumulus** clouds. Fog is really cloud at ground level.

When clouds cannot keep the rain drops up any longer, they fall to the ground. Then we have rain as a shower or as drizzle. If it is very cold, the drops fall as hail, sleet, or snow.

Things to do/The atmosphere

1a Draw each of the diagrams (below).
b For each diagram, write a description of what the sky looks like.

2 Make a list of the following things. Put the one you like best at the top of the list and the one you like least at the bottom.
A rainbow – cumulus cloud drifting through the sky – lightning – overcast sky with drizzle – snow falling – stinging sleet or hail – cloudless sky in summer.

3 Weather maps have special symbols to show the amount of **cloud cover**. The amount of cloud is marked out of 8 – no cloud is $\frac{0}{8}$, a half covered sky is $\frac{4}{8}$, and a completely covered sky $\frac{8}{8}$.

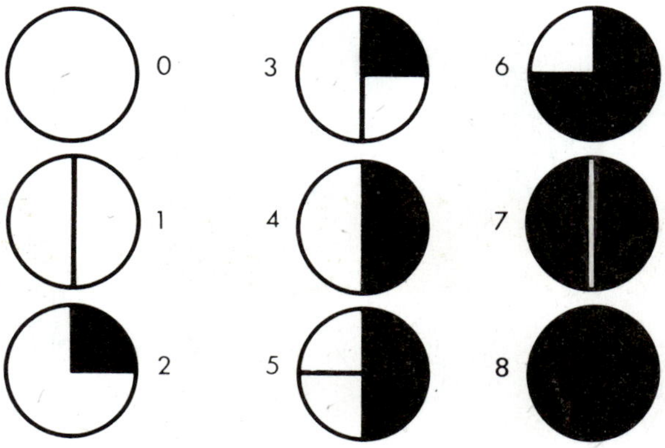

Cloud cover symbols
(In eighths of the sky)

There are also special symbols to show what the weather is like.

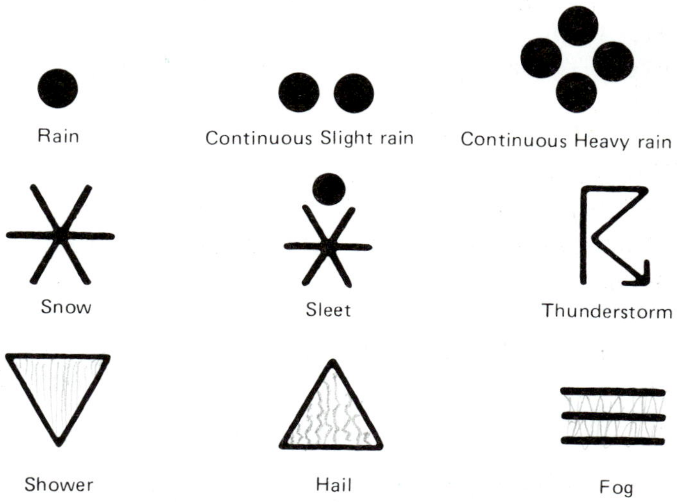

a Draw a series of symbols to show the following –
$\frac{1}{2}$ cloud cover with rain
no cloud cover
$\frac{3}{4}$ cloud cover with hail
completely covered with snow
$\frac{7}{8}$ covered with cloud

Further work

4 Wind speed is measured by the Beaufort scale (given below). For each type of wind condition, draw a cartoon to show what the effect could be.

Beaufort No.	Wind	Speed in Knots	Commonly Observed Effects
0	Calm	0	Smoke goes straight up.
1	Light air	1-3	Smoke starts to drift.
2	Light breeze	4-6	Leaves rustle.
3	Gentle breeze	7-10	Flags wave in breeze.
4	Moderate breeze	11-16	Small branches are moved.
5	Fresh breeze	17-21	Small trees begin to sway.
6	Strong breeze	22-27	Hard to use an umbrella.
7	Moderate gale	28-33	Hard to walk against wind.
8	Fresh gale	34-40	Twigs break off trees.
9	Strong gale	41-47	Chimney pots and slates moved.
10	Storm	48-55	Trees uprooted.
11	Violent storm	56-63	Houses damaged.
12	Hurricane	64-71	Complete towns can be destroyed.

Summary
The Earth is surrounded by a layer called the atmosphere.
Events in the atmosphere are always changing.

Unit 6.2

Space

Look up at the night sky and you will see tiny pinpricks of light. These are the other planets which move around our sun, and the millions of **stars** which make up our **Galaxy** called 'the Milky Way'.

A **star** is a burning ball of gas which gives off heat and light just like our Sun. **Planets** are cold on the outside and can only reflect light. The Earth is one of a group of planets which move around the Sun. A sun is another name for a star. The Sun and planets are called **the solar system.**

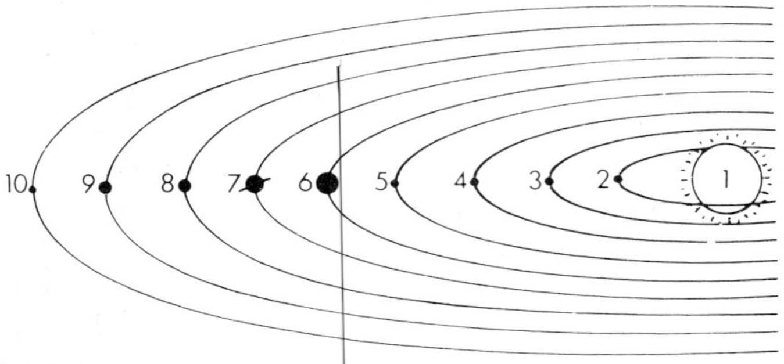

A 1 Sun, 2 Mercury, 3 Venus, 4 Earth, 5 Mars, 6 Jupiter, 7 Saturn, 8 Uranus, 9 Neptune, 10 Pluto

On Earth, the Sun always appears to rise in the East and set in the West. In the British Isles, it is always seen in the Southern part of the sky. As the Earth spins around, the Sun lights up each part in turn giving day and night. Light from the Sun takes eight minutes to travel the 93 million miles to the Earth. Light from the next nearest sun takes 4.2 years to reach us.

B

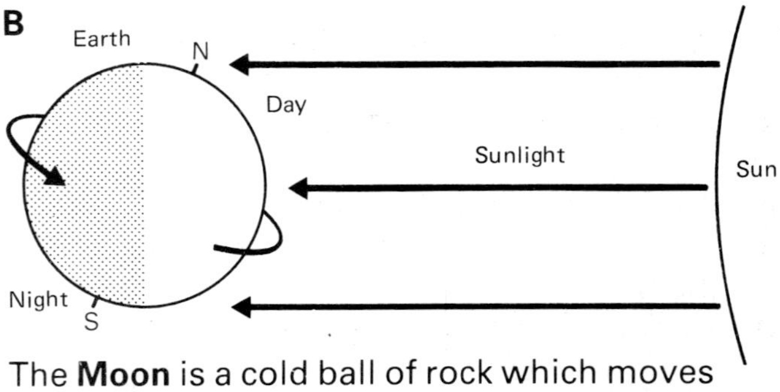

The **Moon** is a cold ball of rock which moves around the Earth. It reflects light from the Sun so it seems to be changing its shape as different parts are lit up. It is only a quarter of a million miles away so it may seem as large as the Sun. Really, it is very much smaller than both the Earth and the Sun.

C

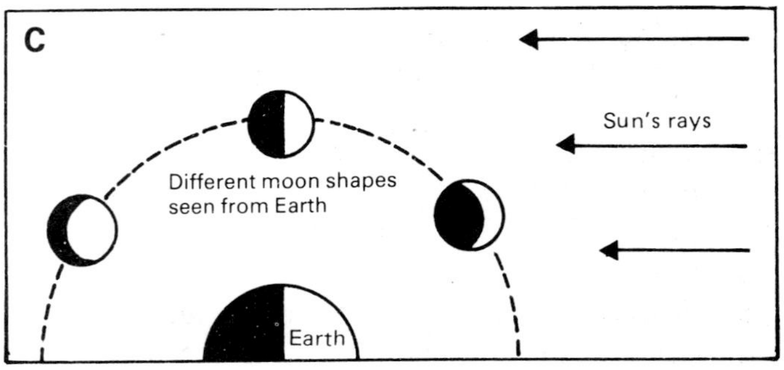

In ancient times, people looked at the stars and tried to explain how they got there. They imagined they saw the shapes of people and animals. These pictures made of stars are called **constellations.** Orion the hunter is one constellation which is easy to find because of the three bright stars which make up his belt.

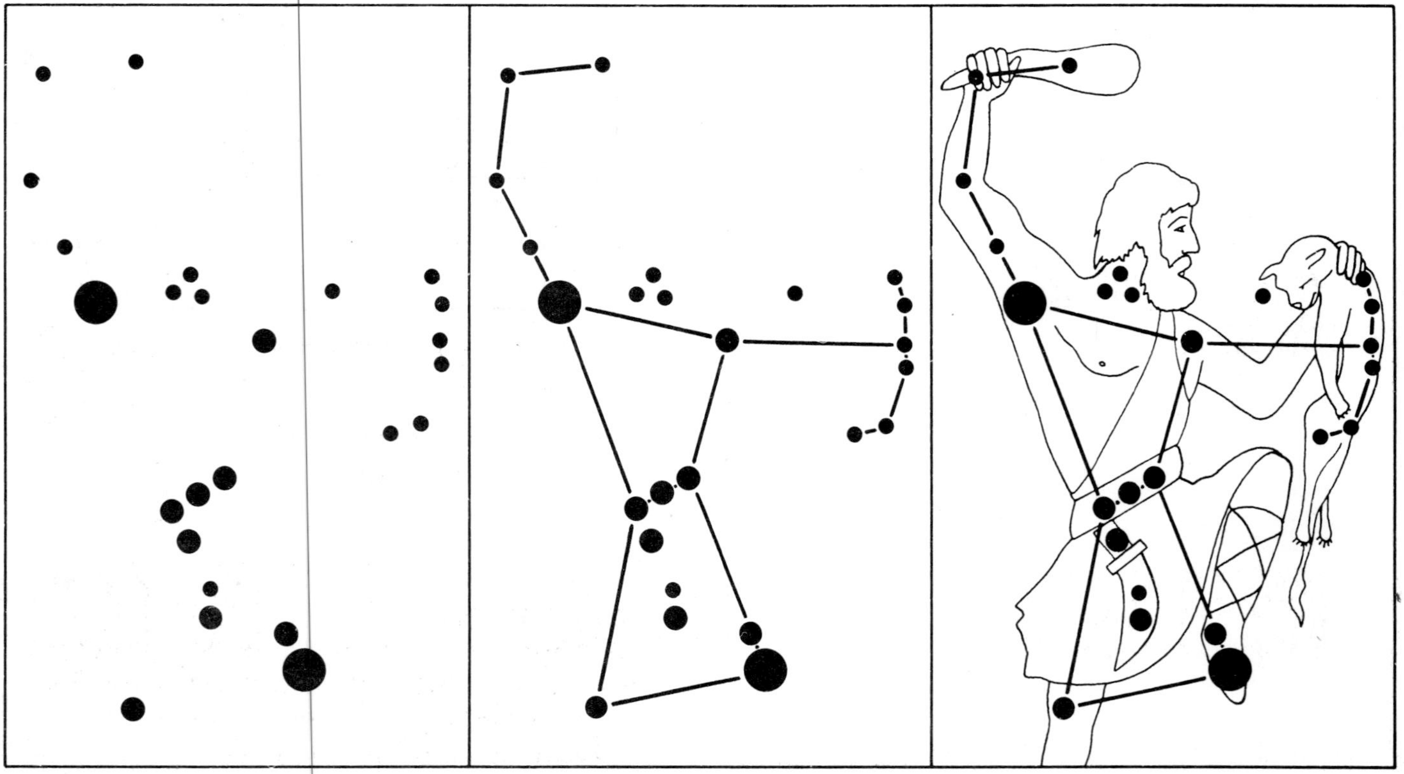

Unit 6.2

Things to do/Space

1 Write out and complete the following sentences –

a A galaxy is made of millions of . . . . . and . . . . .

b A star is made of . . . . . which burns

c The Earth is a . . . . . which moves around the Sun

d Another name for a star is a . . . . .

2 Make a list of the planets. Put the one nearest to the Sun first and the one furthest away last.

3a Copy the sketch B which shows why the Earth has day and night.

b Write your own explanation of the diagram using these words:
turning sunlight shadow

4 The dots in this diagram are of one of the constellations. When joined, they make a picture of a common animal.

a Copy the dots.

b Join up the dots matchstick style.

c Complete the drawing to show how you think it should look.

The answer is given in Recap 6.

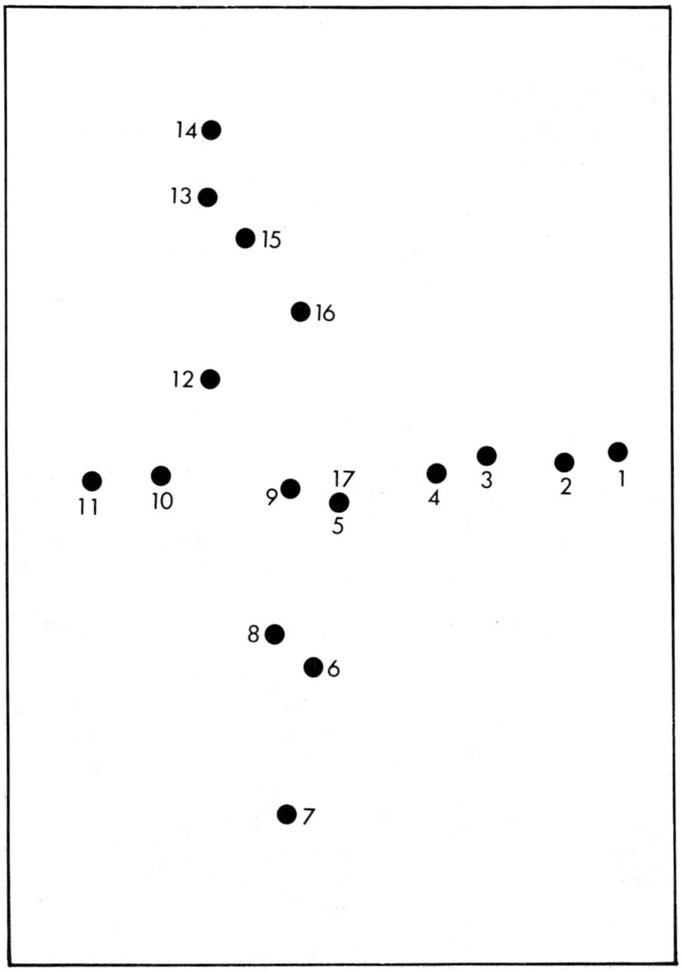

Further work

5 The sketch and map below show a house which has just been bought by a clever architect who likes gardening. You are to help him make up his mind how to use the rooms in the house and the garden outside.

a Where would it be best to plant shrubs which like shade? Site A, B or C?

b Which rooms have the sun shining through the windows in the morning?

c Where should he put a greenhouse so that it gets the sun in the afternoon and evening? Site X1, X2 or X3?

d Which is the best room to have the TV in so that the sun does not shine into the room in the evening?

e Strawberries need sun for most of the day. Where is the best place to plant them? Site A, B or C?

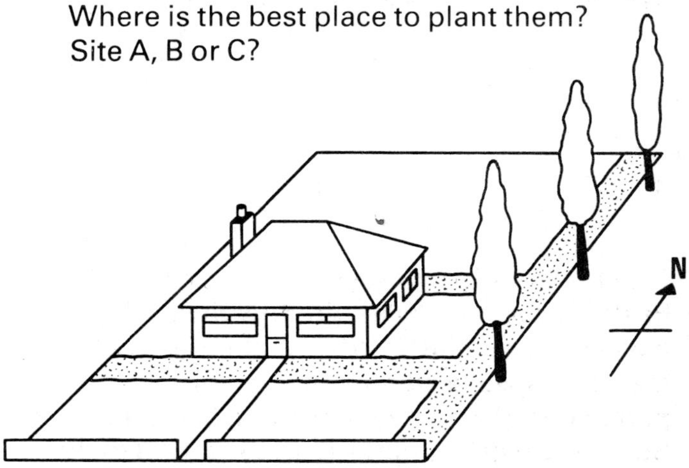

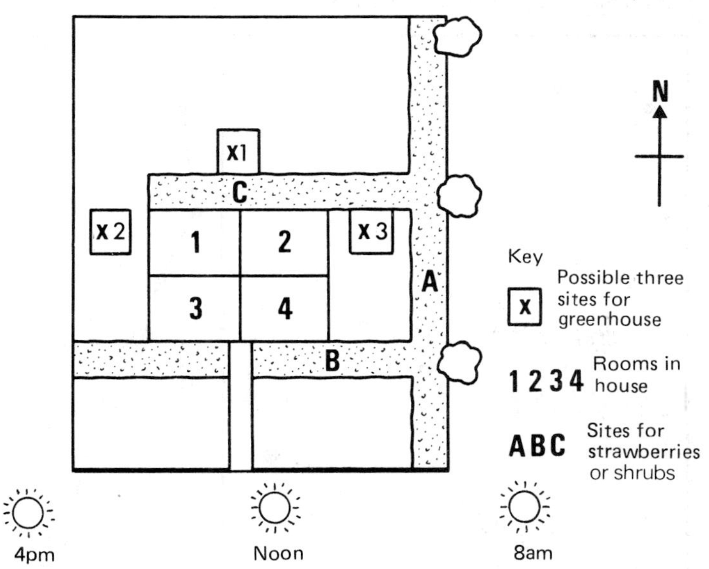

Summary

The Earth is a very small planet set amongst millions of other planets and stars. The Sun is at the centre of our solar system.

Unit 6.3

Dramatic events

Some people believe they have seen flying saucers in the sky. There are many reports of these Unidentified Flying Objects, called UFOs for short. Most of the strange things in the skies can be explained but they can still be very dangerous.

A **blizzard** is a fierce snowstorm which is almost impossible to see through. They are rare and most often found in very cold areas near the North and South Poles.

A **tornado** or **twister** is an upward twisting funnel of air. One was shown near the start of the film *The Wizard of Oz.* They start in the hot summer plains of North America. The wind can reach 300 kms per hour.

Lightning is a giant spark which leaps from a thundercloud to the ground. Thunder is the noise which comes after the lightning. Each spark carries a huge electric shock.

A **hurricane** is a swirling mass of rushing wind. They start over warm sea areas. Winds can be 200 kms per hour on the outside, but the centre or 'eye' is calm.

A **waterspout** is a tornado over the sea. It sucks up water into a thundercloud. It can be over 100 metres high.

Meteors are lumps of rock flying through space. When they enter the earth's atmosphere, they start to burn up. They leave a streak of thin white light in the sky which soon vanishes. They can travel at 100,000 kms per hour, but few reach the earth's surface.

Things to do/Dramatic events

Fishing villages smashed in monster storm

Mystery fire ruins forest

Fishing boat drawn into pillar of water

GIANT HAND PICKS UP BARN

Schoolboy claims he saw alien space ship

Arctic explorer lost, search and rescue impossible

1 Write down these descriptions and beside each, say which type of dramatic event it could be:

a funnel of water moving upwards
a sudden streak of light in the night sky
an electric spark from a cloud
a blinding snowstorm
a corkscrew of air over land
very strong winds rushing in a huge circle over an ocean.

2 Read the newspaper headlines. For each, state what type of dramatic event you think was the cause.

- **a** Fishing villages smashed in monster storm.
- **b** Mystery fire ruins forest.
- **c** Fishing boat drawn into pillar of water.
- **d** Giant hand picks up barn.
- **e** Schoolboy claims he saw alien space ship.
- **f** Arctic explorer lost, search and rescue impossible.

3 Imagine that one of the dramatic events happened to your street.

- **a** Choose a suitable headline.
- **b** Write a description of the event.
- **c** Say what damage would have been caused.
- **d** Draw a sketch or a map to show the damage.

Further work

4 Make a list of the dramatic events which are unlikely to affect the British Isles. For each event you list, give a reason why.

Summary
Some events in the sky happen very suddenly and can cause great damage.

Unit 6.4

The weather forecast

Most of us have been drenched when we were caught in a rainstorm without a coat. Sometimes we put on a sweater then find that the weather turns out to be hot. We do not always know what weather to expect. It is more serious when farmers lose their crops because of rain, or a yachtsman gets into trouble when the wind rises. On TV and radio there is a daily **weather forecast.** Sometimes, the forecast is not completely right as the weather is a very complicated thing.

All day and night, weathermen are collecting information from ships, aeroplanes, weather stations, and satellites. With this information, they can work out what the weather will probably be like during the next few days. Although no two days will have exactly the same weather, some types of weather can be forecast.

When a **barometer** shows a high reading, the weather will be calm. In winter it will be very cold and frosty. In summer it usually means misty mornings and hot sunny days. The weatherman says that a 'ridge of high pressure' lies over the country.

When the barometer reading falls and the weatherman mentions a 'trough of low pressure', look out for rain and strong winds. A low pressure area is sometimes called a **depression**.

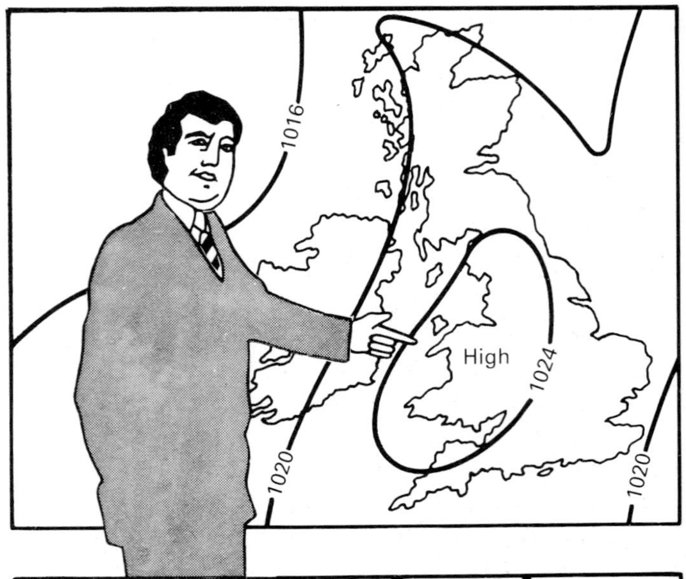

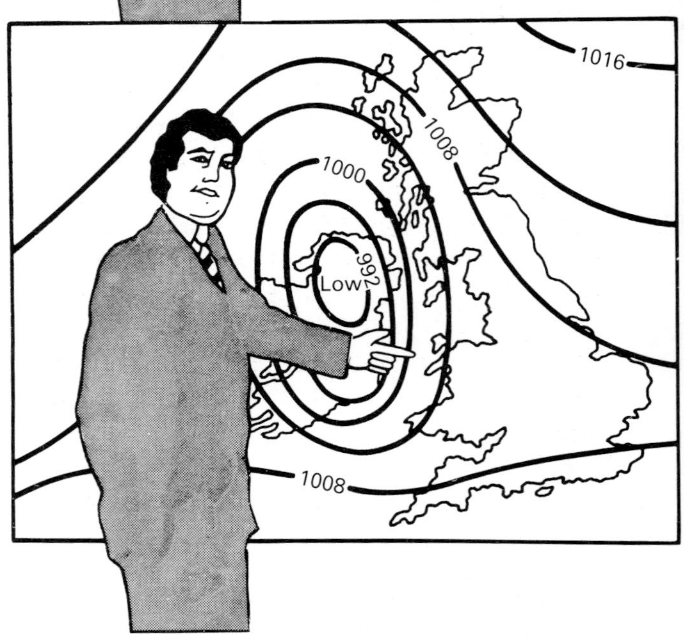

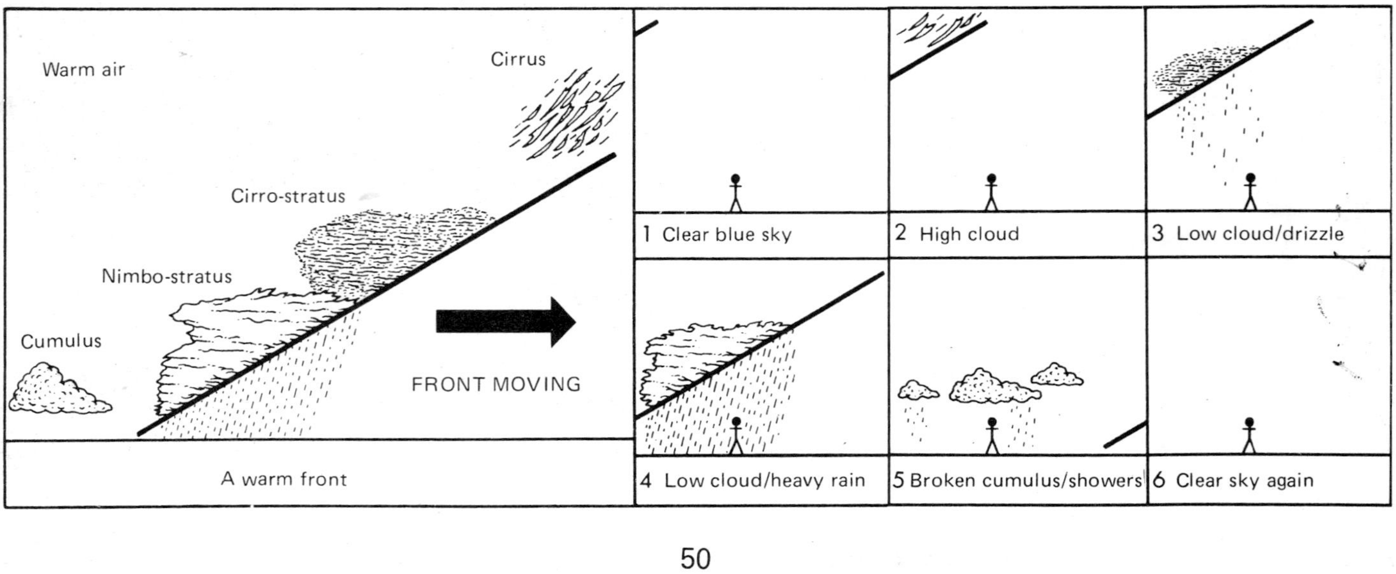

Things to do/The weather forecast

1 Make your own list of people who need to listen to the weather forecast every day. For each person you list explain why they need to know about the weather.

2 What do you think that satellites can see from space which can help predict the weather?

3 Read this passage which tells of a school visit –

'The sky was clear and bright when everyone left home for school. Nobody thought to bring an anorak, not even the teacher. The coach left school at 9.00 am. By then, some cloud had begun to appear. By the time the coach reached the coast, the cloud was quite low and the sun had gone in. Everyone sat shivering on the beach as they drew sketches and made notes. Then the drizzle began and worksheets soon became soggy. Lunch was eaten on the coach as the rain poured down.
After lunch, the rain had stopped and the sun began to appear. The class walked to a farm nearby. Some girls got stuck in the wet mud because they did not bring the right sort of shoes. By 2.30 pm, it had become warmer and there were few clouds to be seen. There was one short shower, but that soon passed.
The coach left at 3.00 pm and by the time school was reached, the weather was dry again.'

a Draw each of the sketches 1 to 6 from the opposite page.
b Beside each sketch, write down what the school party was doing at the time.

Further work

4 Listen to a TV or radio weather forecast for your area. Make notes on what is forecast. The next day, write down what the weather is like and see if the forecast was right.

5 Trace the outline of Britain from the satellite weather photograph below. On your tracing draw the main cloud formations and label the depression, which looks like a catherine wheel.

Summary
It can be important to know what the weather will be like. High and low pressure areas give types of weather which can be forecast.

Unit 7.1

Landforms/River valleys

Some people are said to be as old as the hills. But how old is that? Most hills were once mountains which have been worn down. In turn, the hills will be worn flat. Another word for wearing away is **erosion.**

The photograph shows a small **valley** with a river. Nothing seems to be happening. But if you look into a river, you can see it at work. Each and every day the river picks up tiny bits of rock from its banks and bed and carries them away. It is like a man with a wheelbarrow carrying the rock away then dumping it. At the same time, rain is washing soil down the valley side into the river.

It is hard to believe, but this small stream has carried away every piece of rock that used to be where the valley is now.

Take some sample bottles of river water. Either allow them to stand for a few hours, or filter the water through filter paper. You will see tiny grains of rock which were being carried along by the river. These grains are called **sediment**. A fast flowing river usually carries more sediment than a slow flowing river.

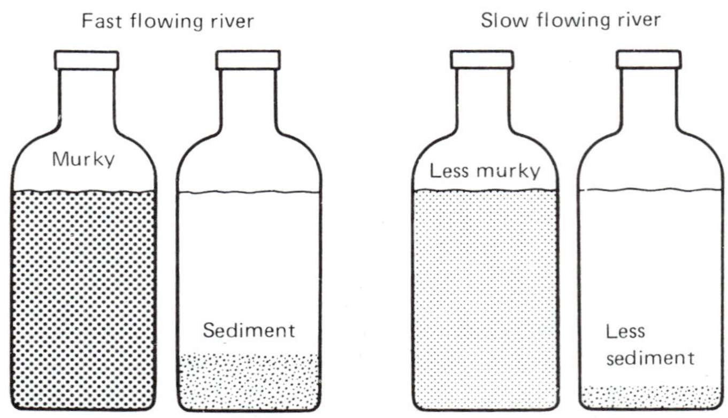

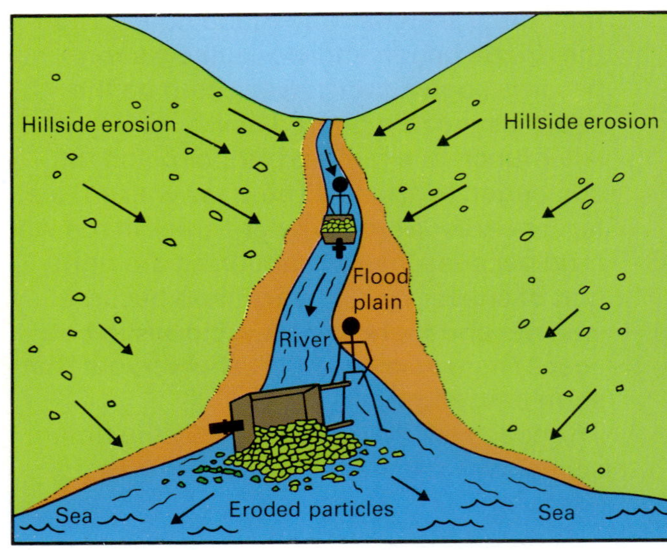

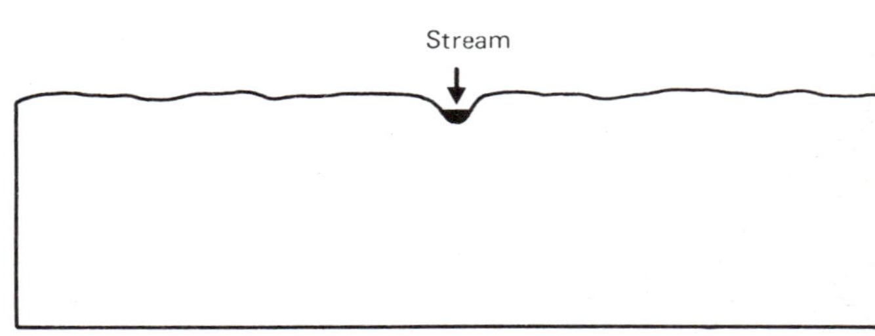

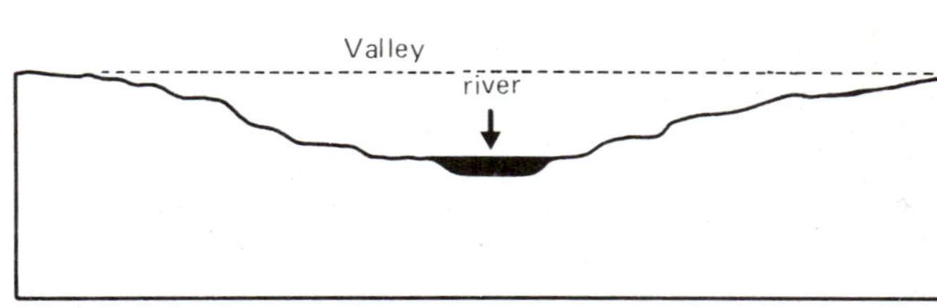

When there is heavy rain, the river can flood. Water spills onto the flat land beside the river. This land is called the **flood plain**.

Things to do/River valleys

1 Make a list of objects you know which are hard, but which are worn down with use, for example, things you wear or play with.

2a Make a copy of the outline of the photograph opposite.

b Label in these terms in the correct place:
river, river bank, valley, flood plain, slopes

3a Write out the sentence which tells you what erosion means.

b Think about the idea of the wheelbarrow moving bits of rock. See if you can think of some better ideas which would describe what happens. What about a bulldozer or a file?

c For one of the ideas you list, draw a cartoon diagram to show how it works.

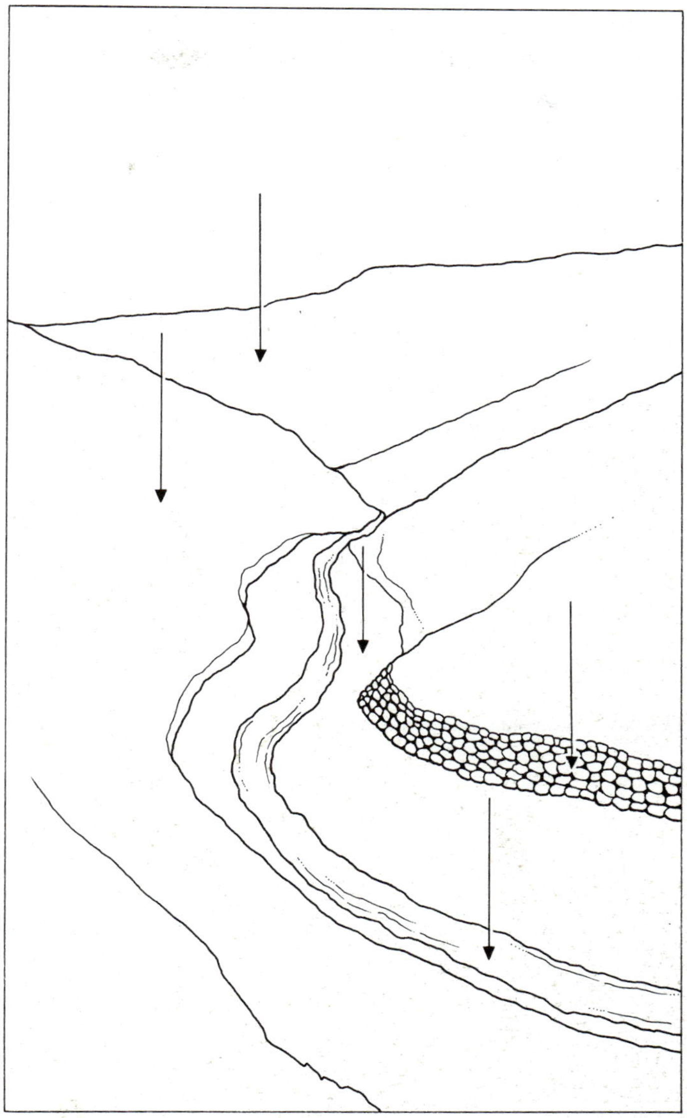

Further work

4 Follow what happens to a grain of rock in the diagram below. Draw each of the diagrams and beside each, say what is happening to the rock.

Summary
The land is being worn away all the time. This is called erosion. Rivers are one way that erosion happens.

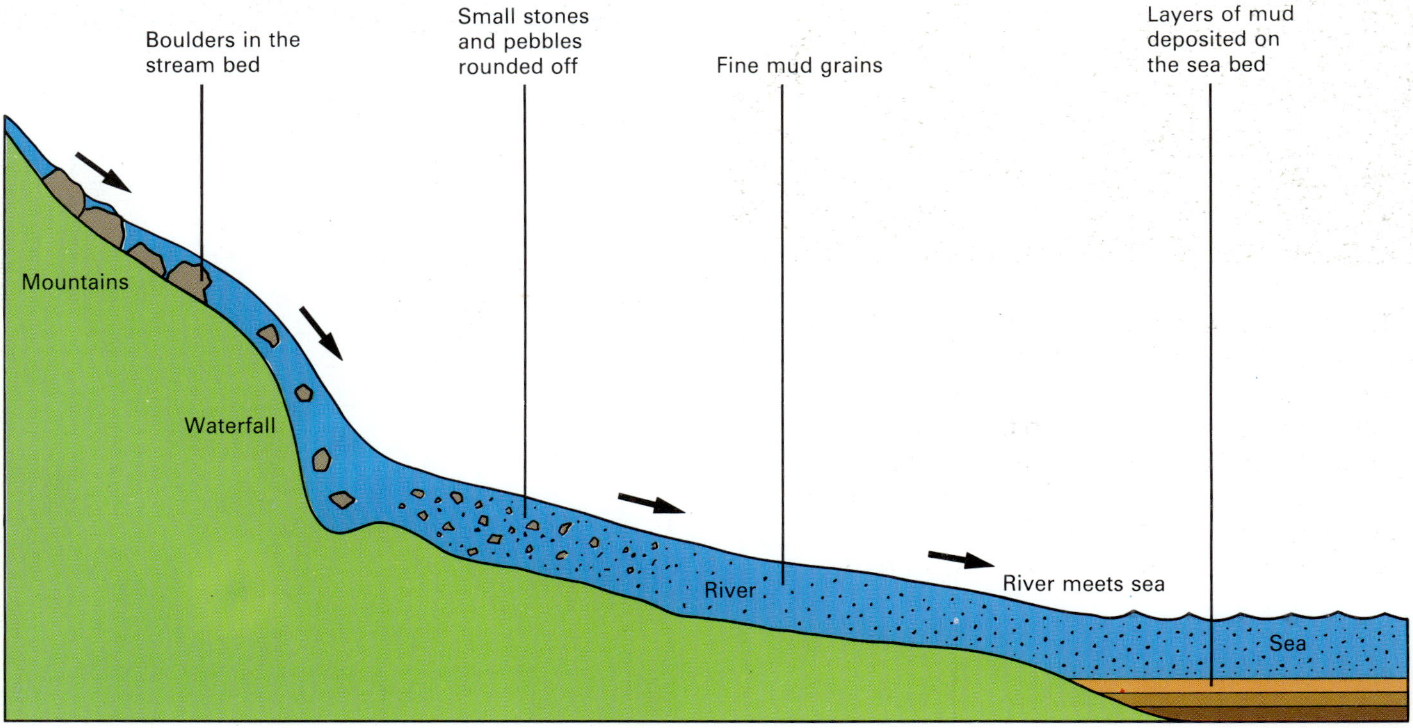

Unit 7.2

Hot desert areas

Deserts are places which have little rain. Because there is so little rain, deserts have a special type of scenery.

In wetter areas, rain helps plants to grow. Plants in turn help make the soil when they rot. The soil covers up the rock beneath, and helps to break it up into new soil. Because there is more soil, more plants will grow.

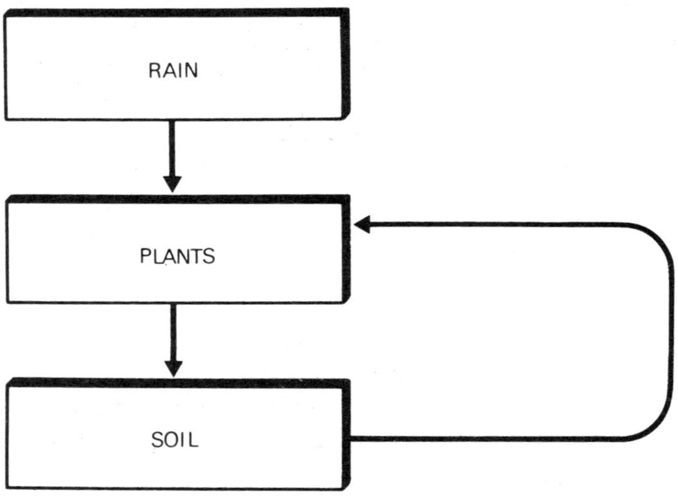

In a desert, plants will not grow. There is not enough water. There is no soil, so the rock is open to the sun, the wind, and frost. The rock is baked then frozen, until it breaks. The bits are blown away to give sand. The breakup of the rock is called **weathering.** Weathering is slow in deserts because they are so dry.

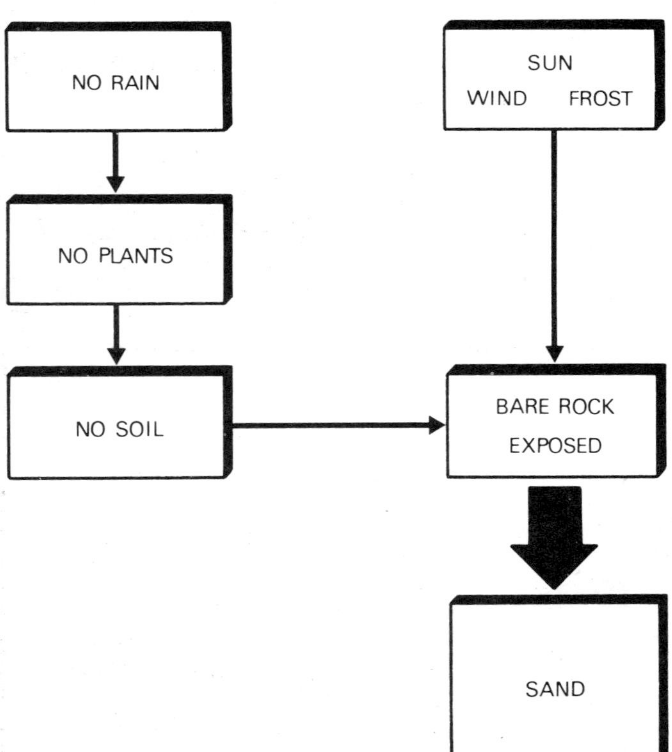

Sand is blown along by the wind leaving bare rock or stones. It builds up into piles called **sand dunes.** These can be under 1 metre or up to 50 metres high, big enough to cover your school and all the playing fields.

There are some strange shapes in deserts. This shape has been made by the wind blowing against the bottom of the rock. Sand in the wind rubs away like sandpaper until the shape is made. A feature like this is called a **mushroom rock.** The arrow on the photograph shows where the sand has worn the rock away.

Things to do/Hot desert areas

1a Make a copy of the sketch below.

b Write out the passage below and fill in the blank spaces.
This is a sketch of a . . . area. There are no signs of . . . to be seen. This is because there is no . . . in the area. The rocks on the ground have been broken off by a process called . . . The rock has been baked by the . . . during the day, then frozen during the . . . The tiny bits of rock are called . . . The wind can make the sand pile up into huge . . .

Use these words:

weathering	sand
desert	soil
sand dunes	life
sun	night

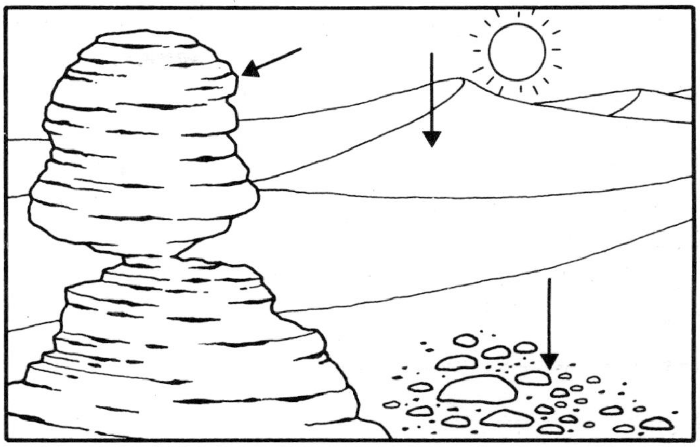

2a Make a copy of this sketch.
b Add your own labels to the features.

3a Find a map of the world in your Atlas which shows deserts.
b Make a list of the main deserts and write down the line of latitude which passes through the middle of each.
c From a map of world rainfall, write down the lowest figure in the key showing very dry areas.

Further work

4a Make a copy of the diagram below and answer the following questions.
b Is area **A** a highland or a lowland area?
c Which direction does the wind blow from?
d On which side of the mountain does rain fall?
e On which side would there be streams flowing?
f Explain why the sand dunes are further east than the rocky area.

Summary

Desert areas have little rainfall. They also have a special type of scenery.

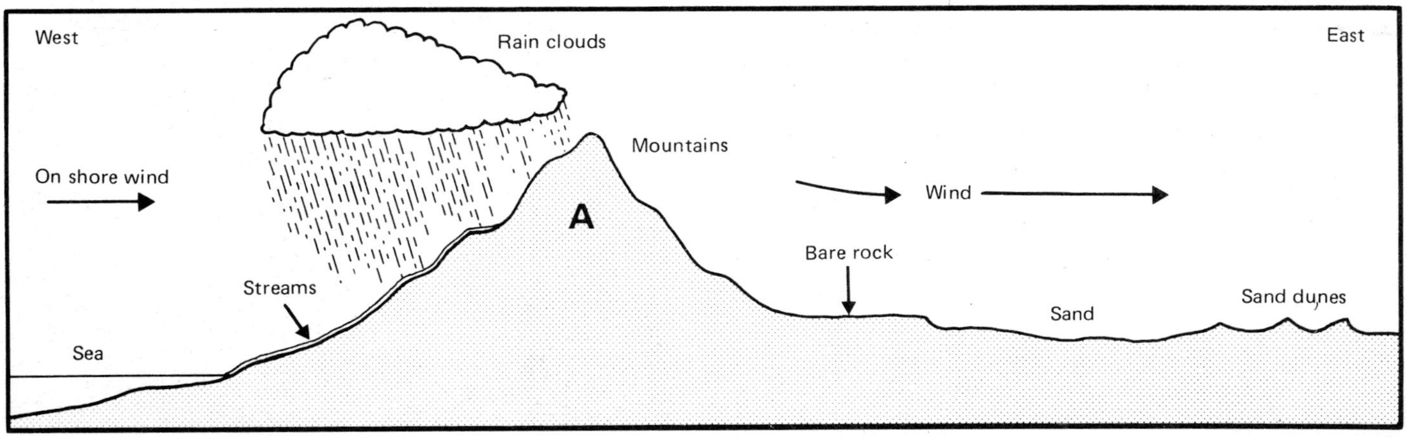

Unit 7.3
The coast

The two photographs below show the sea in very different moods. A quiet sea is flat and calm. An angry sea can batter a ship to bits against the rocks. It can also erode the coast and move bits of rock from one place to another.

A

B

This photograph shows how foolish it can be to build a house too near to a cliff. The cliff will wear back and the house will fall into the sea.

C

Here the opposite has happened. The village used to be by the sea but stones and sand have blocked the bay.

The sea picks up stones from along the coast and throws them at the cliffs. Areas which have softer rock are worn away more easily than areas of hard rock. This is called coastal **erosion** and gives **bays** and **headlands.**

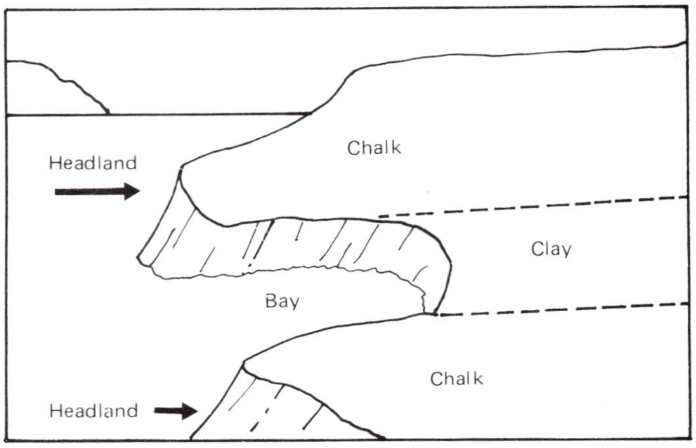

Rock worn away from one part is carried along and dropped somewhere else. This is called **deposition**. Sometimes it forms **beaches** of sand or pebbles. **Spits** can also be made. A spit is a long finger of sand and shingle built up by the sea.

Things to do/The coast

1 Look at the two photographs of the sea **A** and **B**. Write a paragraph to describe the sea in each photograph.

2 Look at photograph **C** showing buildings near the sea.
 a Draw a sketch of the photograph.
 b Say why you think the buildings were put there.
 c Describe what has happened.

3 When scientists write about the moods of the sea, they use figures instead of words. The pressure of the waves tells how much erosion is going on. The greater the pressure, the more erosion.
 a Copy the chart and fill in the last column with the following words (you can use the same words more than once):
 little erosion – greatest erosion – increasing erosion – decreasing erosion.
 b Describe what you think the weather would have been like during the week.

Day	Pressure	Effect on the coast
Monday	5 (tonnes per sq metre)	little erosion
Tuesday	7	–
Wednesday	10	–
Thursday	30	–
Friday	28	–
Saturday	15	–
Sunday	5	–

Further work

4 Study the two diagrams below. They show a coastline as it changed over 500 years.
 a Draw the two diagrams.
 b Describe the differences you notice.
 c Try to explain why the changes were taking place.

Summary
The coastline is always changing its shape. Some parts are being worn away, while other parts are being built up.

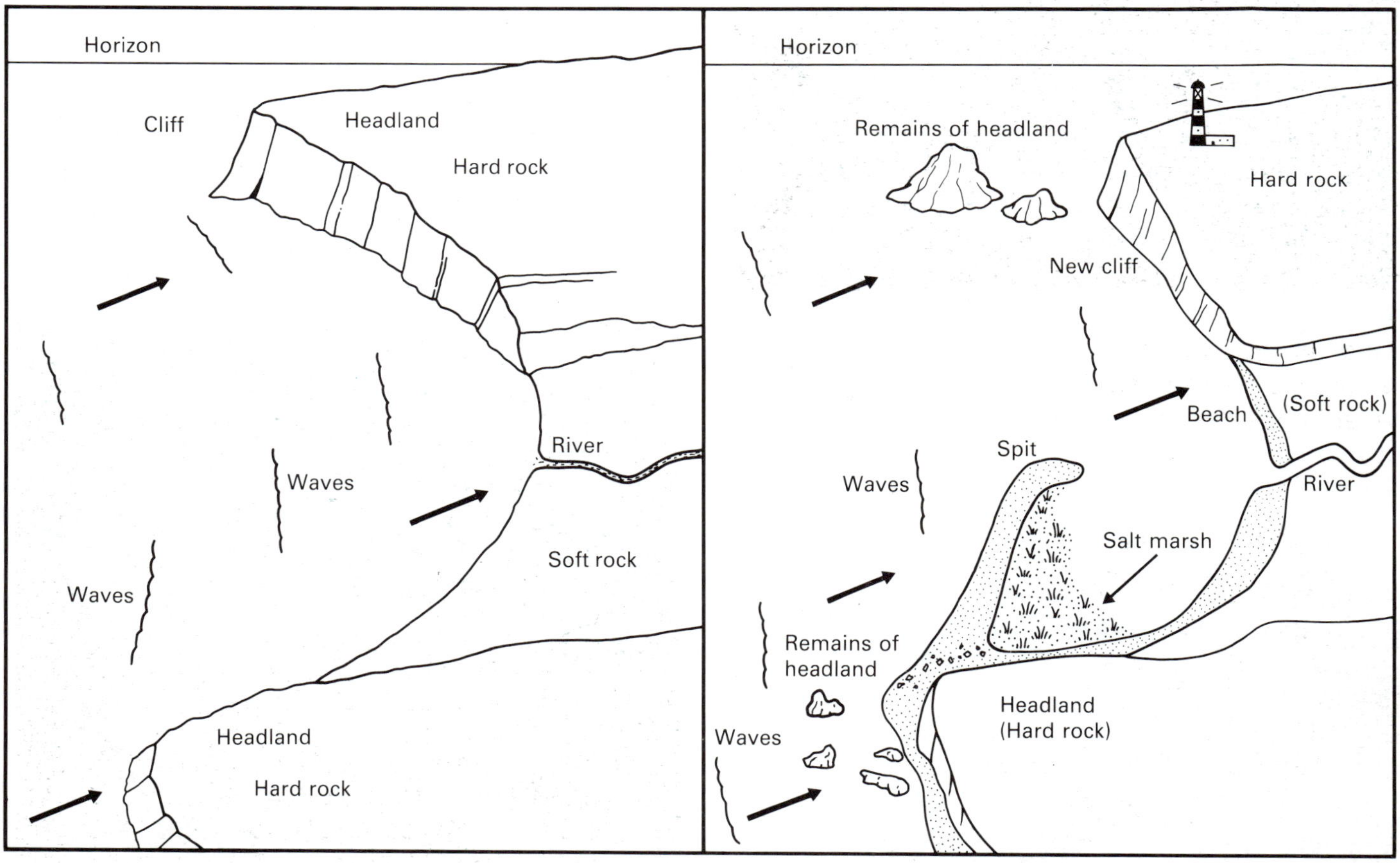

Unit 7.4

Glacial scenery

Every year, the weather seems to be different. Some years have long hot summers and freezing winters. Sometimes, summers are wet and winters are mild.

20,000 years ago, Britain's climate was very different. Most of Europe was covered by **ice sheets** hundreds of metres thick. Valleys were filled with wedges of ice called **glaciers** which moved towards the lowlands. This was the period which is called the **Ice Age**.

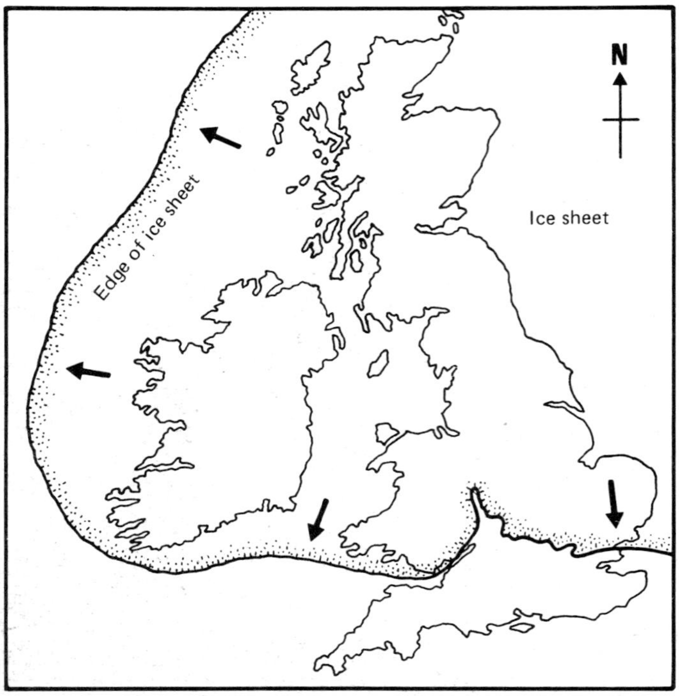

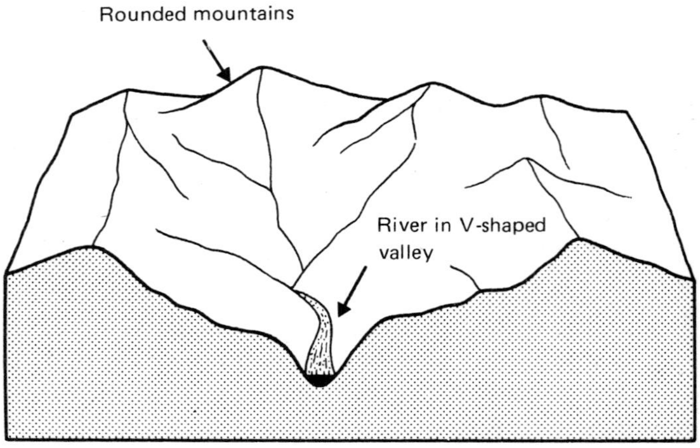

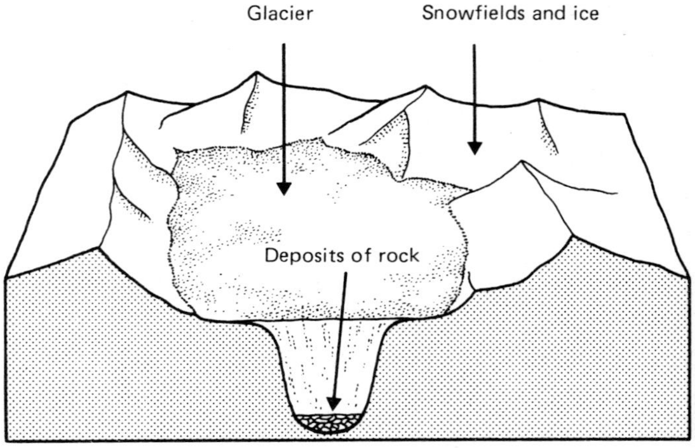

In the mountains, the shape of the land was changed. Rainwater ran into cracks in the rock and then turned to ice which expanded and shattered the rock. In this way, great hollows called **corries** were cut into mountainsides leaving sharp ridges called **arêtes** between them. These corries fed their ice to glaciers which slowly ground their way along old river valleys. Valleys were made deeper and wider as the glaciers moved all before them. When the ice at last melted, the bits of rock were dumped all over the lowlands.

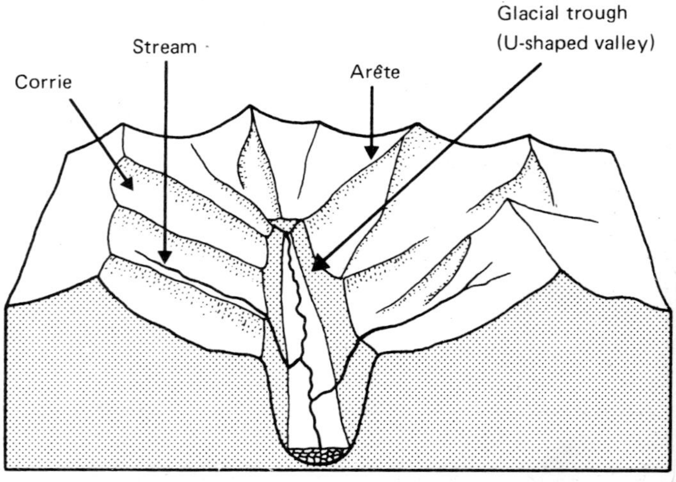

Today, the areas which were covered by ice have huge valleys with smooth rounded slopes. These valleys are called **glacial troughs**. They usually have small streams flowing in them, but these streams are much too small to have carved out the trough. What we can see today in Britain is the result of something which happened thousands of years ago. In many parts of the world, however, ice sheets and glaciers are carving glacial scenery at this very minute.

Things to do/Glacial scenery

1 Describe what happens in Britain today during a very cold winter. Mention the type of weather, the way the scenery changes, and some of the problems we have to face.

2 These countries are used to snow, glaciers and ice sheets.

Switzerland Norway Chile
Austria Greenland Antarctica

a List these countries and using your Atlas, fill in a chart like this;

Country	Mountain or lowland	Near or far from North/South Pole
Switzerland	Mountain	Far from Poles

b About how much of the British Isles was covered by ice during the Ice Age?

c Was the area where you live covered by ice?

3 These two cross sections show an area before and after it has been covered by ice.

a Make a copy of each sketch.

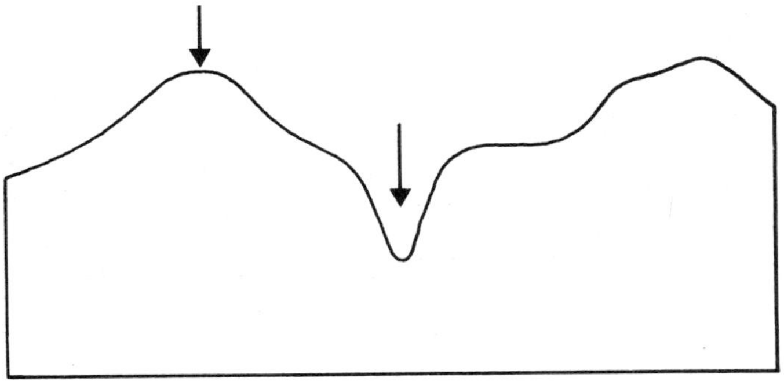

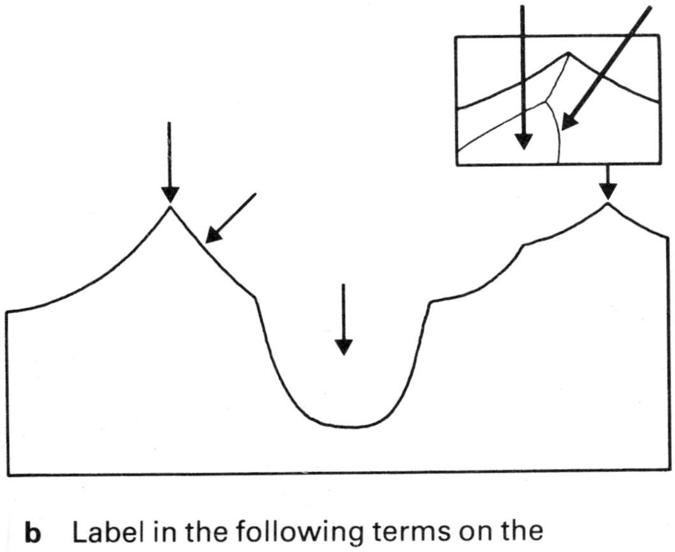

b Label in the following terms on the sketches –

rounded mountain arête ridge
V-shaped valley steep slopes
glacial trough peak

Further work

4 Make a sketch of this photograph. Label in as many features as you can see.

Summary
Many of the features in the landscape were formed thousands of years ago. In Britain, the Ice Age left features which can still be seen today.

Unit 8.1

Settlement/Types of settlement

What do you know about the place you live in? How long ago was it built, and why was it built in the first place? Do you know how it got its name, or even how many people live there? A study of **settlements** can give the answer to questions like these.

These photographs show some of the types of settlements people live in. They come in all shapes and sizes. Small settlements in the country are called **rural** settlements. The word **urban** is used to describe a town or other large settlement.

Gwynedd, Wales – Farms and other buildings standing on their own are called **isolated** places.

Wensleydale, North Yorkshire – A small settlement where there are only a few houses but no shops or other services is called a **hamlet**.

Austwick, North Yorkshire – A larger group of houses with a church and some services we need every day, like shops, is called a **village**.

Bristol, Avon – A **town** has thousands of houses with large shops, factories, as well as cinemas, library, schools and a hospital. A **city** is a large town which has either a university or a cathedral.

Unit 8.1

Things to do/Types of settlement

1a Arrange these settlements in order of size. Put the smallest one first and the largest last –
town, farmhouse, village, hamlet, city.

b Beside each, list the types of buildings you would expect to see there.

2 The map below shows an area where there are many types of settlement. Hamlets and farms are too small to be drawn on a map of this scale.

a Complete this chart by counting up the number of each type of settlement –

Type	Number
Farmhouses	1000
Hamlets	200
Villages	–
Towns	–
Cities	–

b Write out the following sentences using the correct word –
The bigger the settlement, the more/fewer there are.
There tend to be more/less of the smaller settlements.
Small settlements are usually near to/far from other small settlements.
Large settlements are close to/far from other large settlements.

Further work

3 Write a paragraph to compare living in a town to living in a village. Say which you prefer and explain why.

Summary

Settlements are places where people live. There are many types of settlement. There is a link between the size of the settlement and the number of settlements of that size in an area.

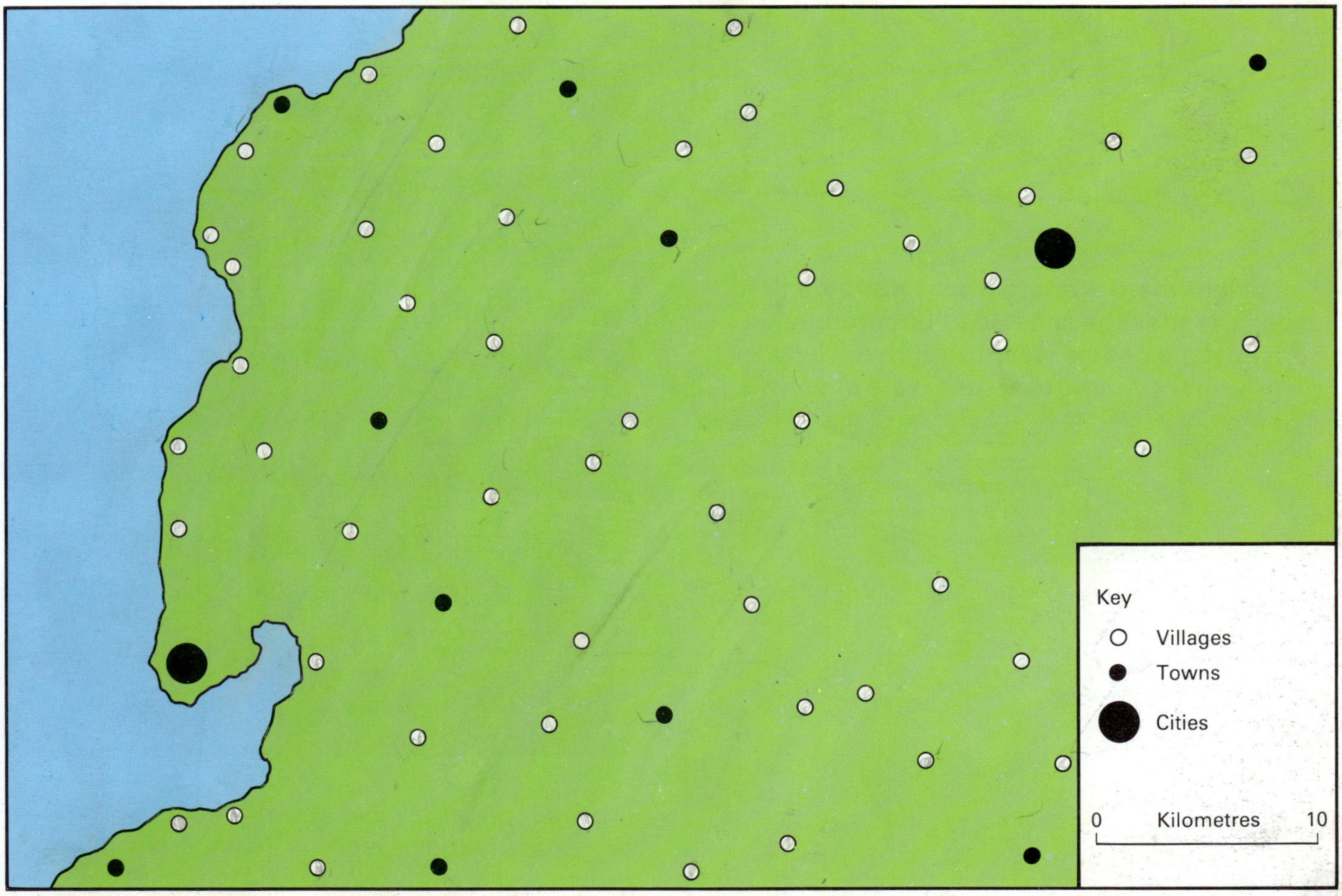

Unit 8.2

Names and sites

There may be a pupil called Smith, Baker or Miller in your school. These names could be traced back hundreds of years to an ancestor who worked as a blacksmith or who made bread.

Names of settlements also have meanings. Different groups of people have invaded Britain in the past. Each group has built settlements and named them in their own language.

Many place names are Anglo-Saxon. Anglo-Saxons lived in England about 1500 years ago. In their language, **ham** was a homestead, **ton** was an enclosure for animals, and **ing** meant a family. The city of Birmingham was Beorm – ing – ham; the homestead of Beorm's family.

The place where the settlement was built is called the **site.** The site had to be carefully chosen if the people were to survive. These diagrams show how two sites were chosen.

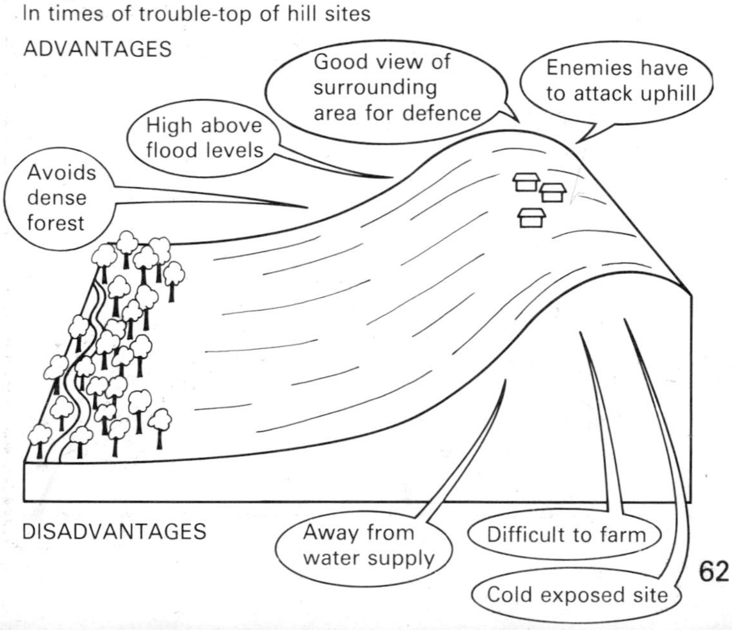

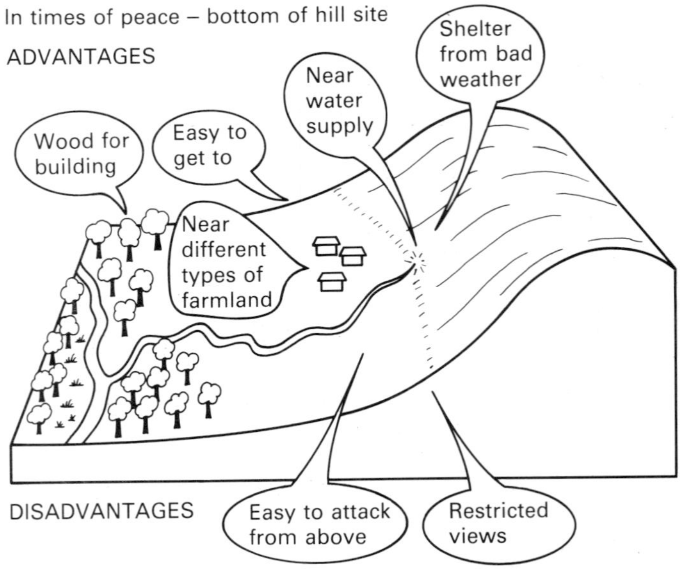

Settlements have also been built where there was something in the ground to be mined. In areas with coal, villages are built to house miners and their families.

Most people today live in settlements which began as villages. Over the years, many have grown and are now towns and cities.

Things to do/Names and sites

1 Make your own list of people's names which could have a meaning. Beside each, say what type of job their ancestor might have done. The spelling may have changed a little over the years.

2 Other common name endings in Britain are as follows:

ford – a river crossing
wick – a cattle or dairy farm
bury – a fortified place
thorpe – a Viking village
by – a Viking homestead

a Using either an Atlas or an Ordnance survey map, mark in and name settlements with these name endings on some tracing paper.

3 You are the scout for a Saxon family which is looking for a site to build homes and farm. The area shown in the sketch is empty and seems to be suitable.

a Draw either a sketch or a map of the area.

b Write a report on the three sites A, B, and C to describe the advantages and disadvantages of each. Mention these things in your report –

water supply – defence – shelter – farmland – dry land.

4 Describe the coal mining village. Say how it would be different from a farming village.

Further work

5a Using your Atlas, name the rivers which these British towns lie beside:

London – Nottingham – York – Shrewsbury – Newcastle.

b Compare a map of population distribution with a physical map of Britain. What do you notice about where most of the people live?

Summary

Place names can tell us about the past. Sites had to be carefully chosen for the settlement to survive.

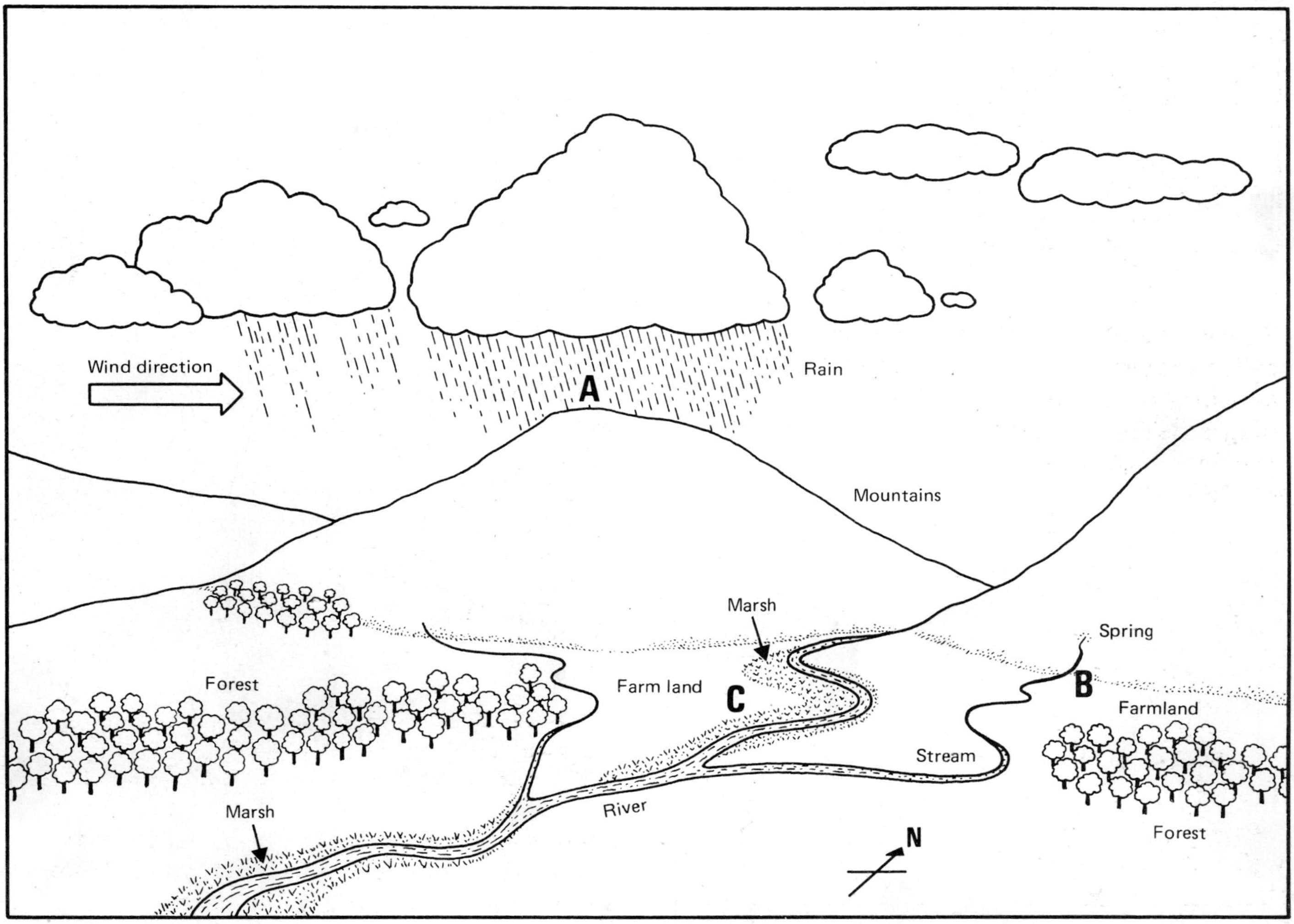

Unit 8.3

Living in towns

Today, eight out of every ten people in Britain live in a town or city. Most people have their job in a town. They do most of their shopping in a town. They also come to a town for their entertainment at night.

No two towns are exactly the same, just like no two people are exactly the same. But like people, towns have many things in common. Some towns are almost like twins. You may think you recognize some of the places shown in these photographs.

In most towns, these different types of buildings tend to be grouped together into separate areas. The word **zone** is sometimes used instead of area. A map which shows these different zones is called a **land use map**. This map shows the main land use zones for a typical city.

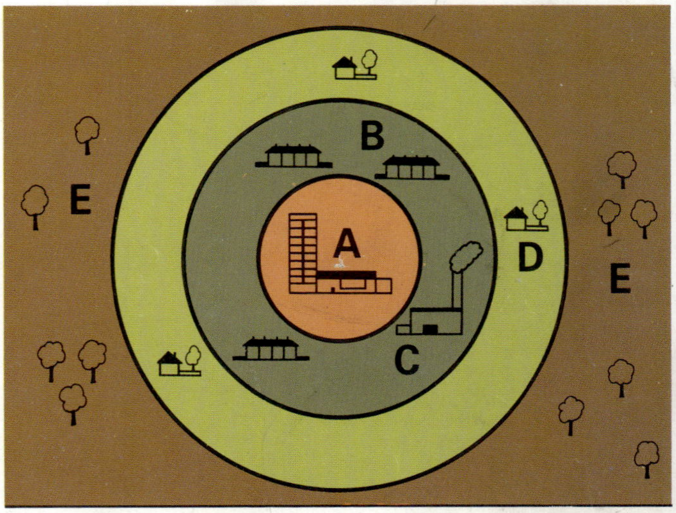

A Shops and offices
B Old houses
C Factories
D Suburbs
E Countryside

Things to do/Living in towns

1 Study the photographs on the opposite page.

a For each photograph, write the name or location of somewhere you know which is nearly the same.

b For each place you have named, say how it is different from the photograph.

2 This list of buildings are those which most people visit at some time:

Post Office	sports stadium	bread shop
hospital	restaurant	cinema
library	furniture shop	newsagents

a Draw a chart to show whether you would expect to find these buildings in a town or in a village

Buildings found in a town	Buildings found in a village

b Write out the list of buildings again. Beside each, say how often you think most people would visit them –
every day . . . once a week . . .
once a month . . . once a year.

3 Write out the two statements from the four below which you think are true:

a More big buildings are found in villages than in towns.

b In the centre of town, you find buildings which you only need to visit once or twice a year.

c Village people always travel to town to buy bread and milk.

d Many village people travel to town to work.

4 Make a copy of the cross section through a city and label in these terms in the correct place:
houses, shops and offices,
factories and houses, countryside.

Further work

5 Outline and then shade in and identify the land use zones in this photograph.

6 Draw an outline map of the main land use zones you can see in this photograph.

Summary
Every town is different, but they do have many things in common. Most people in Britain live in towns.

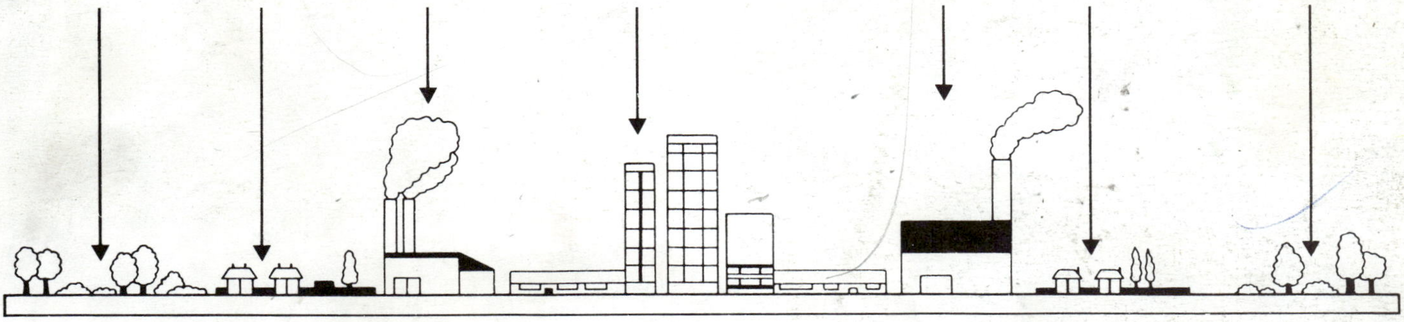

Unit 8.4

Types of houses

Think about the house you live in. Then dream about the house you would like to live in. There are many types of house to choose from. Some are very small and are surrounded by other houses, while others have large gardens with a swimming pool. Some are old while others have only just been built. Most of our dream houses are ones which we could never afford to buy!

The photographs show the main types of houses which people in Britain live in. Each has its good and its bad points.

A **terraced** house is joined to the houses next to it on both sides. They are usually old with a small garden or back yard and two floors. There are also modern terraced houses. Old terraced houses are the cheapest type in most towns.

A **semi-detached** house is joined to one other house but is separated from the next. Most British families live in 'semis'. They usually have a garden at the front and the back and often a garage.

A **detached** house does not touch any other house. It stands alone in its own garden. Many old large detached houses have been divided up into **flats or bed-sitters.** These are one or two rooms in the building which single people or students often rent.

High rise tower blocks can have 15 floors (or storeys). **Low rise blocks** do not have more than four storeys. Both are divided into flats or **maisonettes.** A flat is all on one level. A maisonette has an upstairs and a downstairs. A luxury flat at the top of the building is called a **penthouse.**

A **bungalow** is a house which has only one floor.

Terraced houses

Maisonettes

High rise tower block

Detached

Semi-detached

Bungalows

Things to do/Types of houses

1 Draw two sketches, one of the house you live in, and one of your dream house.

2 Write a sentence to explain the meaning of each of these terms:

terraced;	high rise tower block;
flat;	penthouse;
maisonette;	detached;
semi-detached;	bungalow.

3 For each of the people shown below, say what type of house you think they might live in. Give a reason to explain your answer.

a Mr Brown and Mrs Brown have five small children. He has saved some money and wants somewhere for his children to play.

b Mr Singh has not been in Britain for long so he has not yet saved much money. He and his wife want their own house for their family of two children. They do not have a car.

c Mr and Mrs Murphy nave just soid their large detached house. They are both over 60 and found the house too big. It was expensive to heat and there were too many stairs. They like their new home.

d Miss Jones is single and has moved to the city to become a nurse. She wants a few rooms for as little money as possible.

e Mr. MacNeil is a business tycoon. He wants a home with a good view of the city centre. He will pay whatever is asked to get the best.

Further work

4 Write out this description of a house for sale from a newspaper. Try to find out what exactly it means:

S-det. 3 bdrm. 50's hse,
2 receps. lge gdns. gar. freehold.

Summary
There are many different types of houses to suit people with different needs.

Unit 9.1

Industry and our needs/A quarry

Most of the things you use come from rocks under the ground. Your house is made of stone, brick, or concrete which all come from rocks. The pen and pencil you write with have parts which come from rocks. The work of getting things out of the ground is called **extractive industry.** (Remember that to extract something means to take it out, like teeth!)

The photograph shows a quarry where a rock is being dug up. This rock is **limestone.** Other rocks which are quarried at different places are granite, slate, and sandstone. Rocks which have metals in them like iron or copper, are called **ores.** The iron or copper has to be melted out of the **iron ore** or **copper ore.**

This cross section through a quarry shows what has to be done. Explosives break up the rock. This is called **blasting.** The bits are fed into a **crusher** which breaks them up even more. A conveyor belt takes the bits to a **grader** where sieves sort out the bits into different sizes, or grades. The graded bits are put into **storage bins.** Lorries drive under the bins and are loaded up. The rock is then taken away either to be used as it is, or to be turned into something else. Limestone is used for building roads, helping crops grow, building houses, and in making steel.
Quarrying is called a **primary industry** because it is a first stage and gives **raw materials** for other industries.

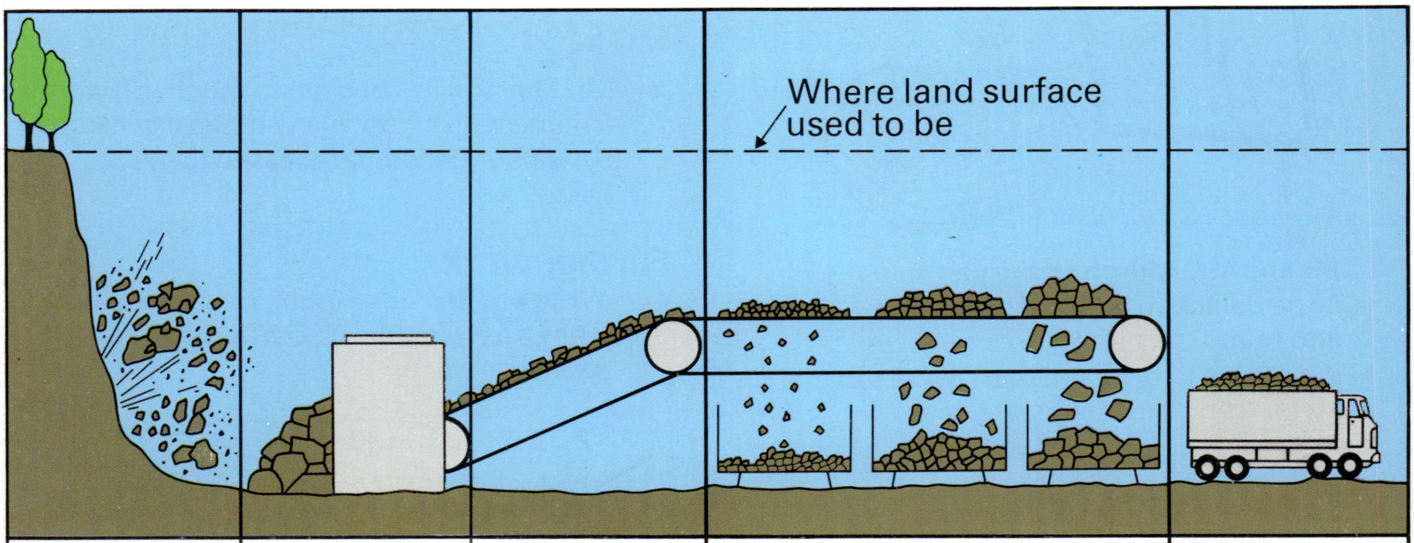

1 Blasting	2 Crusher	3 Conveyor belt	4 Grader/Storage bins	5 Lorry

Things to do/A quarry

1 Try to imagine your day so far without metals or other things made from rocks. Write a short story to describe how your day would have been different.

2a Make a copy of the sketch below. It shows the area in the photograph on the opposite page.

b Complete the labels using words from the opposite page.

3 The steps taken in getting the limestone from the ground are shown in the diagram on the opposite page. Copy this diagram and under each section describe what is going on.

4 Answer these questions:

a What might the land have been used for before the quarry was dug?

b Why might quarrying be a dangerous job?

c What method of transport could be used to carry the rock away, other than lorry?

d What do you think should happen to the hole left by the quarry workings when all the rock is gone?

Further work

5 Find a map of rocks in Britain in your Atlas. This is called a **geology** map. Trace or copy an outline of Britain and shade in all the areas which are made of limestone rock.

Summary

Quarrying is an important industry. Many of the everyday things we use are made from rocks. Quarrying is called an extractive industry. Raw materials are provided for other industries.

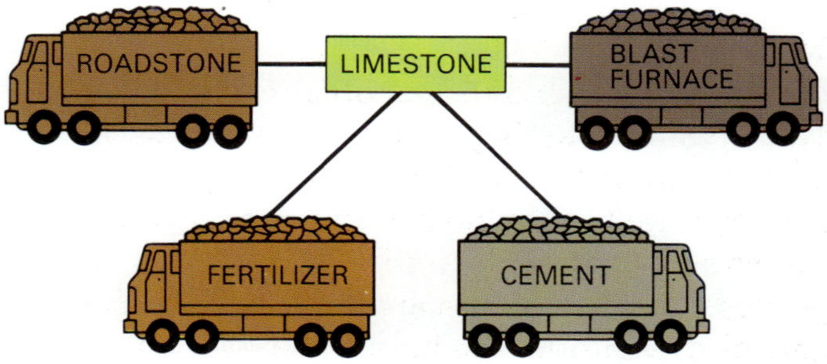

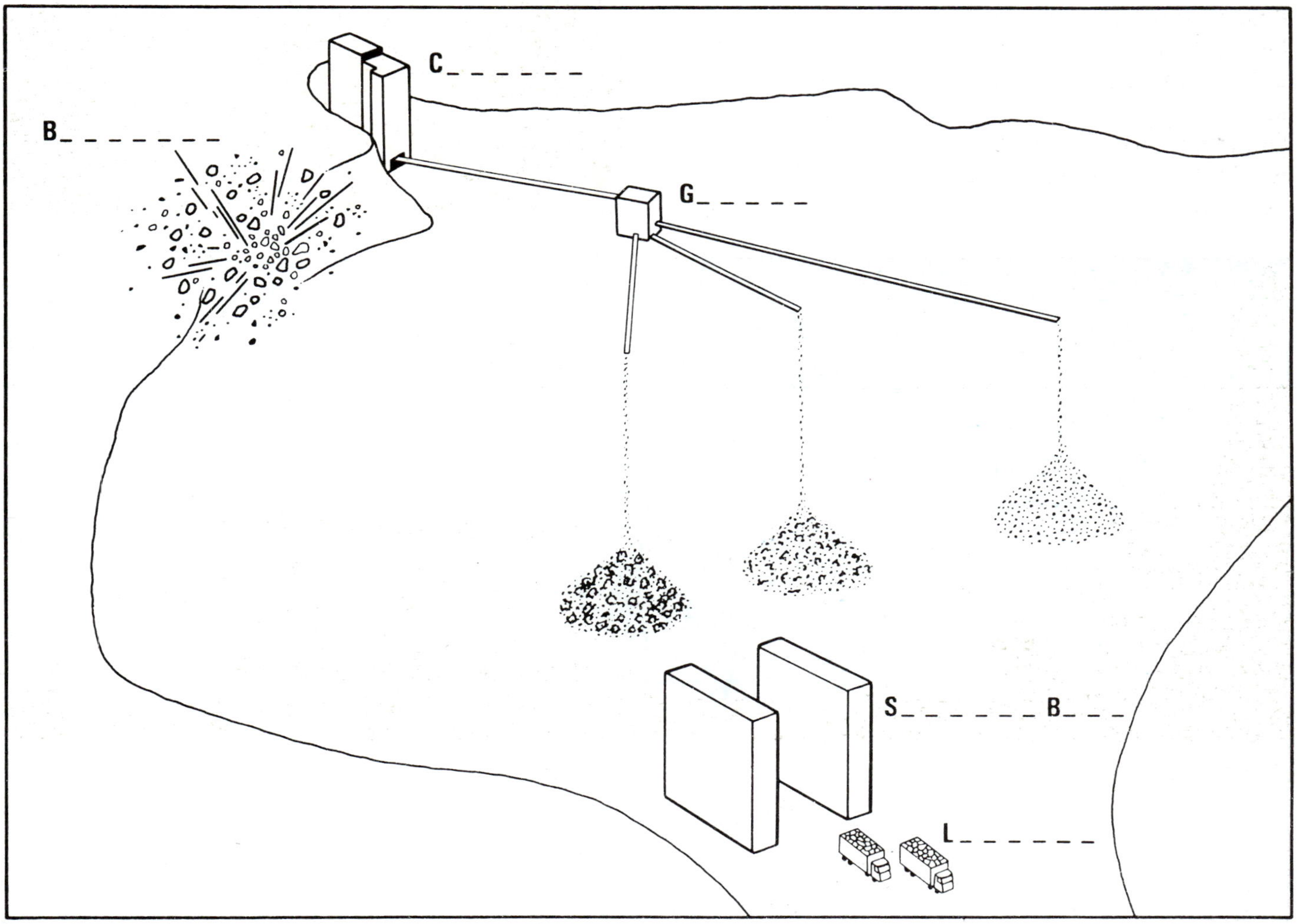

Unit 9.2
A farm

The photograph shows a small farm which tries to meet our needs by growing things. Chickens are an important food in Britain as you will see in any supermarket. Flowers are always in demand for special occasions. Growing flowers for sale in shops is called **horticulture.**

Compared to other types of farm, this one is very small. Nothing can be left to chance. Because the sun does not always shine at the right time, and because it often rains at the wrong time, all the flowers are grown in **glasshouses.** The glasshouse is heated by hot water pipes to keep the temperature the same. An oil fired burner heats the water. A special **artificial soil** is used to control the growth of the flowers. When ready, the flowers are picked and packed, then immediately taken away to shops all over the country.

The chicks are bought when one day old. They are put into a **broiler house** which is also kept warm so that the chicks will grow more quickly. They are fed on specially made up foods. When they reach 4lbs weight, they are sold to a factory where they are killed and packed. The farm in the photograph has about 50,000 chickens.

The farm can be run like a factory because the conditions can be controlled. Although it is expensive to build the greenhouses and broiler sheds and to keep them heated, the farmer could soon go broke if he kept everything out of doors.

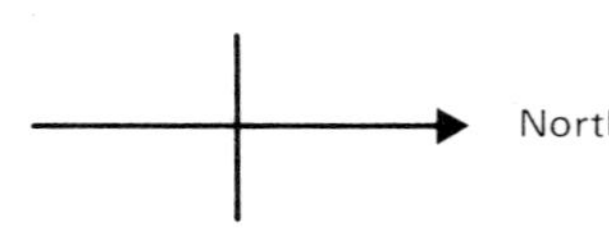

Key	
1	Garden and houses
2	Workshops and storage
3	Chicken houses
4	Flower glasshouses
5	Packing shed
6	Broiler house
7	Oil tank
8	Land for new water reservoir

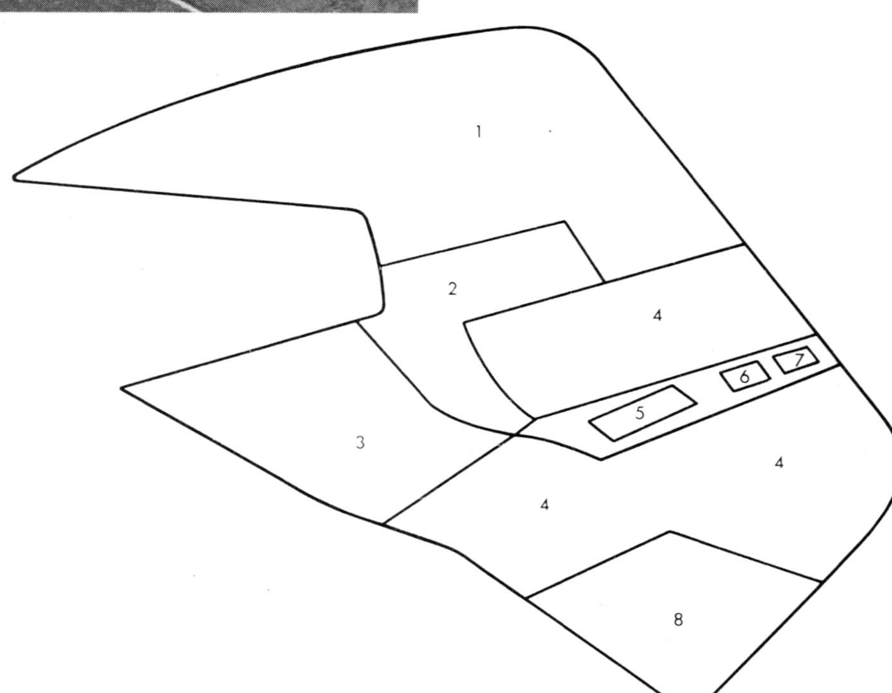

Things to do/A farm

1a Make a list of the occasions when flowers are used.

b For each of these types of flower, give the occasion they are usually used on –
carnations roses daffodils
mistletoe lillies

c What are some of the problems which gardeners have growing flowers out of doors in Britain?

d Write down the different ways chickens can be cooked and eaten.

e What would happen if the farmer let the chicks run loose around the farm buildings?

f Why do you think the farmer does not get worried about killing all the chickens?

g Why do supermarkets like to have chickens all at the same weight?

2a Copy out and complete these figures for a farm in 1980.

Costs per year (1980)	£	Returns from Sales	
Buying chicks	50 000	Chickens	100 000
Flower cuttings	100 000	Flowers	150 000
Wages	40 000	**Total Sales**	?
Heating oil	20 000	Subtract total costs	?
Electricity and Water	10 000		
Repairs and insurance	10 000	Subtract tax	10 000
Total costs	?	**Net profit**	?

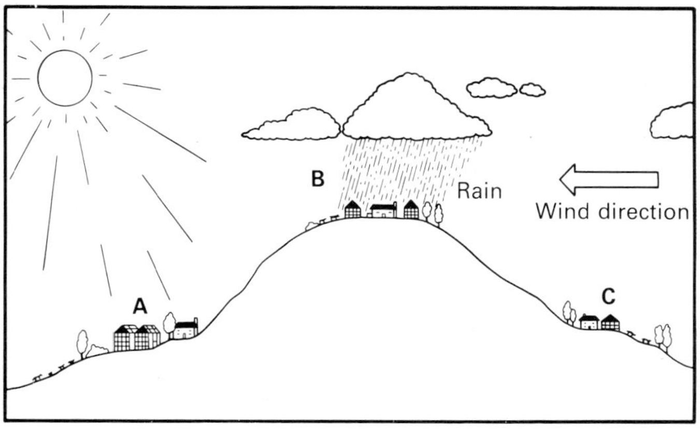

b What is the most expensive thing the farmer has to buy?

c What would it cost the farmer if the price of oil doubled and he paid his workers twice as much?
What does the farmer earn most of his money from?
Make a list of the things which the farmer might do with the net profit which he makes.

Remember that he may need to save some money in case the weather is bad one year and he has to spend more on heating.

Further work

3a Make a copy of the diagram below.

b If you were going to begin growing flowers for sale, which of three farms would you buy? Explain your choice.

4 Look at the table showing the 1985 figures. Write a paragraph to describe the changes which the farmer has made.

Costs per year (1985)	£	Returns from sales	£
Buying chickens	50 000	Chickens	125 000
Buying flower cuttings	50 000	Flower blooms	65 000
*Buying flower blooms from abroad	90 000	Selling imported blooms	130 000
Wages	60 000	**Total sales**	320 000
Heating (oil)	14 000		
Electricity and Water	8 000	Total costs	280 000
Repairs and insurance	8 000	Gross profit	40 000
		Subtract VAT	24 000
		Subtract Tax	6 000
Total costs	280 000	**Net profit**	10 000

* Imported by air from Israel and Colombia.

Summary

Farming is a business just like any other industry. Some things are best grown indoors where conditions can be controlled.

Unit 9.3
A chocolate factory

Chocolate cannot be grown on a farm. It must be made in a **factory.** This photograph shows one factory where chocolates and sweets are made. This type of work is called **manufacturing.**

The **raw materials** which make chocolate are cocoa, milk and sugar. The factory must be built where these three raw materials can be brought together and **processed.** The chocolate then has to be wrapped and the finished **product** delivered to the shops. The word **market** is used to describe the people the finished product is sold to. An industry which makes something from raw materials is called a **manufacturing industry**.

Some factories like the one above are clean and do not disturb the people who live nearby. Others are dirty and cause a nuisance. This nuisance is called **pollution.** Here are some examples of pollution.

People need factories to make goods and to provide jobs. We do not need pollution which can damage our health. A factory should try to make things at a profit and cause as little pollution as possible.

Things to do/A chocolate factory

1 There are many kinds of chocolates and sweets. Make a list of the different raw materials which are used to make different types. A sweet wrapper may help.

2 Write a sentence to explain what each of the following terms means:

raw materials manufacturing industry
pollution market
product

3 Study these three photographs below. They show very different kinds of factory.

a Describe what each factory looks like.

b Describe any types of pollution which you think each factory might be causing.

Further work

4 Raw materials can come from our own country, or they may need to be brought in from other countries. Goods brought in from abroad are called **imported goods**.

a On a simple world outline, mark in the following places and join them to Britain with arrows –

Cocoa from Ghana
Sugar from the West Indies
Wool from Australia
Oil from Saudi Arabia
Coffee from Brazil
Wood from Sweden

Summary
Factories are buildings where raw materials are brought together to be turned into a finished product. Factories can cause pollution of many different kinds.

Unit 9.4

An airport

Travel is something we all need to do almost every day. Some distances, like from home to school, are short. Holidays are times when we travel much further. Business people need to travel all year round, and factory products must be delivered on time. The fastest way to travel the greatest distance is by aircraft. Most large cities have an **airport** which looks like the one shown in the photograph.

Passengers arrive and park in the car park. Tickets, luggage, and passports are checked in at the **terminal building.** When the flight is called, they walk onto the **apron** where the aircraft is waiting. The **control tower** tells the pilot when it is clear to take off. The aircraft moves to the end of the **runway** then the engines are revved up. The aircraft leaps down the runway and soon the ground is left far behind and the landscape looks like a toy.

The people who work at the airport have one thing in common. None of them make anything. The baggage porters, air traffic controllers, clerks, even the pilots, are all providing a service. An airport is an example of a **service industry.** The term **tertiary industry** is sometimes used to describe work where people do not make anything.

Unit 9.4

Things to do/An airport

1 These jobs all have something in common, except one. Write down the odd one out and give a reason for your answer:
nurse postperson carpenter
lawyer waitress

2 The area shown in the map below has been bought for an airport to be built. The buildings and runways need to be planned.

a Study the information provided then draw your own airport plan. Try to keep aircraft away from the houses. Use the symbols shown below.
Three runways: the longest should face the main wind direction
Hangars for the aircraft
A terminal building with apron near the main road
A car park near the terminal

b Write a report on your plan, saying why you think it is best.

Further work

3 The timetable shows the destination of flights throughout the day from an airport in southern England.

a On an outline of western Europe, draw in a line from southern England to each of these places.

Destination	Departure Time	AM	PM
Frankfurt	0915		
Majorca	0930	9-30	
Paris	0945		
Malta	1000		
Belfast	1200		
Amsterdam	1230		
Edinburgh	1430		2-30
Rome	1600		
Dublin	1730		
Barcelona	1815		
Nice	2040		

b Write out the timetable and complete the column with am and pm times.

c Why do you think so many flights go to the Mediterranean coast?

d What sort of person might want to fly to Frankfurt?

Summary

An airport is an example of a service industry. People who work there provide a service for other people. Nothing is made at an airport.

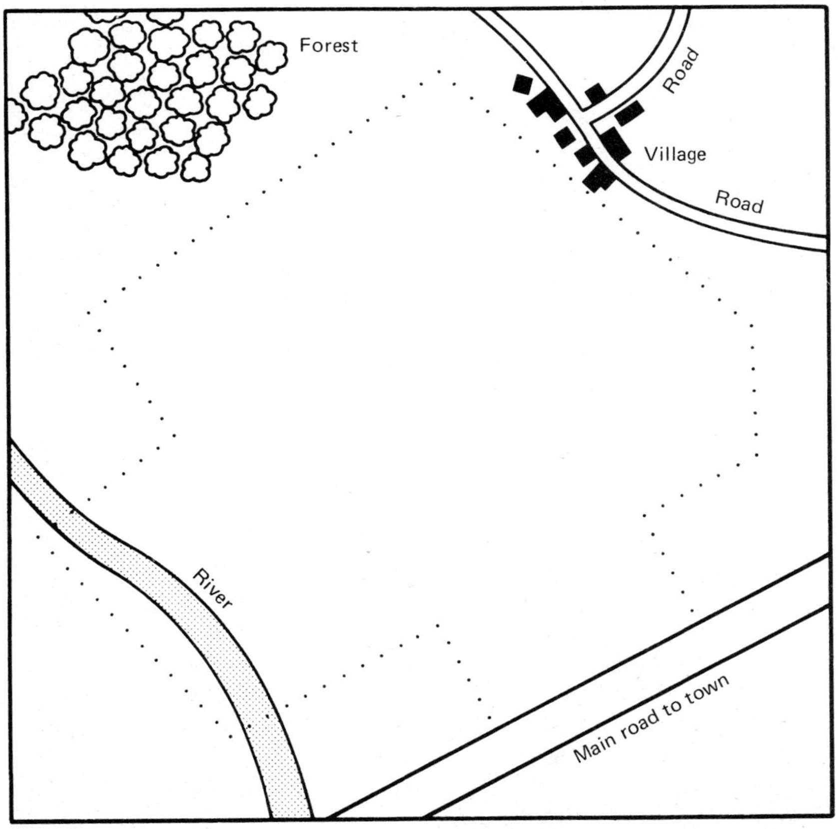

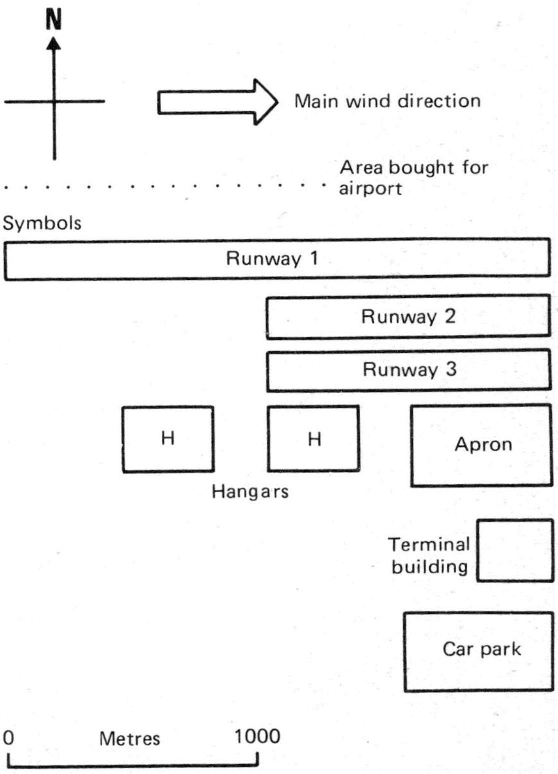

Unit 10.1

Routeways and transport/The shortest route

Signs like these usually stop people getting from one place to another in a straight line. A straight line distance should be the quickest between two points, but in real life, this is not always possible.

The headmaster in this school wants to keep the grass growing so that the school will look nice. Thousands of feet would soon turn the short path into a muddy track.

Concorde makes a supersonic bang when flying at top speed. It must not fly over countries who object to the noise. Instead, it tries to fly over areas of water where nobody will be disturbed. The extra speed makes up for the extra distance it has to travel.

Sea **routes** must go around land areas. The Suez canal was built to shorten and straighten the route between Europe and the Far East. The largest ships still have to go the long way around Africa because the canal is not deep enough.

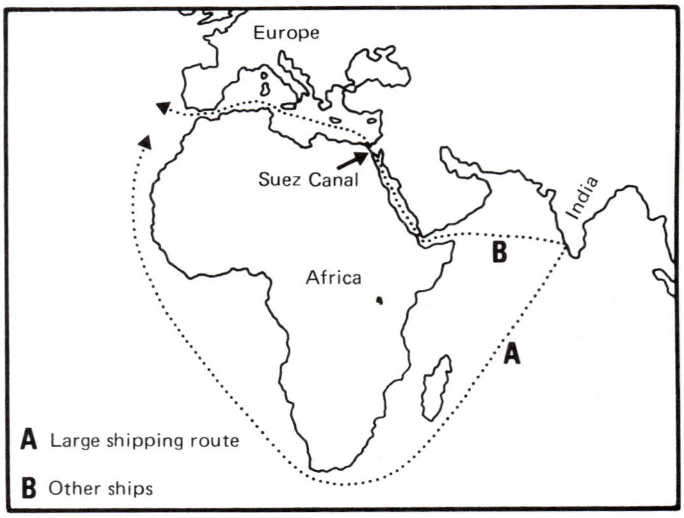

Roads are sometimes built to go around a village when the old road becomes too crowded. It would be wrong to knock down the houses to widen the road. A new wider road to **by-pass** the village is better.

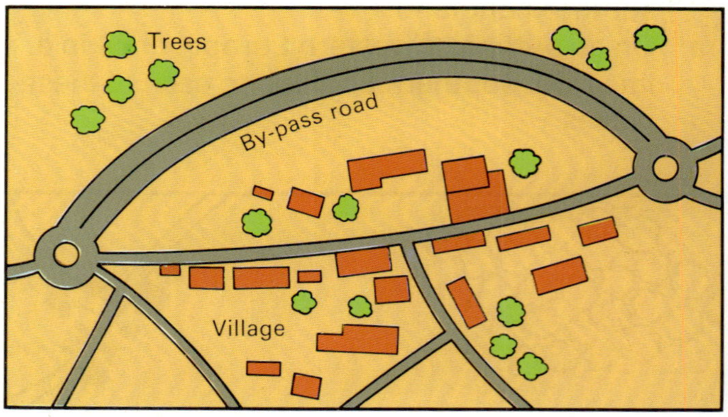

Railway engines cannot go up steep slopes with a heavy load. Tunnels and embankments can be built to keep the line flat. Trains cannot take any tight corners so lines are built as straight as possible. The word **gradient** is used to describe the slope.

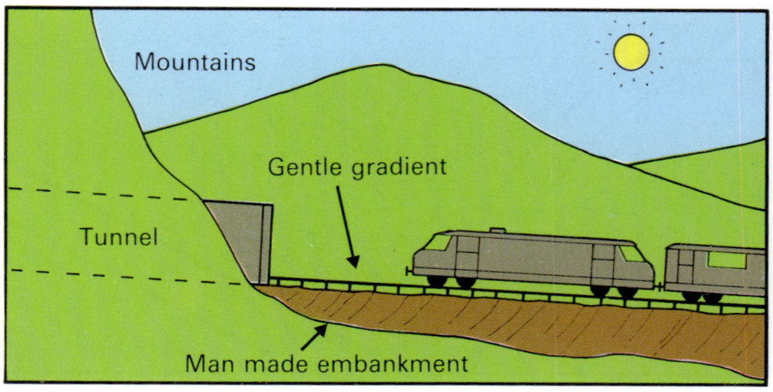

Unit 10.1

Things to do/The shortest route

1a Draw a sketch map to show your route to school.

b Draw on your map the things which stop you travelling in a straight line.

2 Are there any places in your school where the shortest route is not possible? Describe or sketch these places. If possible, measure the straight line distance and compare it to the actual distance you have to travel.

3 Four spies at the hut shown on the map are given a job. A foreign agent is hiding at the farm. He must be killed. To make sure the job is done, each spy takes a different route.

a Make out a chart to show how long each spy took to get to the farm. Each travels at 5km/hr approximately.

Example: Hannay
Basic time (50kms÷5) 10 hrs
Private estate 3
River 1
Total time ? hrs

b Which spy would reach the farm first?

c What was the greatest obstacle in each of the routes?

d Which was the longest route in kms?

e What happened to Arbuthnott ?

f Why did the spy who took the shortest route not get there first?

Further work

4 Explain why it is that the shortest route is not always the fastest. Give examples from the page opposite.

Summary

Routes are the paths that link one place with another. The route can be a footpath, road, sealane, airway, railway. A straight route is not always possible.

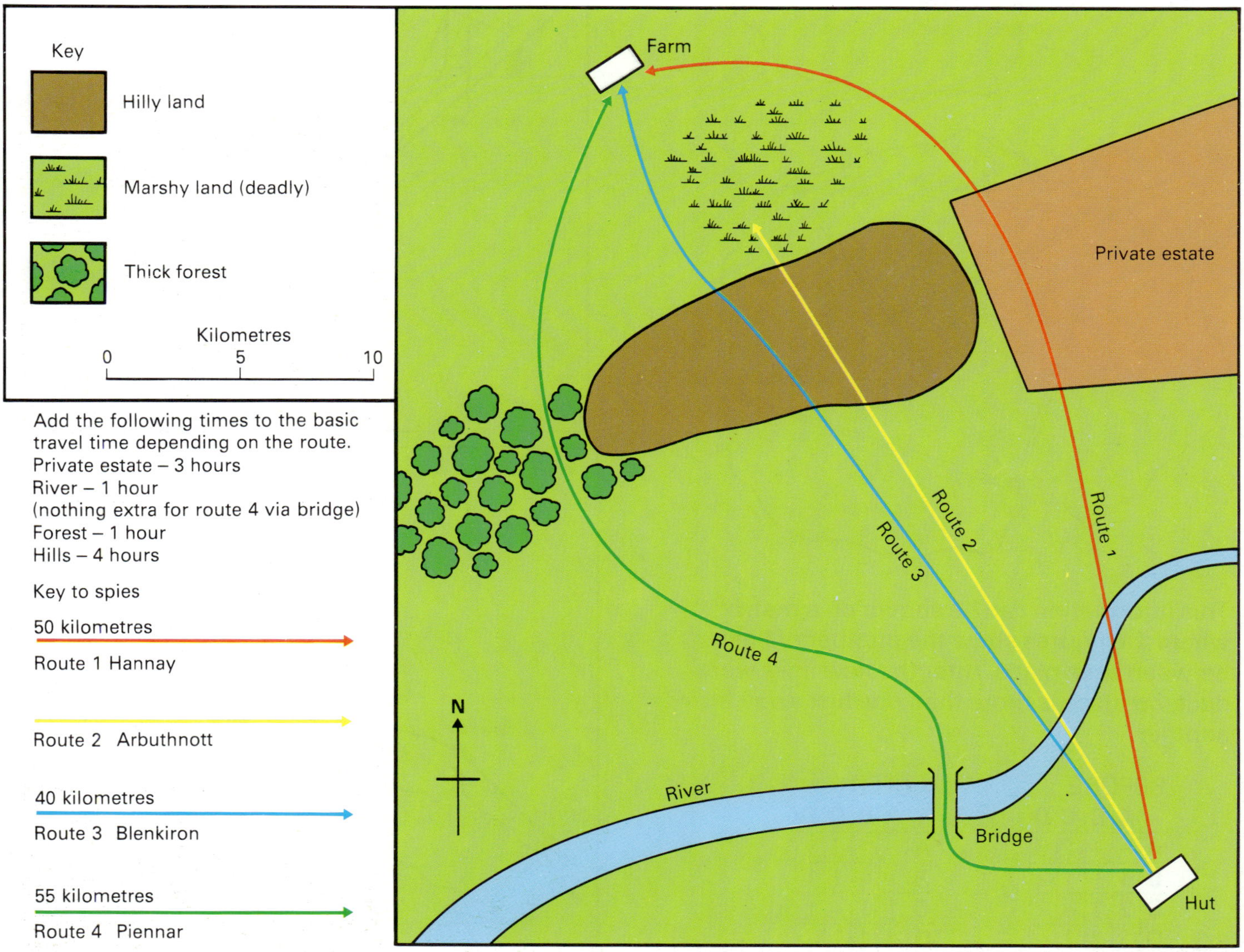

Unit 10.2

Networks

Imagine a country without routes. Nothing could move so nothing could be made or sold. Nobody could travel to work or go on holiday.

When routes are linked with other routes, a **network** is made. A country which has a good route network will find it easier to become rich.

On this small island, the four towns are linked by a single route. It is difficult to get from A to C or to D. By building three new roads, the network can be improved.

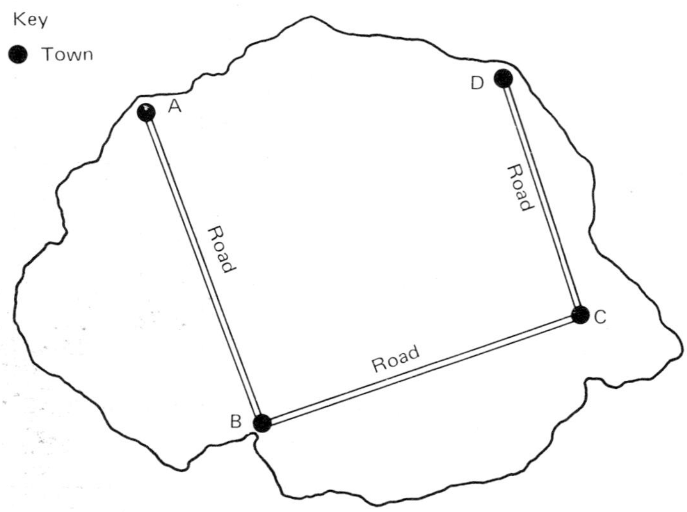

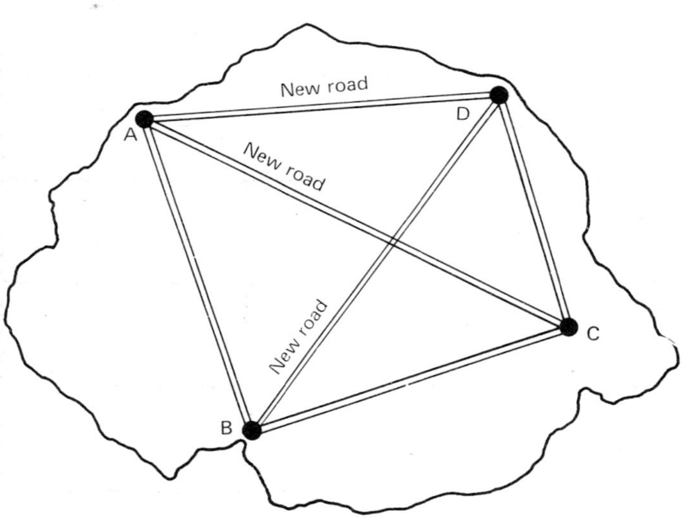

This information can be shown on a **matrix** where the figures show the number of **links** between each place. After the new links were built, no place is more than one link away from another.

BEFORE

	A	B	C	D
A	–	1	2	3
B	1	–	1	2
C	2	1	–	1
D	3	2	1	–

AFTER

	A	B	C	D
A	–	1	1	1
B	1	–	1	1
C	1	1	–	1
D	1	1	1	–

Sometimes a bridge can improve the network. These maps show the roads around the Severn Estuary before and then after the Severn bridge was built.

Distances between each place are shown.

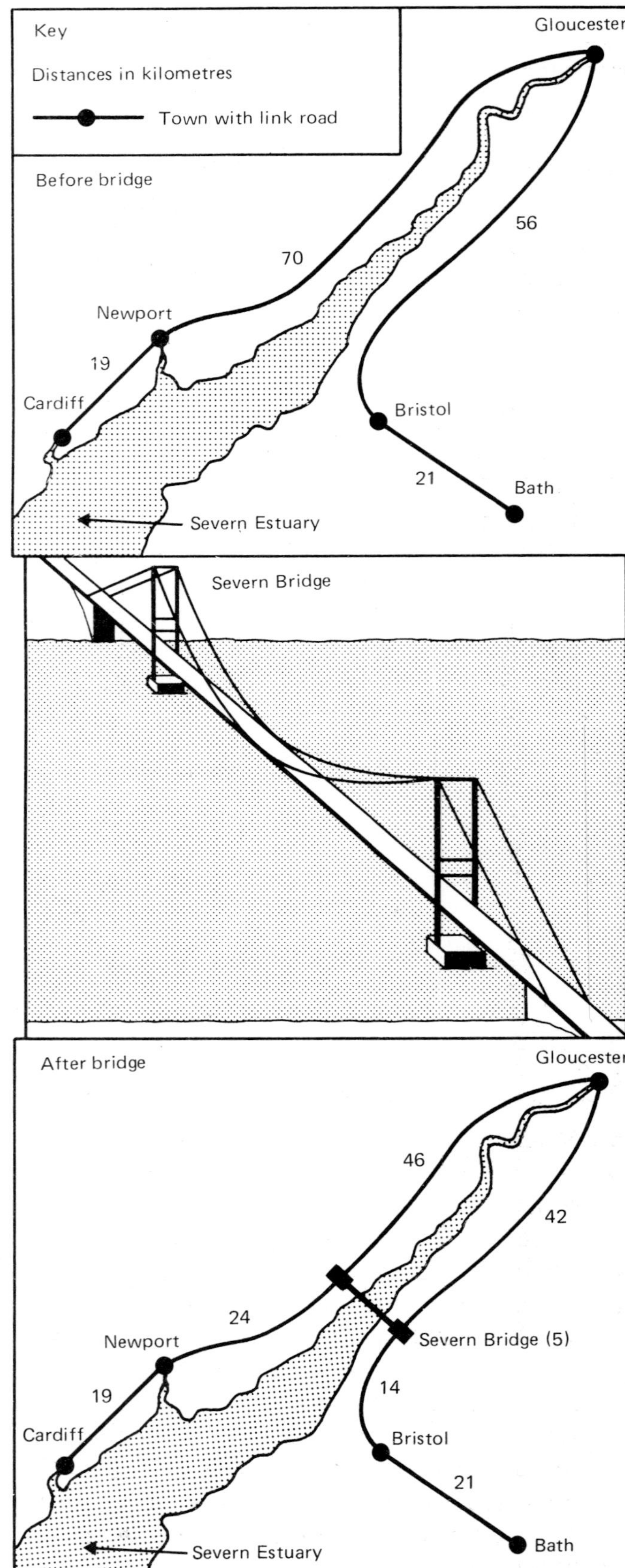

Things to do/Networks

1 These maps show the road networks in two countries, Britain and Ghana.

Ghana

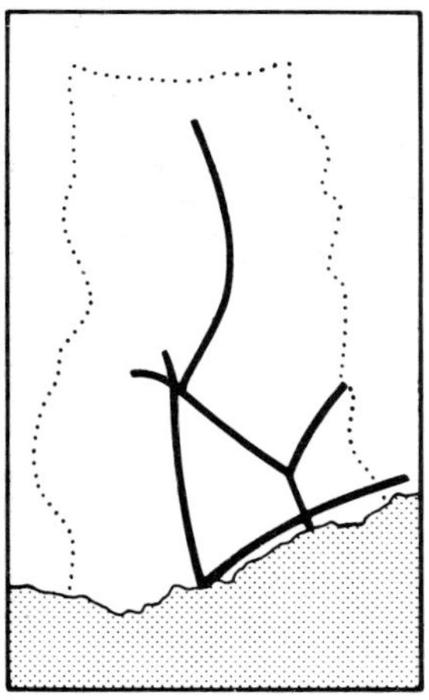

a Which country has the best network?
b Why do you think the difference might exist?

2 On this island, there is only one road. The government want to improve the network by building new roads.

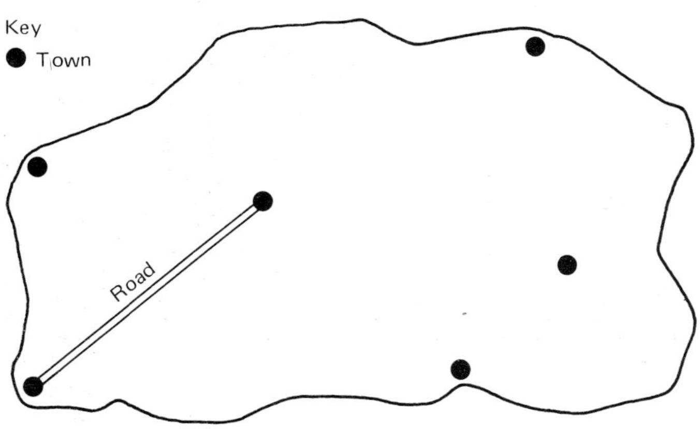

a Make a copy of the map.
b Using a coloured pencil, draw in a set of new roads so that each town is linked directly to at least one other town. This can be done by building four new roads.
c Using a different colour, draw in more roads so that each town is directly linked to at least two other towns. Another three roads should be all that is needed.
d Draw a ring around the town which has the most links joining onto it. This will be the most **accessible town** on the island because it is the one most people will be able to get to most easily.

3 Study the maps which show the effects of the Severn bridge.
a Draw two copies of this distance matrix.
b Fill in the distances between each place for before and then after the bridge was built.

DISTANCE MATRIX	BRISTOL	BATH	GLOUCESTER	NEWPORT
BATH	21			
GLOUCESTER				
NEWPORT				
CARDIFF				

c For the following routes, fill in the distance which the bridge has saved.

ROUTES	DISTANCE SAVED
BRISTOL – NEWPORT	
BRISTOL – CARDIFF	
BATH – NEWPORT	
BATH – CARDIFF	

Further work

4 Make two tracings of the railway network for two countries shown in your Atlas. Say which country you think has the best network.

Summary

When routes are joined, a network is made. Networks can be improved by building new links.

Unit 10.3

Which way to travel

Students and teachers travel to school in many different ways. Some walk, some come by bicycle, and some come by car. The choice depends on the distance to be travelled, the cost, and how much has to be carried.

Aircraft and ships can both carry people and goods (freight). They each have advantages and disadvantages.

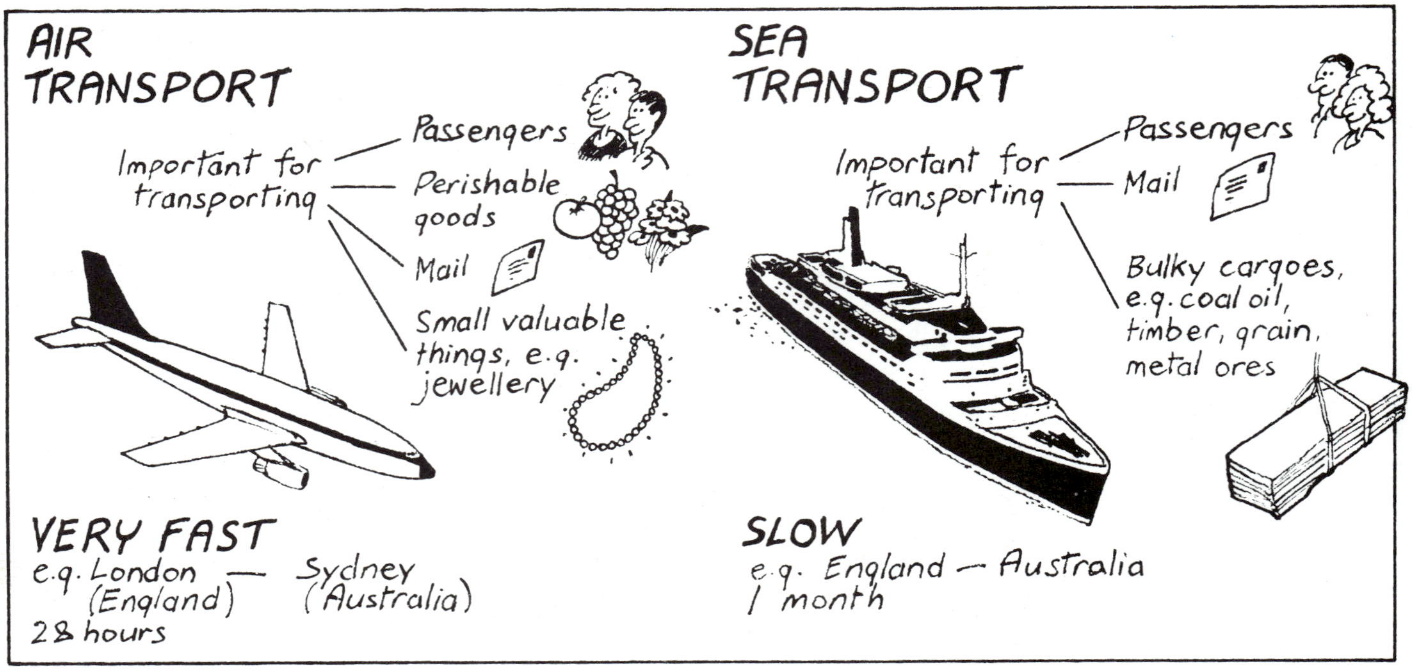

The map shows some of the most important air and sea routes around the world. The routes go between places where there are large cities and much industry. The routes between cities near each other are usually busier than between cities far apart.

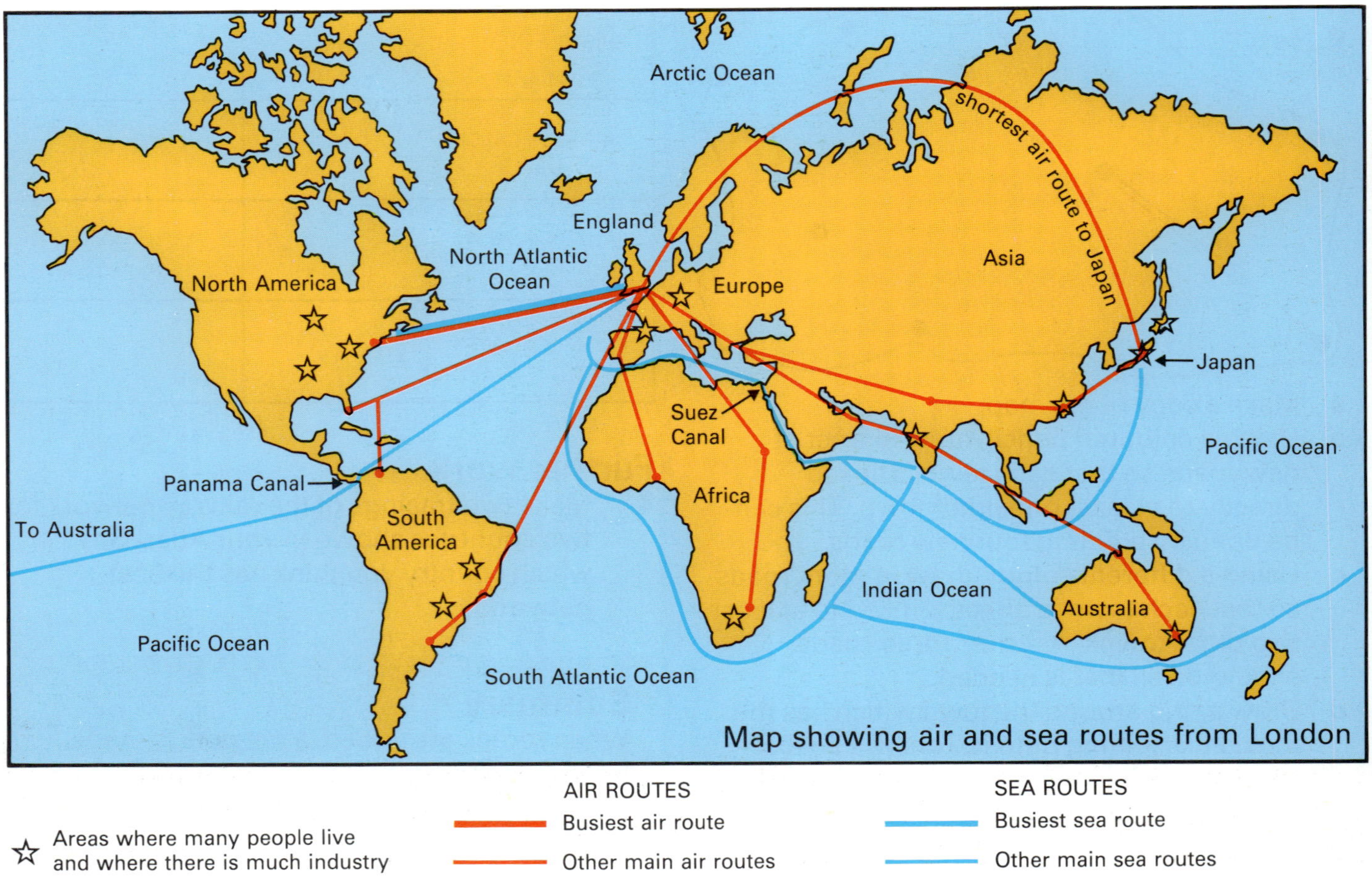

Things to do/Which way to travel

1 Study the world map showing main air and sea routes from London.
Complete these sentences:

- **a** The busiest air and sea routes cross the . . . Ocean.
- **b** The busiest routes go between places which have cities and . . .
- **c** One reason why the route between England and Japan is not so busy is because Japan is . . . . than the USA.
- **d** The two canals which can shorten sea distances are the . . . . . canal and the . . . . . canal.
- **e** The air route to Japan is not drawn straight because the Earth is really . . . . . and not flat.

Use these words:
industry – further away – Atlantic – Suez – round – Panama

2 The Acme Freight Company will look after any transport problem. They will arrange transport of anything to anywhere in the world. They use a points system to decide whether to send each job by air or by sea.

- **a** Copy the scoring chart in your exercise book.
- **b** For each of the 'cargoes' given in the letters, make a scoring chart and decide whether you should send it by air or sea.

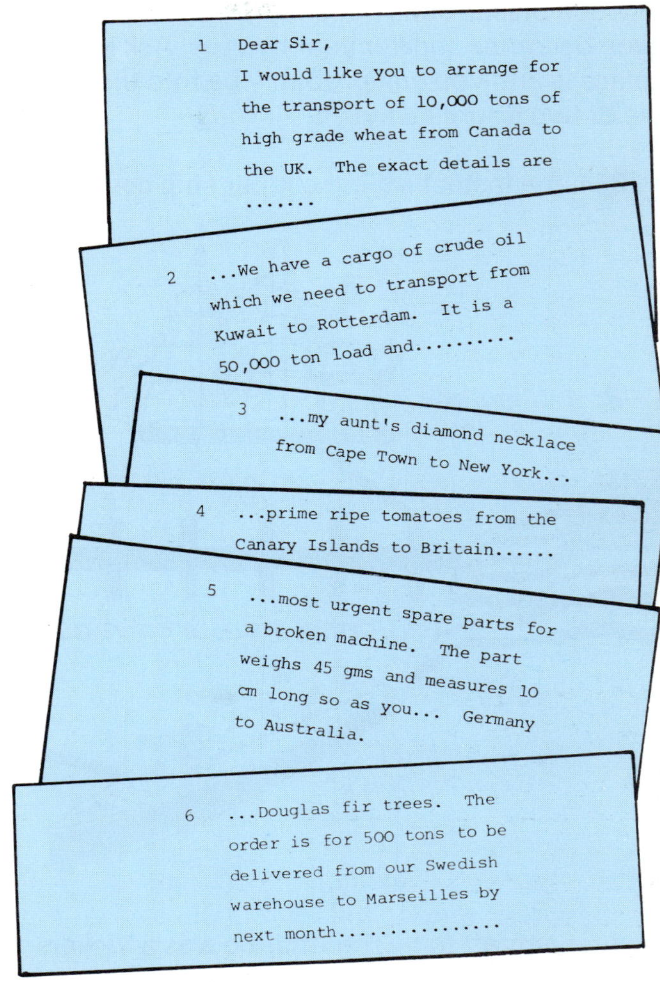

1 Dear Sir,
I would like you to arrange for the transport of 10,000 tons of high grade wheat from Canada to the UK. The exact details are ....

2 ...We have a cargo of crude oil which we need to transport from Kuwait to Rotterdam. It is a 50,000 ton load and.........

3 ...my aunt's diamond necklace from Cape Town to New York...

4 ...prime ripe tomatoes from the Canary Islands to Britain......

5 ...most urgent spare parts for a broken machine. The part weighs 45 gms and measures 10 cm long so as you... Germany to Australia.

6 ...Douglas fir trees. The order is for 500 tons to be delivered from our Swedish warehouse to Marseilles by next month...............

Scoring

Score from 1 to 10 on these questions:
1 Is it small (1) or big (10)?
2 Is it light (1) or heavy (10)?
3 Will it rot (1) or keep well (10)?
4 Is it fragile (1) or strong (10)?
5 Add 5 points if it is not urgent.
Cargoes which score 0 – 20 go by air.
Cargoes which score 21 – 45 go by sea.

Example: tomatoes

Q	Score
1	4 (because boxes are quite small)
2	4 (boxes are fairly light)
3	2 (they rot quickly)
4	3 (quite fragile)
5	5 (not urgent)
	18 goes by air

3a Make a class survey to find out how each person travels to school.

- **b** A second survey could be made to find out how parents travel to work.
- **c** Draw a bar graph of the results of the surveys. Comment on the findings shown by the graph.

Further work

4 On an outline map of the world mark in the following:

- **a** The main areas of industry.
- **b** One important city in each industrial area.
- **c** The busiest air and sea routes.
- **d** Three different routes a ship could take between Australia and England.

Summary

Different types of transport are suited to different types of freight. Busy routes go between areas with cities and industry.

Unit 10.4

Distance and time

The world seems to be shrinking. The distance between places does not change, but the time taken becomes shorter year by year. Ask how far a place is and you will probably be told that it is one or two hours away!

In 1854, the fastest sailing clipper ship could cross the Atlantic in 12 days if the wind was right. By 1907, the steam ship Mauretania completed the crossing in four and three quarter days. Today, Jumbo jets make hundreds of crossings every day in under six hours. Some people say that the Atlantic Ocean has shrunk to become the Atlantic 'river'.

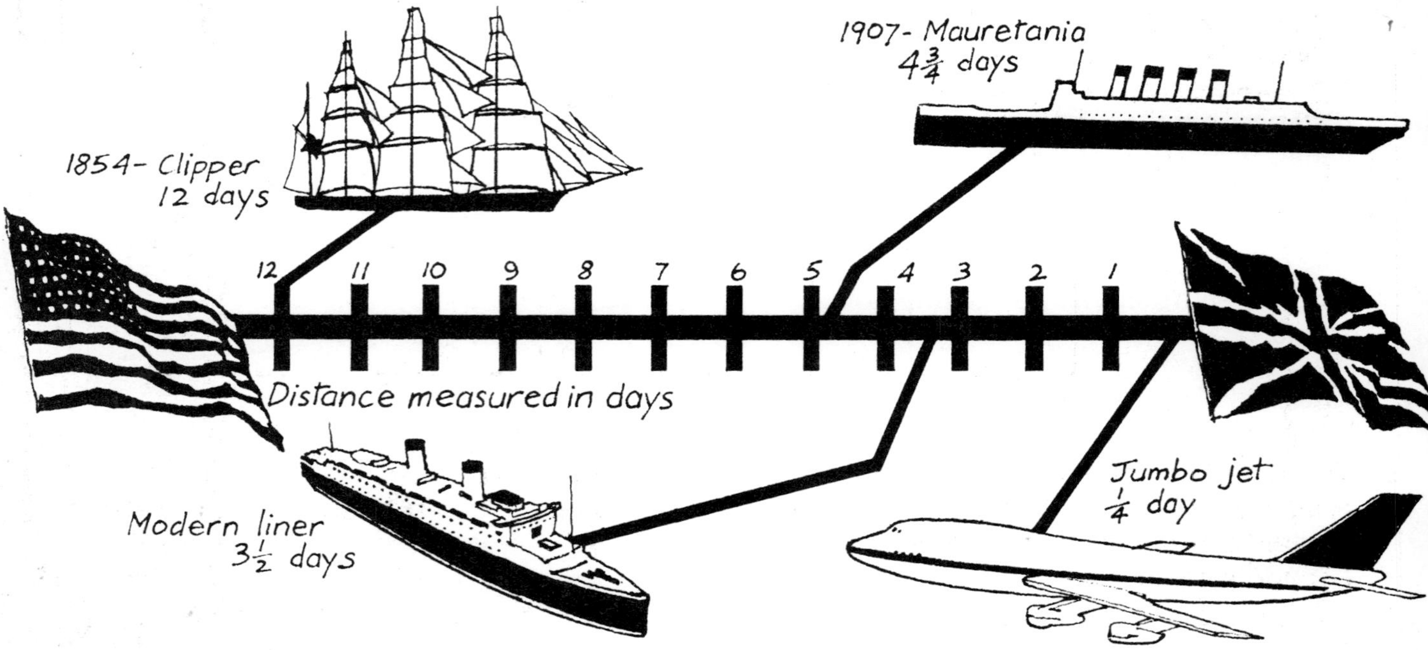

The first aircraft to fly the Atlantic was a Vickers Vimy. It took 16 hours and 27 minutes to cross at an average speed of 200 kph. Today, supersonic Concorde can cross the same distance in 3 hours 30 minutes flying at 2500 kph. The trouble is that it uses nearly its own weight in fuel to do so.

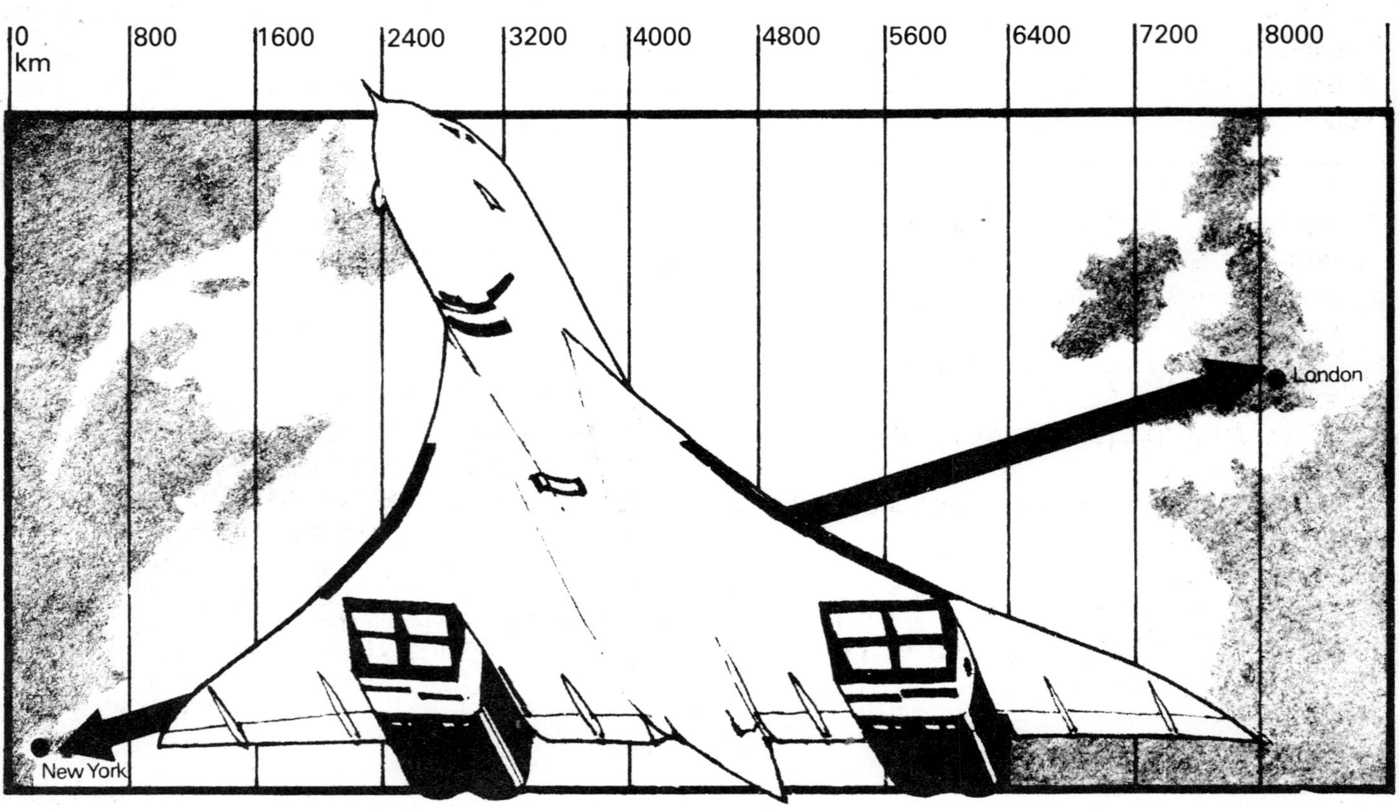

Things to do/Distance and time

1a Copy this world map. Make sure the size is exactly the same.

b Mark in the following cities –
Tokyo
Sydney
Buenos Aires
New York
Mexico City
Johannesburg

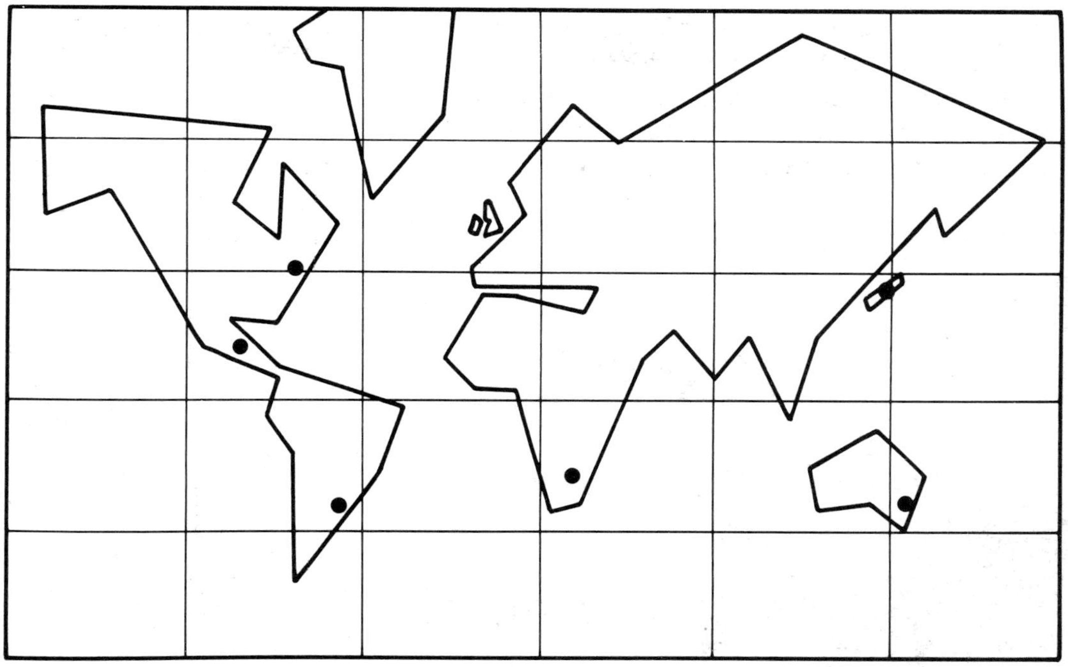

c This table shows the times taken by ordinary sub-sonic passenger aircraft from London compared to the time which Concorde could take.

	Time taken		
Route from London	**Sub-sonic**	**Concorde**	**Saving**
Tokyo	14.30	8.40	5.50
Sydney	28.30	15.00	13.30
Buenos Aires	16.25	9.50	6.35
New York	7.05	3.30	3.35
Mexico City	13.05	6.35	6.35
Johannesburg	12.10	7.20	4.50
Total	?	?	?

d Add up the total times sub-sonic flights would take.

e Add up the total times which Concorde would take.

f Divide both answers by 6 to give an average.

g What is the difference in time between the two averages?

h By about how much would Concorde reduce the times taken?

Further work

2 Concorde has shrunk the world by about half. Copy the grid outline below and complete a simple world outline of the continents. Draw lines to join London to each of the cities mentioned on the table opposite.

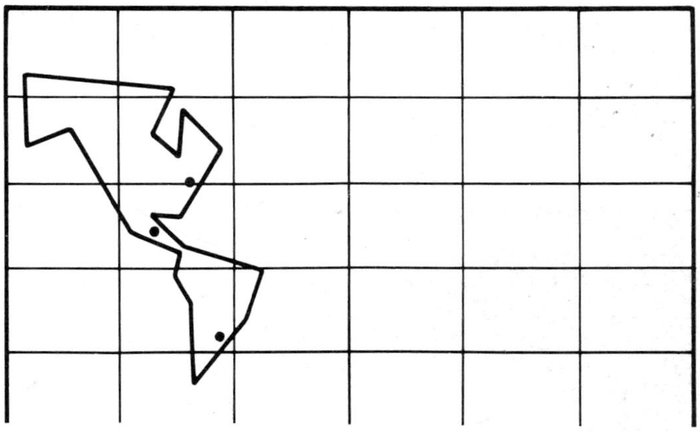

Summary

The time taken to complete a distance has become as important as the number of miles between each place. New means of transport can make many places more accessible.

Unit 1

Recap

The best way to learn about a place is to go there. Most of the time this is not possible. Geography tries to describe and explain places no matter where they are.

1 Learning about places can be important as well as being interesting. List as many reasons as you can why you should learn about places. Think about these things before you answer:
people we meet – holidays – jobs we do – general interest – the news – things we buy.

2 A map can show a great deal of information about a place if it is drawn properly. Map **A** was drawn by a five-year old boy. It shows his journey from Canada to England.

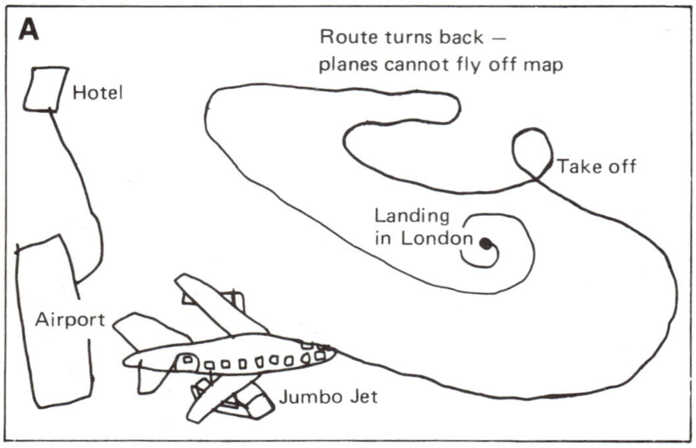

a Make a list of the important things which he left off the map.
b Suggest some ways in which the map could have been improved to make it more accurate.

C

3 Map **B** and the photograph show a village near the coast.
a In what direction was the camera pointing to take the photograph?
b How far is it from Bossington to the sea?
c Make a list of the things which you can see on the map but not on the photograph. For each, explain why you cannot see it.
d What does the photograph tell you about the area that the map does not show?
e Draw a sketch of the photograph. Using the map, add labels to show what is there.

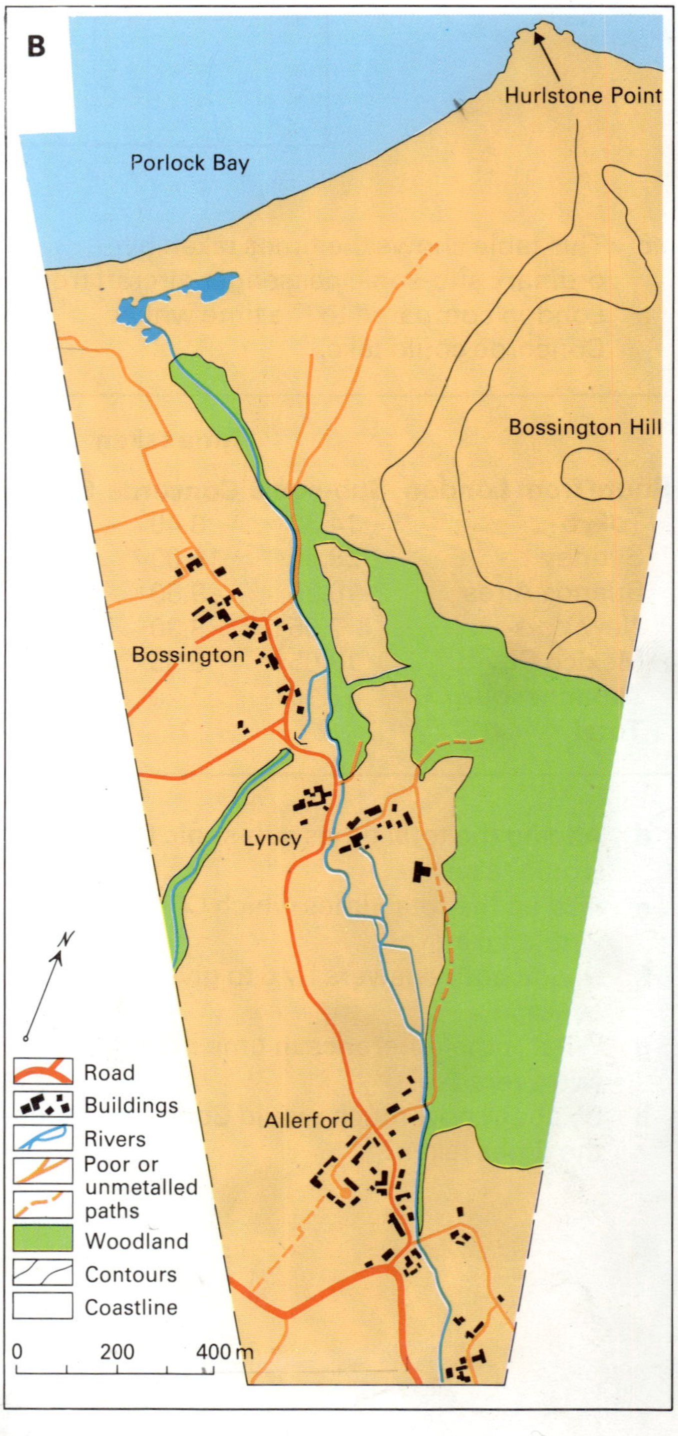

Recap

Collecting and recording information about a place can be done in several different ways. No single way will give the complete picture. Written descriptions would need to be very long to give every detail. Maps can show where places are but have to miss out a great deal. A photograph can only show part of the area for one moment in time. Graphs and figures are accurate, but give a very limited amount of information.

This information about Iceland uses a variety of methods used in geography to show what the place is like.

Written description

Iceland is an island which lies just south of the Arctic circle. Most of the island is high land and mountain. There are several areas which are covered by ice. Most of the rocks are very recent. There are still active volcanoes which pour out new rock when they erupt. Many of the houses are heated by hot water from the volcanic areas. Fishing and farming are important occupations. New industries, like plastics and making electrical goods, are being built up.

Graphs and statistics

Population	231,000
Size	103,000 kms²
Capital city	Reykjavik
Highest point	2119 metres

Temperature

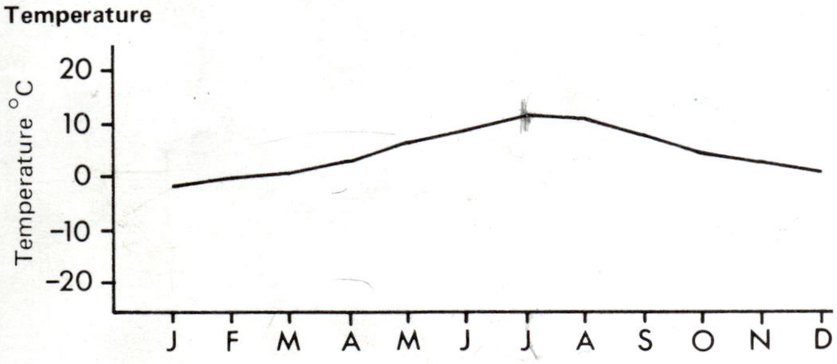

Occupations

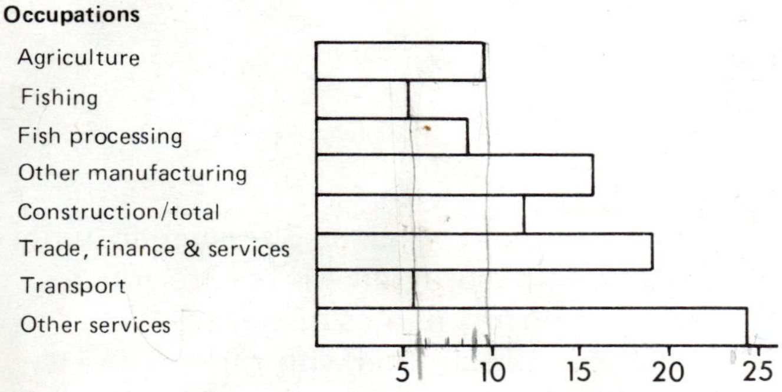

Photograph

Map

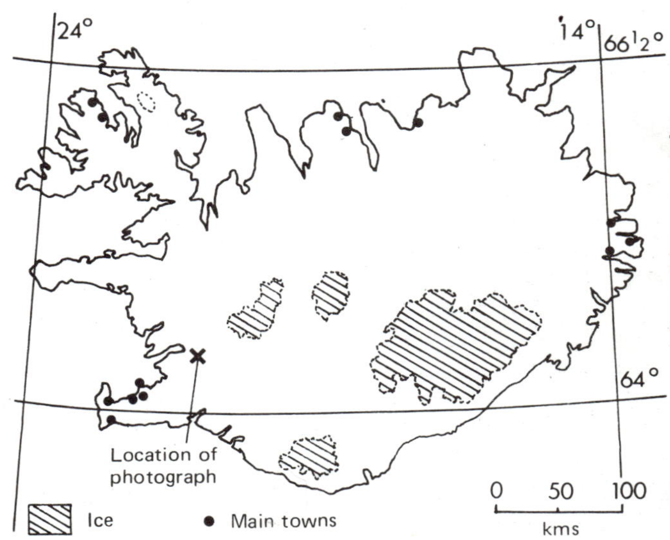

1 Make a list of the pieces of information included in the written description which are not mentioned elsewhere.

2a Draw a simple outline sketch map of Iceland to show its general shape.

b Make a more accurate copy of the map using a grid. Mark on main towns and inlets.

c What do all the towns have in common?

d Say what sort of work people in the towns probably do.

3 Write down which of the following the graphs and statistics give information on: temperature, vegetation, rainfall, jobs, population, volcanoes, rivers, towns.

4 Write a full description of the photograph. Its location is marked on the map above.

Unit 3
Recap

Maps show where places are and how to get there. Symbols can be used to show what can be found at each place. Information about height, for example, can help complete the picture. Grid lines help pinpoint different places on the map. Maps have many uses in everyday life and knowing how to read a map can be very useful.

1 Think about some of the maps you have seen outside school. Make a list of where you saw them and what type of information they gave.

2 Make a copy of the grid square. You can make it several times larger.
Using the symbols provided, draw the following features on the outline:
- a straight road from 0191 to 0294
- a village along the road in 0293
- a wood in 0392
- a disused windmill at 022921
- a battlefield site at 045945

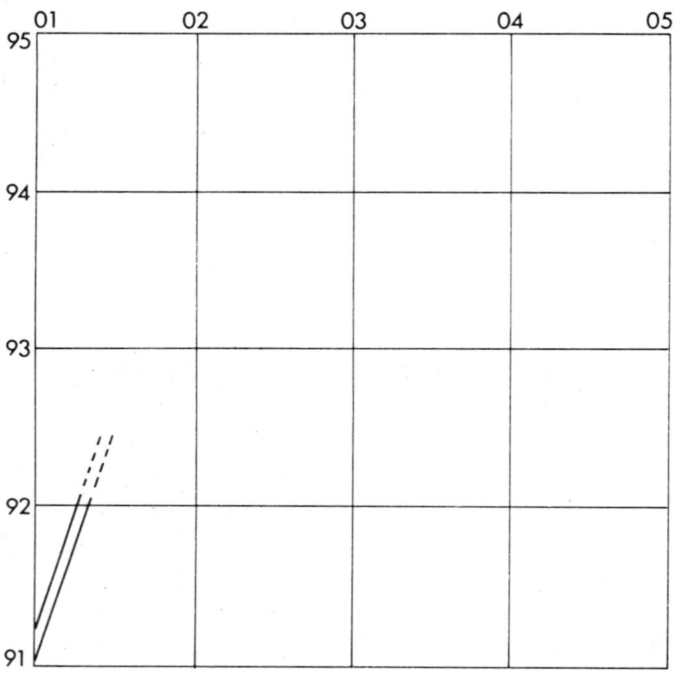

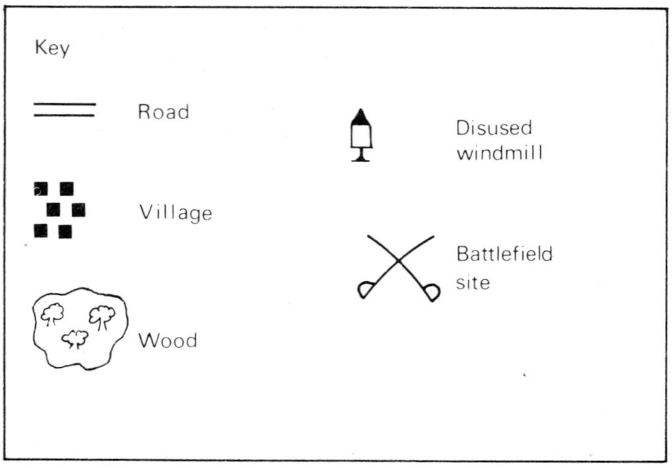

3 Somewhere on the map below there is an ancient buried treasure. To find out where it is follow the instructions carefully. You could draw the map and mark on your route.

- **a** Start at the village with two churches.
- **b** Take the East road.
- **c** After 1 km turn North.
- **d** Pass through the wood and keep going North.
- **e** When you meet a road again, go north.
- **f** At the old mill, turn East.
- **g** Climb to the top of the hill.
- **h** From the top of the hill, the treasure lies ½ km to the South-East.
- **i** At which of these places is the treasure buried?

Bleeton church	Bleeton wood
Lowood farm	Thoxted wood
Old mill at 104438	
Old mill at 123439	

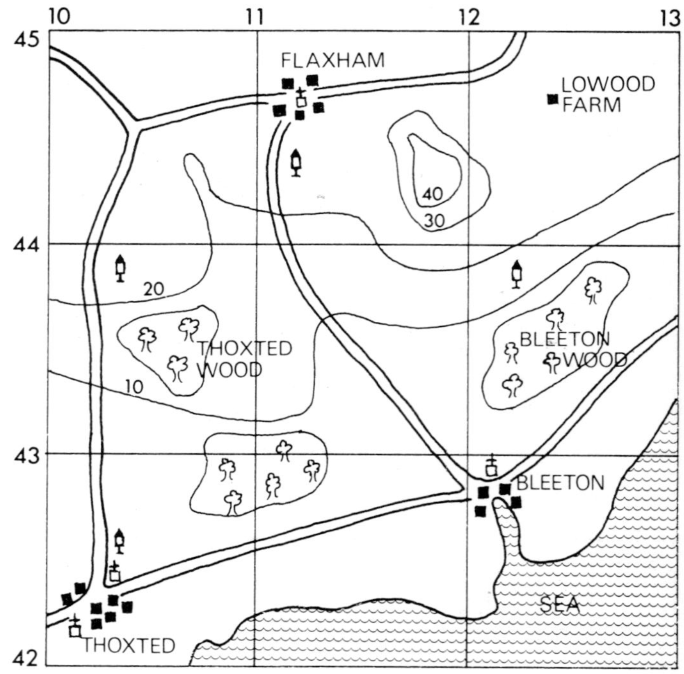

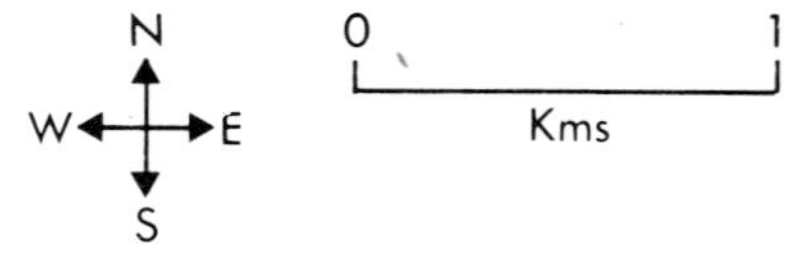

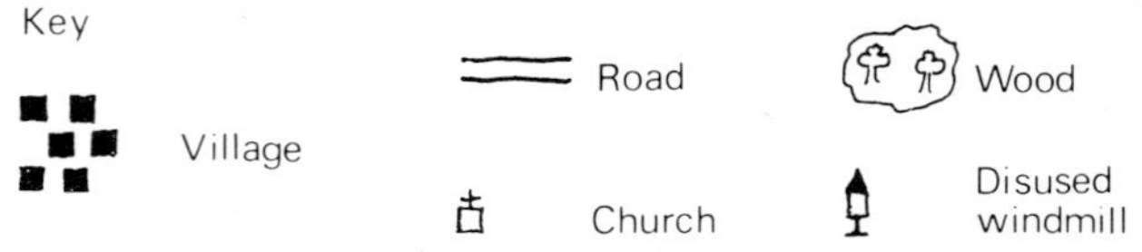

4 Using a proper Ordnance Survey map, write your own treasure trail. Make sure you do not mention any names of places.
Swap your description with a friend and try to find each other's treasure.

Recap

Your atlas is an encyclopedia of places. It has few words except the names of places. Information is given by using maps with symbols.
Finding out where places are and what is there is an important skill in geography. The Contents and Index pages, together with the latitude and longitude grid, can make finding places easy.

1 Diagrams **A** and **B** show the world drawn in two different ways. The latitude and longitude grids are drawn on each.
Pair up the latitude and longitude positions in the list below with the correct letter on the maps. For example:

20°S 20°E(C)	60°N 120°E
20°N 80°W	40°S 140°E
40°S 60°W	20°N 20°E

A

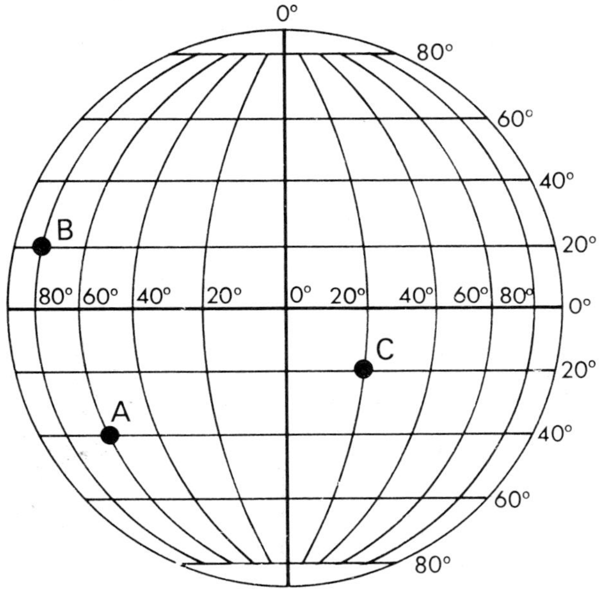

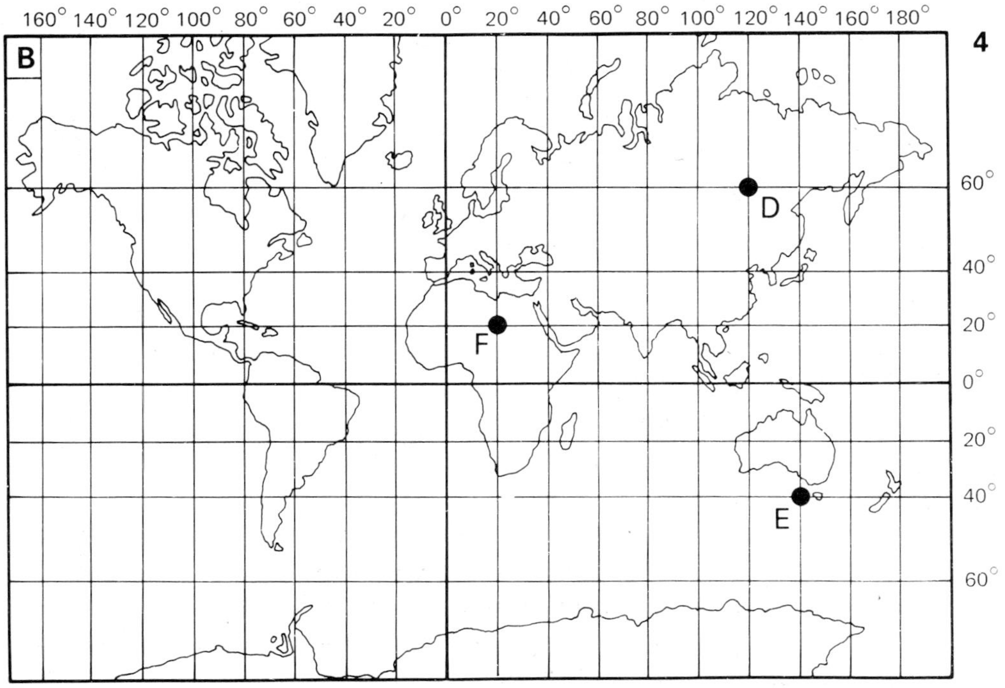

2 Find out what information your atlas gives about the town or area you live in. The list below includes some of the things the maps in your atlas may be able to tell you.

how high the land is
the relief of the area
the names of rivers
temperature and rainfall
the type of rock
name of the county
population total or density
roads and railways
nearest airport

Your atlas may have many more special maps where more information can be found.

3 Copy the following paragraph filling in the gaps with the words given underneath.

The Earth is divided by lines which go from . . . to West called lines of . . . Lines are also drawn from North to . . . called lines of . . . Lines of longitude all meet up at the . . . Pole and the South Pole. Lines of . . . never join up with other latitude lines. Latitude lines are always either North or . . . of latitude 0. Another name for latitude 0 is the . . . Lines of longitude are always either . . . or West of longitude 0. This line passes through . . . near London.

south equator east latitude east latitude
north south longitude Greenwich

4 Use your Atlas to find the city at each of the following positions. It will help if you look at a world map first to find out what country the place is in. The name of the city begins with the letter in brackets.

51°N 0° (L)
29°N 95°W (H)
5°N 0° (A)
35°S 138°E (A)
43°N 132°E (V)

Recap

The earth's surface is divided into large areas of water and land which are called oceans and continents. Currents move the water around in giant circles. Man will need to find out much more about the ocean bed in future years. Continents are difficult to describe quickly. They are very large and have many different kinds of scenery. Some parts are difficult to live in. The people in these parts remain poor and lead lives very different to our own. Other parts are more suitable for farming or industry so more people live there.

1 Imagine that you are the first scientist to discover and map a new planet. It lies 80 million miles away from its sun and has areas of land and water just like Earth.

- **a** Make a copy of map **A** and divide it up into oceans and continents.
- **b** As the discoverer, you must think of suitable names for the oceans and continents. Write these onto the map. This planet seems like the earth in more ways than one!

2 Find a set of maps of Australia in your atlas. The physical map will look like map **B**:

- **a** Make a copy of the cross-section beneath the map.
- **b** Label in the following terms in the right place:
  mountain, plain, ocean, plateau.
  (the same term may be used more than once).
- **c** What does the atlas tell you about the actual landscape over much of western Australia?

3 Study map **C** showing the distribution of population in Australia. Your atlas may have a map like this or a political map which will show the main cities.

- **a** Describe where most people seem to live.
- **b** Think of some reasons why so much of Australia has few people living there. Other maps of Australia in your atlas may give some clues.

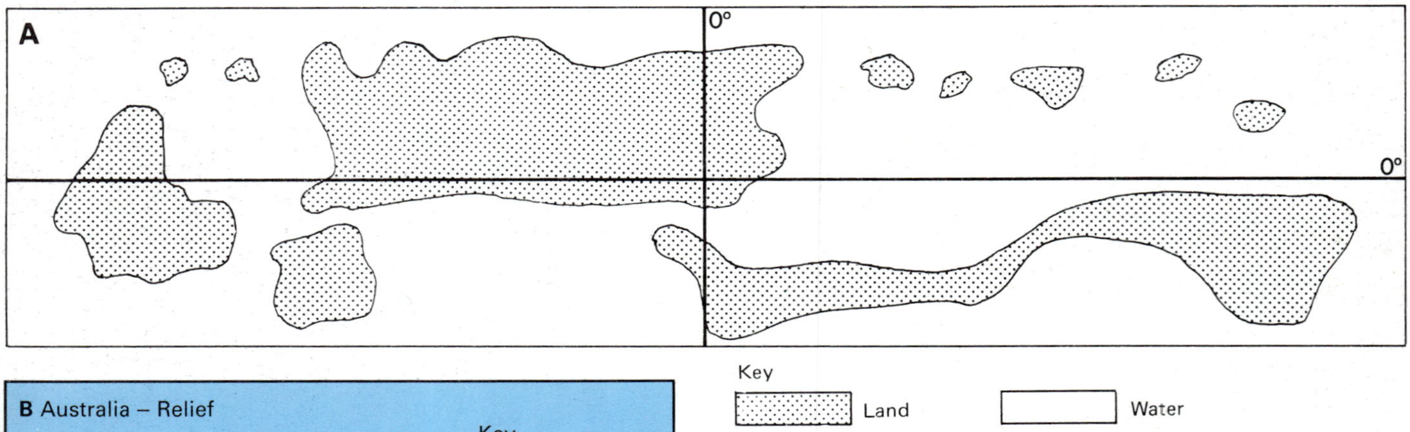

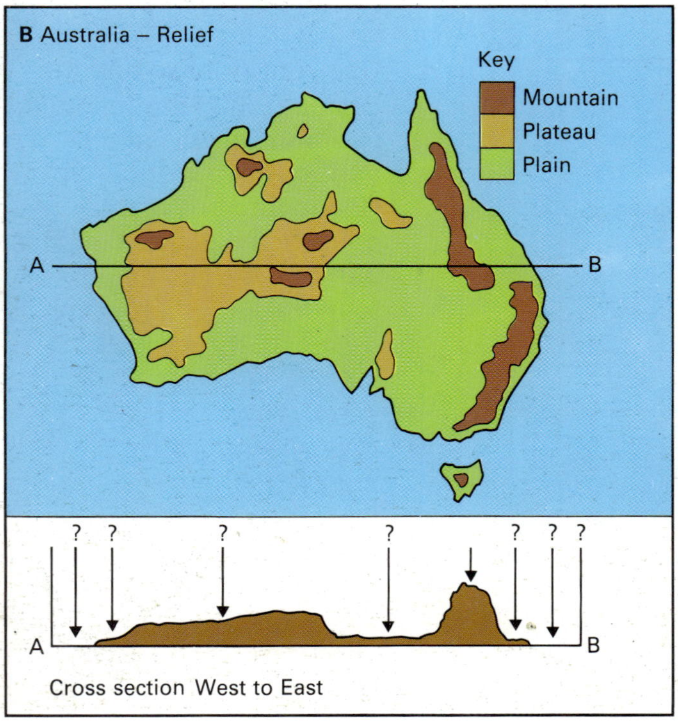

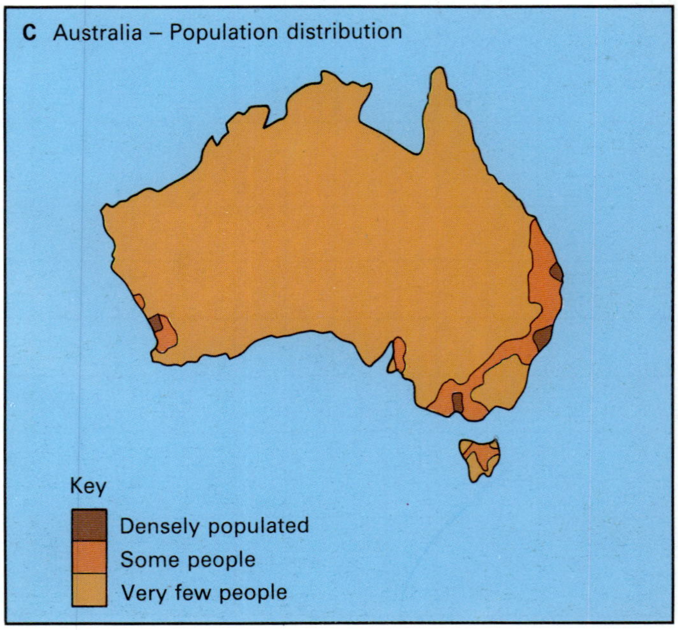

Recap

Life on earth depends on the layer of gases called the atmosphere, which surrounds it. Our position in the solar system is also important. Planets which are further from the sun would be too cold for us to live on without protection. Planets nearer to the sun would be too hot. Movement of air in the atmosphere gives our daily weather. We depend on the weather for many things. Sometimes the weather can be very violent and damage is caused.

1 Describe some of the ways in which the weather has recently affected things you wanted to do.
  - a Describe what has happened in the photograph below and how the weather has been to blame.
  - b What sort of damage has taken place?
  - c From what you have noticed yourself, what are some of the effects of the weather on each of the following:
    rivers, plants, soil, sea.

2 Make a sketch of the photograph of the sky with clouds.
  - a Label in the different types of cloud with the correct term. Estimate what height they are at.
  - b What do you think the weather on the ground might be like with this type of cloud in the sky?

The answer in 6.2 Q4 is 'The Swan'.

Unit 7

Recap

The landscape around us is slowly changing. When a volcano erupts or when there is a flood, it is easy to see the changes. New land either appears or is washed away almost overnight. Most of the changes take place over a very long time and cannot be seen day by day. Things we see in the landscape have not been made by accident. The weather, rivers and glaciers have made them that way.

1 The diagram shows how the 'erosion machine' works on the landscape. Study it carefully to see how and why it works.

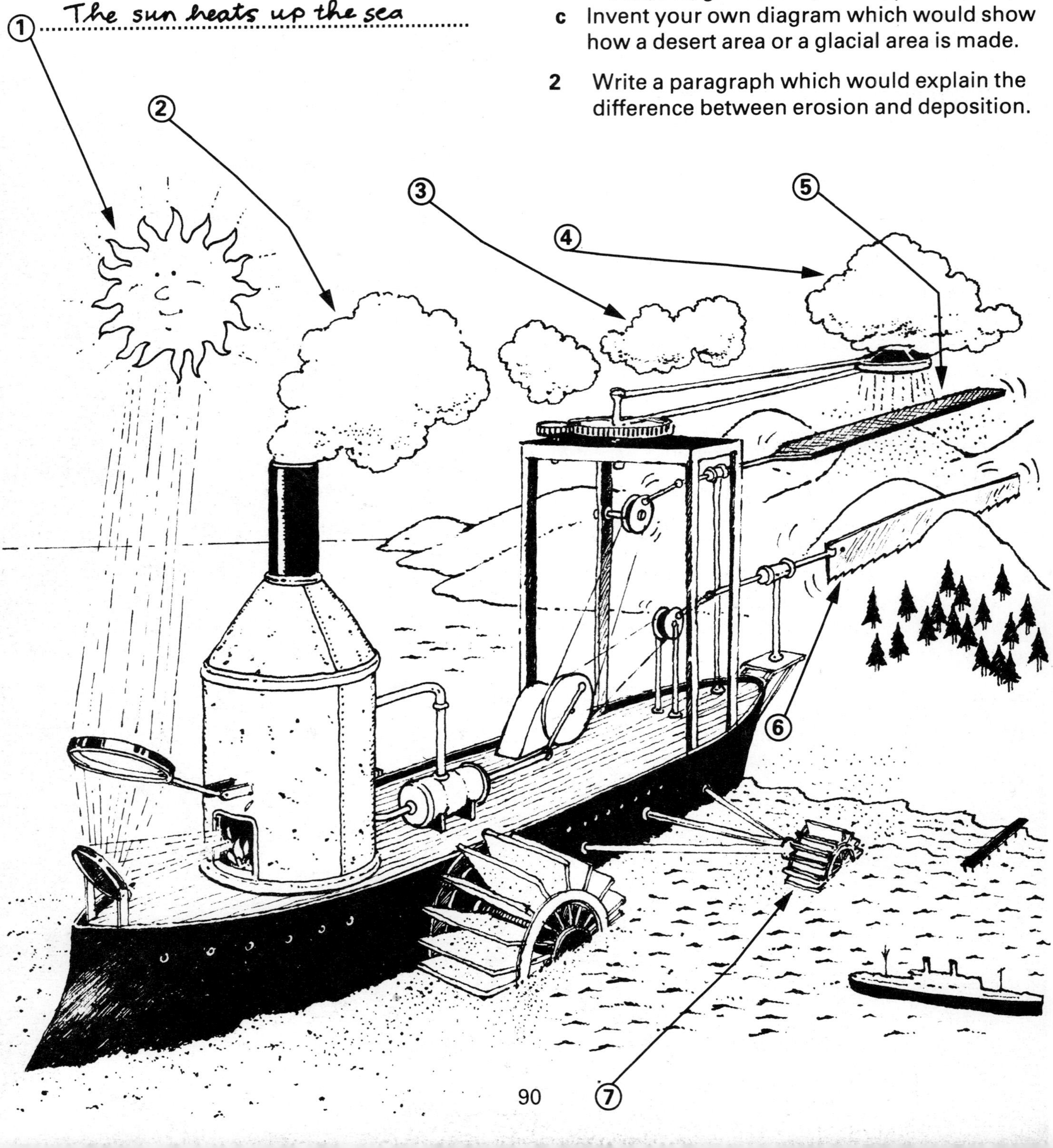

a Pair up the following list of events with the numbers on the diagram, then list them in the right order. For example:

1 *The sun heats up the sea* is first.
Clouds bring rain to the mountains
Rivers cut valleys
Waves wear away the coastline
Rainwater wears away the land
Clouds form over the heated sea
The sun heats up the sea
Clouds are blown over the land

b Use the following terms to describe how the land in the diagram is being worn away:
saw, file, grindstone, boiler, paddle, cutter.

c Invent your own diagram which would show how a desert area or a glacial area is made.

2 Write a paragraph which would explain the difference between erosion and deposition.

Recap

Most people live in groups of buildings called settlements. Settlements come in many shapes and sizes from hamlets to cities.

Different settlements often have things in common. This is sometimes because they were built at the same time or for the same reason.

Small settlements tend to look after the needs of a few people who live nearby. Cities are centres for industry and shopping and serve a much larger surrounding area.

1 Study the four lists below. Each list has one 'odd man out'. Write down which one is 'odd' and explain why.

city factory village hamlet	Brixham Luton Nottingham Derby	factories shops and offices port houses	semi-detached bungalow zone maisonette

2 The photograph below shows a small settlement in a rural area.

a What type of settlement is this?

b Make a list of the buildings you can see other than houses. Add to your list any other buildings you think the settlement probably has.

c How many main roads meet at this settlement?

d How many people live here? Guess how many people would live in each house and work out a rough total.

e Draw sketches of some of the houses and say what type of house they are.

f What do you think most of the people do for a living?

3 This photograph is of a quite different type of settlement.

a What type of settlement is this part of?

b In which part of the settlement would you expect to see an area like this, in the centre or towards the edge?

c What are the main differences between the houses and other buildings in this area compared to those in the rural area?

d Imagine what it would be like to live in each of the areas shown in the photographs. What would be the advantages and disadvantages of living in each?

Recap

Look around your bedroom at all the things that you use or own. Without some of them, life would be difficult. Some of your possessions are luxuries you could do without.

Most of these things have been made in factories or on farms, then sold in shops. Hundreds of people may have been involved in making what seem to be very simple things.

1 The diagram shows what is involved in making one everyday item, a shoe.
 a Make a sketch of one of your shoes and label in the different raw materials which have been used.
 b Make a list of some of the jobs people have to do to get the raw materials for a shoe.
 c How do you think the raw materials are transported?
 d What must be done to the raw materials before they reach the shoe factory?
 e What are the different types of work which go on inside the shoe factory?
 f How are the shoes transported to the shops?
 g About how many people work in an average shoe shop and what jobs do they do?

2 Decide on something you use for a game or hobby, and study it carefully. Make a sketch of it and label in the different raw materials which have been used. Draw a diagram like the one below to show what is involved in making it. How does a diagram like this help to explain why some things seem to cost so much?

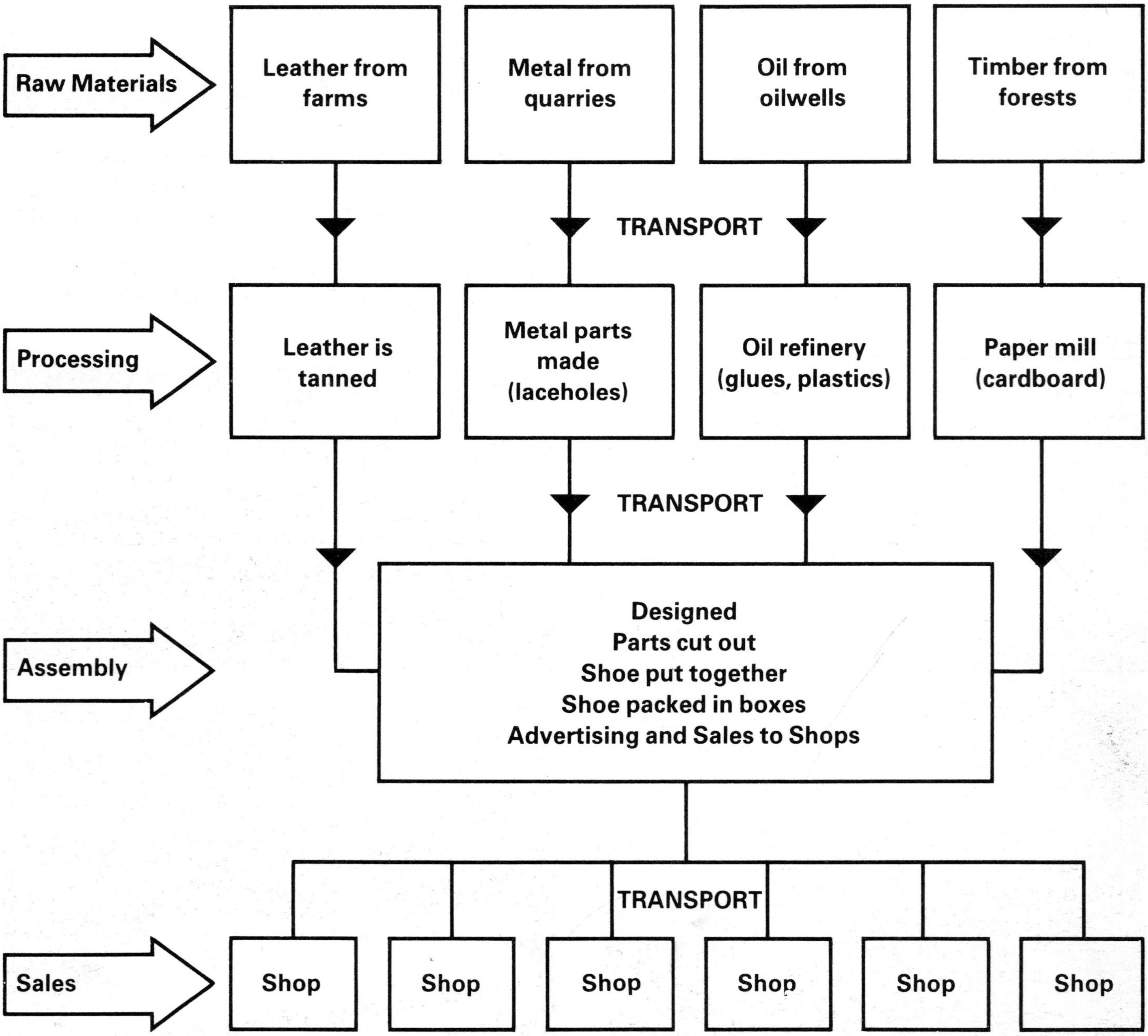

Recap

Transport is the link which allows people and goods to move about. Many new types of transport have been invented and travel has become easier. Travellers now have a wide range of routes and methods of travel to choose from.

Routes between Britain and mainland Europe have become important. More people want to go abroad on holiday in their own car. Britain is part of the EEC and wants trade with the other European countries to increase.

The map shows the routes which one shipping company operates between Britain and Europe. The map also shows the times taken and the number of sailings per day in August (in brackets).

1 Draw up a chart and fill in the following information:

a List all the routes shown on the map

b Name the country each European port is in

c Measure the distance travelled on each route

d Write down the time taken for each route.

Route	European country	Distance in km	Time taken
Felixstowe/ Zeebrugge	....	....	....

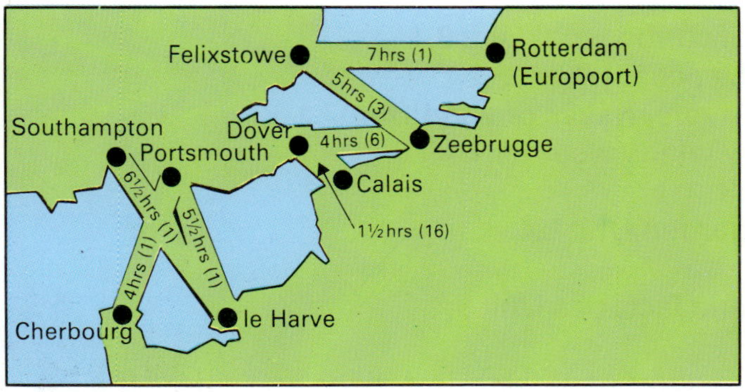

2 Draw a copy of the map outline below and mark in the ports.

a Draw a series of lines between the ports to show the number of sailings per day for August. Do this by ruling one line to represent one sailing. Try not to leave any space between the lines. The Dover/ Zeebrugge route will be six lines thick.

b Compare your finished map with the times taken and the distance for each route. Describe what you notice about which routes are the busiest.

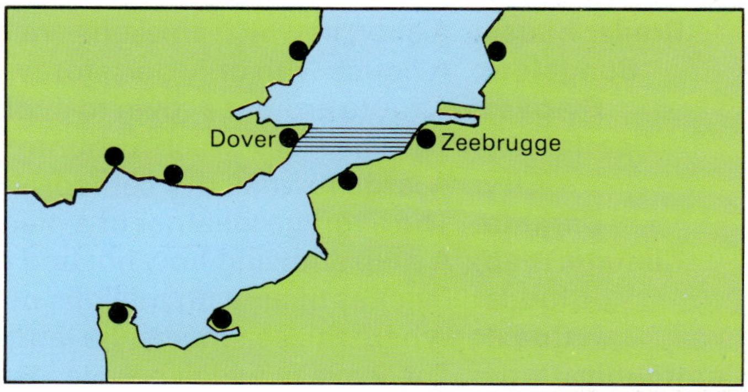

3 These photographs show three different ways of getting from Britain to Europe.

a Describe the advantages and disadvantages of each method.

b Say how you think a Channel tunnel which links Britain to Europe might improve the present situation.

Glossary

Accessible : Easy to get to/Unit 10.2
Air photograph: A photograph taken from an aircraft/Unit 1.4
Airport: A place where aeroplanes land and take off/Unit 9.4
Anglo-Saxon: Old English language which gave rise to most of our place names/Unit 8.2
Arête: A sharp ridge between two corries in glacial scenery/Unit 7.4
Atlas: A book of maps/Unit 4.1
Atmosphere: The layer of gas around the Earth/Unit 6.1
Barometer: An instrument for measuring whether air pressure is low or high/Unit 6.4
Bay: Part of the coast where the sea has worn away the land into a curved inlet/Unit 7.2
Beaches: Sand or pebbles found where the sea meets the land/Unit 7.2
Beaufort Scale: A scale for measuring wind speed by looking at things like smoke and trees/Unit 6.1
Bed-sitter: A one or two room flat, usually for one person/Unit 8.4
Blizzard: A fierce snowstorm/Unit 6.3
Broiler house: A shed in which chickens are reared in controlled conditions/Unit 9.2
Bungalow: A house with only one storey/Unit 8.4
By-pass: A route around a town to avoid traffic jams/Unit 10.1
Capital city: The city from which a country is governed/Unit 4.3
City: A large town with a cathedral or university/Unit 8.1
Climate: The average weather of a place/Unit 2.3
Climatic map: A map showing how hot and dry or cold and wet a place is/Unit 4.4
Clouds: Patches of air with millions of tiny water droplets floating in them/Unit 6.1
Coast: Where the sea meets the land/Unit 7.2
Communications: The ways in which people or ideas travel from place to place/Unit 2.3
Conclusions: The final ideas we have about a place/Unit 2.3
Concorde: The British and French built supersonic airliner/Unit 10.4
Constellation: Imaginary shapes of people and animals in the night sky/Unit 6.2
Contents page: A page in the front of a book (or atlas) showing page numbers for items/Unit 4.1
Continental shelf: The ocean bed bordering the continents covered by shallow water/Unit 5.2
Continents: The seven very large areas of land on the earth's surface/Unit 5.1
Contour lines: Lines on a map which join up places that are the same height/Unit 3.4
Control tower: The tower at an airport where air flights are controlled and kept safe/Unit 9.4
Corries: Great hollows dug by frost and ice into glaciated mountain sides/Unit 7.4
Cross-section: A diagram which seems to show a slice cut out of the ground/Unit 3.4
Cumulus cloud: Clouds which look like huge balls of cotton wool/Unit 6.1
Currents: Vast masses of moving water (in the ocean) /Unit 5.2
Deposition: The dropping of rock sediment by rivers, waves or wind/Unit 7.2
Depression: A low pressure system giving rainy windy weather/Unit 6.4
Desert: A place which has little rain/Unit 7.3
Detached house: A house which stands alone in its garden/Unit 8.4
Developed country: A country with many roads, cities and factories/Unit 5.4
Developing country: A country with a small but growing number of factories, roads and cities/Unit 5.4
Distribution of population: The pattern of where people live in an area/Unit 5.1
Drainage: Rivers and streams which drain water from the land/Unit 2.3
Drizzle: Gentle rain/Unit 6.1
Equator: The imaginary line of latitude 0°, through the middle of the tropics/Unit 4.2
Erosion: The wearing away of land by nature/Unit 7.1
Extractive industry: The work of getting minerals out of the ground/Unit 9.1
Factory: A place where things are made from raw materials/Unit 9.3
Farm: Land used for growing food or rearing animals/Unit 9.2
Flat: A home which is only part of a building and is on one storey/Unit 8.4
Flood plain: Flat land bordering a river/Unit 7.1

Fog: Cloud at ground level/Unit 6.1
Fold mountains: Highlands which have been folded by pressure in the Earth into great ranges/Unit 5.3
Four figure reference: Four numbers (eg 1023) which show where a map square is/Unit 3.3
Freight: Goods which are carried by water, air, road, or rail/Unit 10.3
Galaxy: A star system. Ours is the Milky Way. /Unit 6.2
Geography: The study of people and places/Unit 1.1
Geology: The study of rocks/Unit 9.1
Glacial scenery: Scenery affected by ice action/Unit 7.4
Glacial trough: Huge valleys in mountain areas carved by glaciers/Unit 7.4
Glaciers: Slow but powerful rivers of ice/Unit 7.4
Glasshouses: Glass buildings where plants are grown in controlled conditions/Unit 9.2
Gradient: The slope of the land or along a routeway/Unit 10.1
Graph: A mathematical diagram showing how one thing is related to another/Unit 2.4
Greenwich meridian: Longitude 0° which passes through Greenwich, London/Unit 4.2
Grid: A network of lines/Unit 2.2
Grid reference: A set of 4 or 6 numbers which shows where a place is on a map/Unit 3.3
Ham: Anglo-Saxon word for a homestead. (As in BirmingHAM.)/Unit 8.2
Hamlet: A small settlement with homes but no services/Unit 8.1
Headland: Part of coast which sticks into the sea/Unit 7.2
Height: How high or low a place is/Unit 3.4
High rise tower block: A block of flats or offices which rises high in the sky/Unit 8.4
Horticulture: Growing flowers for sale/Unit 9.2
Human features: Things in a landscape made by people/Unit 4.4
Hurricane: A huge swirling tropical sea storm/Unit 6.3
Ice age: When N. Britain and N. Europe were covered with ice/Unit 7.4
Ice sheet: Layer of ice hundreds of metres thick/Unit 7.4
Index: A list of items at the back of a book (or atlas) giving page numbers/Unit 4.1
Ing: Anglo-Saxon word meaning 'family'. (As in Nott**ing**ham.)/Unit 8.2
Isolated settlement: Homes on their own, well away from anyone else/Unit 8.1
Jungle: Dense forest found in some wet tropical areas/Unit 5.3
Key: A list of symbols on a map, showing what they mean/Unit 3.1
Key words: Important words to write down when taking notes/Unit 2.1
Landform: A natural feature with a recognisable shape, like a hill/Unit 7.1
Latitude: The number of degrees a place is north or south of the equator/Unit 4.2
Layer shading: Shading or colour used to show heights on a map/Unit 3.4
Lightning: A giant spark from thundercloud to earth in a storm/Unit 6.3
Limestone: A common rock often quarried to make cement and roadstone/Unit 9.1
Location: Where a place is/Unit 2.3
Longitude: The number of degrees a place is east or west of the Greenwich meridian/Unit 4.2
Low-rise blocks: Flats or offices in blocks but with few storeys/Unit 8.4
Maisonette: A small house or flat with an upstairs and downstairs/Unit 8.4
Manufacturing industry: Work to make things from raw materials/Unit 9.3
Map: A plan of part of the earth's surface with symbols and key/Unit 1.2
Market: The place where goods are sold, or the collection of people who buy them/Unit 9.3
Matrix: Information placed in a simple set of boxes/Unit 3.2
Meteor: Lumps of rock, flying through space, sometimes burning up in our atmosphere as shooting stars/Unit 6.3
Mist: Thin cloud at ground level/Unit 6.1
Moon: Ball of rock which moves round the Earth/Unit 6.2
Mushroom rock: A rock eroded or weathered more at the bottom than the top/Unit 7.3
Network: A pattern of routes which cross each other to form a net/Unit 10.2
Ocean: The great sheets of salt water which cover most of the earth/Unit 5.2
Ocean floor: The bottom of the ocean/Unit 5.2
Ores: Rocks which have useful metals in them/Unit 9.1

Panama Canal: Canal linking the Atlantic and Pacific Oceans in Central America/Unit 10.3
Penthouse: A luxury flat at the top of a building/Unit 8.4
Physical features: Things in the landscape formed by nature/Unit 4.4
Place names: Names of places which are usually made up from old names/Unit 8.2
Planet: Balls of rock or gas which move around the sun/Unit 6.2
Plateau: The flat top of an upland area/Unit 5.3
Political maps: Maps which show countries with their main cities and towns/Unit 4.3
Pollution: Dirt or noise produced by people which spoils an area/Unit 9.3
Population: The number and type of people who live in a place/Unit 2.3
Primary industry: Work which produces raw materials. (As in quarrying.)/Unit 9.1
Profit: The money made by a firm after it has paid all its costs/Unit 9.2
Quarry: A place where rock is dug out of the ground/Unit 9.1
Raw material: A thing which other things can be made out of, such as iron ore/Unit 9.1
Relief: The shape of the land/Unit 1.3
Ridge of high pressure: Calm weather, usually clear and sunny/Unit 6.4
River basin: The land drained by a river and its tributaries/Unit 5.3
Routeways: The line of a journey/Unit 10.1
Runway: The tarmac or concrete path for aircraft taking off or landing/Unit 9.4
Rural: To do with the countryside and country life/Unit 8.1
Sand dunes: Piles of sand deposited by the wind/Unit 7.3
Scale line: A line on a map which shows how far real distances are/Unit 3.2
Sediment: Tiny grains of rock which settle to the bottom of river or sea/Unit 7.1
Semi-detached house: A house joined to one other house/Unit 8.4
Settlement: Places which people build to live in/Unit 2.3
Shrinking world: As speeds get faster places seem to be closer together/Unit 10.4
Site: The land on which a settlement is built/Unit 8.2
Six figure reference: Six numbers (eg 534782) which find a point on a map/Unit 3.3
Sketch: A drawing of a place/Unit 1.3
Sketch map: A simple map showing only a few things about a place/Unit 2.2
Solar system: Our sun and its nine planets/Unit 6.2
Space: The regions above our atmosphere, between the earth and other planets/Unit 6.2
Spits: A long finger of sand or shingle deposited by the sea/Unit 7.2
Spot height: A point on a map with a number giving its height/Unit 3.4
Stadium: A large sports ground with seats for spectators/Unit 1.4
Star: A burning ball of rock and gas in space which gives out heat and light/Unit 6.2
Stratus cloud: Clouds which cover the sky like a blanket/Unit 6.1
Suez Canal: Canal linking Mediterranean Sea and Red Sea in the Middle East/Unit 10.3
Symbol: A small simple drawing used to save space on a map/Unit 3.1
Terminal building: The building at an airport where passengers wait for aircraft/Unit 9.4
Terraced house: A house joined to houses on either side/Unit 8.4
Ton: Anglo-Saxon word meaning enclosure for animals. (As in BrighTON.)/Unit 8.2
Tornado: An upward twisting funnel of air causing great damage/Unit 6.3
Town: A settlement with thousands of homes and services/Unit 8.1
Trenches: The deepest parts of the oceans/Unit 5.2
Trough of low pressure: Weather system giving stormy weather/Unit 6.4
Urban: To do with cities and city life/Unit 8.1
Valley: A long narrow hollow in the earth's surface/Unit 7.1
Vegetation: The plant life of a place/Unit 2.3
Village: A settlement with homes and some services like shops and churches/Unit 8.1
Volcanoes: Mountains formed by molten rock from deep in the earth/Unit 5.3
Weather forecast: What people think the weather will be like/Unit 6.4
Weathering: The breakup of rock by nature/Unit 7.3
Work: What people do for a living/Unit 2.3
Zone: An area. (As in 'urban land uses zone'.)/Unit 8.3